MANAGEMENT, WORK & ORGANISATIONS SERIES

Series editors: **Gibson Burrell**, School of Management, University of Leicester, UK
Mick Marchington, Manchester Business School, University of Manchester and Strathclyde Business School, University of Strathclyde, UK
Paul Thompson, Strathclyde Business School, University of Strathclyde, UK

This series of textbooks covers the areas of human resource management, employee relations, organisational behaviour and related business and management fields. Each text has been specially commissioned to be written by leading experts in a clear and accessible way. The books contain serious and challenging material, take an analytical rather than prescriptive approach and are particularly suitable for use by students with no prior specialist knowledge.

The series is relevant for many business and management courses, including MBA and post-experience courses, specialist masters and postgraduate diplomas, professional courses and final-year undergraduate courses. These texts have become essential reading at business and management schools worldwide.

Published titles include:

Maurizio Atzeni
WORKERS AND LABOUR IN A GLOBALISED CAPITALISM

Stephen Bach and Ian Kessler
THE MODERNISATION OF THE PUBLIC SERVICES AND EMPLOYEE RELATIONS

Emma Bell
READING MANAGEMENT AND ORGANIZATION IN FILM

Paul Blyton and Peter Turnbull
THE DYNAMICS OF EMPLOYEE RELATIONS (3RD EDN)

Paul Blyton, Edmund Heery and Peter Turnbull (eds)
REASSESSING THE EMPLOYMENT RELATIONSHIP

Sharon C. Bolton
EMOTION MANAGEMENT IN THE WORKPLACE

Sharon C. Bolton and Maeve Houlihan (eds)
SEARCHING FOR THE HUMAN IN HUMAN RESOURCE MANAGEMENT

Peter Boxall and John Purcell
STRATEGY AND HUMAN RESOURCE MANAGEMENT (3RD EDN)

J. Martin Corbett
CRITICAL CASES IN ORGANISATIONAL BEHAVIOUR

Susan Corby, Steve Palmer and Esmond Lindop
RETHINKING REWARD

Ian Greener
PUBLIC MANAGEMENT (2ND EDN)

Keith Grint
LEADERSHIP

Irena Grugulis
SKILLS, TRAINING AND HUMAN RESOURCE DEVELOPMENT

Geraldine Healy, Gill Kirton and Mike Noon (eds)
EQUALITY, INEQUALITIES AND DIVERSITY

Damian Hodgson and Svetlana Cicmil (eds)
MAKING PROJECTS CRITICAL

Marek Korczynski
HUMAN RESOURCE MANAGEMENT IN SERVICE WORK

Karen Legge
HUMAN RESOURCE MANAGEMENT: ANNIVERSARY EDITION

Patricia Lewis and Ruth Simpson (eds)
GENDERING EMOTIONS IN ORGANIZATIONS

Patricia Lewis and Ruth Simpson (eds)
VOICE, VISIBILITY AND THE GENDERING OF ORGANIZATIONS

Alison Pullen, Nic Beech and David Sims (eds)
EXPLORING IDENTITY

Jill Rubery and Damian Grimshaw
THE ORGANISATION OF EMPLOYMENT

Hugh Scullion and Margaret Linehan (eds)
INTERNATIONAL HUMAN RESOURCE MANAGEMENT

John Walton and Claire Valentin (eds)
HUMAN RESOURCE DEVELOPMENT

For more information on titles in the Series please go to **www.palgrave.com/business/mwo**

Series Standing Order

If you would like to receive future titles in this series as they are published, you can make use of our standing order facility. To place a standing order please contact your bookseller or, in case of difficulty, write to us at the address below with your name and address and the name of the series. Please state with which title you wish to begin your standing order.

Customer Services Department, Macmillan Distribution Ltd,
Houndmills, Basingstoke, Hampshire, RG21 6XS, UK

WORKERS AND LABOUR IN A GLOBALISED CAPITALISM

Contemporary Themes and Theoretical Issues

Edited by

Maurizio Atzeni

Lecturer in Labour and Industrial Relations and Marie Curie Research Fellow, School of Business and Economics, Loughborough University, UK

palgrave
macmillan

First published 2014 by
PALGRAVE MACMILLAN

Palgrave Macmillan in the UK is an imprint of Macmillan Publishers Limited,
registered in England, company number 785998, of Houndmills, Basingstoke,
Hampshire RG21 6XS.

Palgrave Macmillan in the US is a division of St Martin's Press LLC,
175 Fifth Avenue, New York, NY 10010.

Palgrave Macmillan is the global academic imprint of the above companies
and has companies and representatives throughout the world.

Palgrave® and Macmillan® are registered trademarks in the United States,
the United Kingdom, Europe and other countries.

ISBN 978–0–230–30317–1

This book is printed on paper suitable for recycling and made from fully
managed and sustained forest sources. Logging, pulping and manufacturing
processes are expected to conform to the environmental regulations of the
country of origin.

A catalogue record for this book is available from the British Library.

A catalog record for this book is available from the Library of Congress.

Printed and bound by CPI Group (UK) Ltd, Croydon, CR0 4YY

CONTENTS

ABBREVIATIONS

AFL	American Federation of Labor
AFL-CIO	American Feberation of Labor-Congress of Industrial Organizations
BRIC	Brazil, Russia, India and China
CA	*Companha do Aco*
CGT	Confédération Générale du Travail
CIO	Congress of Industrial Organizations
CNU	Cameroon National Union
ECB	European Central Bank
EWC	Excluded Workers Congress
FLOC	Farm Labour Organizing Committee
GATT	General Agreement on Tariffs and Trades
HRM	Human Resource Management
ICE	Immigration and Customs Enforcement
ILO	International Labour Organization
IMF	International Monetary Fund
IRCA	Immigration Reform and Control Act
ITUC	International Trade Union Confederation
IWW	Industrial Workers of the World
JIT	just in time
LIUNA	Laborers' International Union of North America
NAFTA	North American Free Trade Agreement
NEC	New European Countries
NGO	non-governmental organisation
NICs	newly industrialising countries
NIT	New Information Technology
NLRA	National Labor Relations Act
NOWCRJ	New Orleans Workers Center for Racial Justice

OECD	Organisation for Economic Co-operation and Development
PCP	Petty Commodity Producers
ROI	Return on Investment
SEIU	American Service Employees' Industrial Union
SMU	Social movement unionism
SMVR	Sindicato dos Metalúrgicos de Volta Rodonda
TNCs	Transnational Corporations
ULRs	Union Learning Reps
USAID	United States Agency for International Development
WTO	World Trade Organization

CONTRIBUTORS

Maurizio Atzeni is Marie Curie Research Fellow at Loughborough University, UK and at CEIL/CONICET in Buenos Aires, Argentina. His research focuses on forms and processes of workers' resistance and organisation. He is the author of a book on workplace conflict and collective action (*Workplace Conflict, Mobilisation and Solidarity in Argentina*) and editor of *Alternative Forms of Work Organisation*. He has also published journal articles and book chapters on mobilisation theory, workers' self-management and trade unionism in Argentina.

Sheila Cohen is a trade union researcher and writer. She is Senior Research Fellow at the Work and Research Unit (WERU), University of Hertfordshire. She is the author of *Ramparts of Resistance: Why Workers Lost Their Power and How to Get It Back*, and most recently a history of the main trade union branch at Ford Dagenham in the UK, *Notoriously Militant*.

Ralph Darlington is Professor of Employment Relations at the University of Salford, UK. His research is concerned with the dynamics of trade union organisation, activity and consciousness in Britain and internationally within both contemporary and historical settings. He is author of *The Dynamics of Workplace Unionism, The Political Trajectory of J.T. Murphy, Syndicalism and the Transition to Communism, Radical Unionism*, co-author of *Glorious Summer: Class Struggle in Britain, 1972* and editor of *What's the Point of Industrial Relations? In Defence of Critical Social Science*.

Silvia Federici is Emerita Professor at Hofstra University (Hempstead, New York, USA). She is the author of many essays on political philosophy, feminist theory, cultural studies, and education. Her published works include: *Revolution at Point Zero, Caliban and the Witch: Women, the Body and Primitive*

Accumulation and *A Thousand Flowers: Social Struggles Against Structural Adjustment in African Universities* (co-editor).

Gregor Gall is Professor of Industrial Relations at the University of Bradford, UK. He held the same positions at the Universities of Stirling and Hertfordshire. He has written extensively on union organising and anti-unionism. Amongst his books are *Tommy Sheridan: From Hero to Zero? A Political Biography* and *An Agency of their Own: Sex Worker Union Organising.* He has edited *New Forms and Expressions of Conflict at Work.*

Marcel van der Linden is the Research Director of the International Institute of Social History and Professor of Social Movement History at the University of Amsterdam, in the Netherlands. He is the author of *Workers of the World: Essays toward a Global Labor History.*

Massimiliano Mollona teaches political and economic anthropology at Goldsmiths College, University of London, UK. His interests focus on the anthropology of labour, class and political economy. Based on his mixed disciplinary background in anthropology and economics he conducted fieldworks in Italy, Britain and Brazil mainly in 'steel towns', where he explored local patterns of work and politics associated with trajectories of industrialisation and de-industrialisation. He has published extensively on issues of class and labour, including the volumes *Made in Sheffield: An Ethnography of Industrial Work and Politics* and *Industrial Work and Life: An Anthropological Reader,* co-edited with Johnny Parry and Geert De Neve.

Immanuel Ness is Professor of Political Science at the Brooklyn College of the City University of New York, USA. His research focuses on labour organisation and mobilisation, migration, resistance and social movements. He is author of *Guest Workers and Resistance to US Corporate Despotism* and *Immigrants, Unions, and the U.S. Labor Market* and editor of the peer-review quarterly journal, *Working USA: The Journal of Labor and Society.*

Beverly Silver is Professor of Sociology and Director of the Arrighi Center for Global Studies at the Johns Hopkins University, USA. Her research focuses on various facets of the dynamics of historical capitalism. Among her most noted publications is the prize-winning *Forces of Labor: Workers' Movements and Globalization since 1870,* which has been translated in over ten languages.

David A. Spencer is Professor of Economics and Political Economy at Leeds University Business School, University of Leeds, UK. His general research interests lie in the economics and political economy of work, employment relations/work studies, the history of economic though and political economy. He has authored numerous articles in these areas and is the author of the book *The Political Economy of Work.*

INTRODUCTION: NEO-LIBERAL GLOBALISATION AND INTERDISCIPLINARY PERSPECTIVES ON LABOUR AND COLLECTIVE ACTION

Maurizio Atzeni

WHY THIS BOOK?

The effects of the current world economic crisis on employment and working conditions have put to the fore, once again, the role of workers in resisting, coping with or finding alternatives to a changed, unfavourable context. In the field of industrial relations and the sociology of work, after decades in which non-conflictual visions of work associated with Human Resource Management seemed to be the dominant pattern of work relations, researchers' attention is now shifting back to workers and labour. Studies of migrant workers, of exploitative working conditions in the developing world, of gender discrimination, of work relations in the growing service sector, of emotional labour, are all important recent additions to the field in which the role of workers is pivotal. While these new studies aim to spread more light on issues that have more powerfully emerged in a context dominated by post-Fordism and globalisation, there has also been a revitalisation of more traditional workplace studies concerned with issues of workers' organisation, collective action, trade unionism, the labour process and workers' self-management. In other overlapping disciplines, such as social anthropology, labour geography, social history and political economy, a focus on labour has been central to explain patterns of exploitation in the informal sector and of illegal immigrants in the global cities; to envisage strategies of resistance across space and societies; to link labour unrest to historical patterns of capitalist development; to re-open the crucial debate about gendered, unpaid work and social reproduction; and, overall, to redefine the concepts of work and of the working class.

In a nutshell, what all these streams of research emphasise is a commitment to a more socially compromised research, one in which the activities of people at work, the struggles they engage in and the organisational and political strategies they produce assume a central status, according to the position workers have in capitalism. In the current academic and social context, labour has thus regained centrality in explaining contemporary processes and issues, becoming a subject of study in itself.

Considering the renewed importance of labour and workers studies, the aim of this book is relatively straightforward: to provide a comprehensive set of theories, themes and issues coming from different disciplines that can help reflect upon the centrality of labour within the contemporary process of globalisation. Changes in the international division of labour and technological innovations have altered previously established patterns of work and labour relations, have put into question accepted dichotomies such as that between formal and informal work or between productive and unproductive work, and have consistently changed the social framework within which working classes have historically formed. How have these changes, that marking a new era in the structure of work, been addressed within the literature? Are these changes fundamentally calling for a new conceptualisation and understanding of labour and the working class within capitalism? Does workers' resistance within capitalism remain the central category, the building block for social change? What forms can resistance take? More generally, can we make/provide a theoretical framework for the importance of workers' resistance within global capitalism?

These questions are the threads linking and cutting across all the chapters of this book. Within its pages the latter question is divided into three main parts. The first explains the continued centrality of labour within capitalism, focusing on aspects related to class, social reproduction and work organisation as mediated by different geographical and historical contexts. The second focuses on labour as an actor for social change and aims to explain strategies, forms and processes of workers' resistance to work within capitalism, both in terms of formal organisation by trade unions and workers' own activity. The third considers how globalisation has, on the one hand, made more precarious the conditions of work for the majority of the world's population, across the North/South and the formal/informal divide but, on the other hand, how forms of workers' resistance and self-organisation have appeared from different groups of workers in different sectors of the economy.

In the first part of this Introduction the aim is to give an overview of the structural changes imposed by the process of neo-liberal globalisation and what these have meant in terms of typology and quality of work. The second part will consider how these changes have been addressed, particularly within the sociology of work literature, pointing to the limitations of the discipline in the conceptualisation of workers' collective action. The final part will give an overview of the chapters included in the book, how they are linked to each other and how they contribute to the overall aims of the book.

NEO-LIBERALISM AND GLOBALISATION

The changes in the world of work that have occurred over the last three decades on a global scale cannot be understood just in terms of societal responses and adaptations to massive technological innovations and developments, particularly in the transport and communication systems, that have changed production, exchange and distribution in the world market. While the introduction of new technology has speeded up, supported and made real certain processes, as with flexibility and de-localisation, these have not been 'natural' consequences of the way in which the market economy evolves and adapts itself to change. Rather, what we call today globalisation can be seen as directly linked to the imposition, by political and economic elites, of neo-liberalism as the new political economic model for the world order. In this sense globalisation has been the result of a project, starting in the 1970s, which in the shadows of a discourse that viewed market reforms as common sense, aimed to re-establish conditions for capital accumulation and restoration of class power (Harvey 2005).

The post-second world war social compact of the industrialised capitalist centres, based on the so-called Fordist model of production, has been put into question. This model, promoting mass labour, mass production and consumption, had guaranteed, in many parts of the industrialised world, relatively higher standards of living, consistently reduced for many years the level of unemployment, and provided the basis for the development of the welfare state. But it had also strengthened the associational and institutional power of trade unions, giving them a fundamental role in collective bargaining and working conditions negotiation, overall contributing to effectively raise the interests of workers vis-a-vis the interests of capital. This empowerment of labour together with the centrality of the State in the management of the economy was evident also in the South of the world, even though here the application of the Fordist system had been less homogeneous compared to the developed countries. However, when promoted by 'developmentalist' regimes, as for instance in Argentina and Brazil, the industrialisation process based on the Fordist system had been able to produce consistent improvements for workers, either through expanding their consumption capacity or raising standards of living and education and promoting the enlargement of the middle classes (Amin 2008).

The imposition of neo-liberalism, with its discourse on the thaumaturgy of the market in getting efficient and quality-based production and distribution, has been in reality, since the beginning, targeted to break the redistributive model that dominated in the post-war period and thus to reduce workers' power in society. This was obtained not just by cutting rights and curbing trade unions' power, but also by reducing the role of citizenship in determining the political and economic model of the state and opening up previously regulated spheres of the economy to the market (with the correspondent loss of national economic sovereignty and increasing power of transnational financial capitals and institutions).

Analyses of the changes imposed by neo-liberalism vary greatly between countries. Neo-liberal reforms have been introduced at different historical moments, under different political regimes, in geographically diverse economic contexts, and have also been accepted or opposed by workers and societies in different forms and degrees, even between countries with similar history, culture and patterns of economic development (Atzeni et al. 2011). This diversity, makes it even more important to underline the political, economic and class-based character of the neo-liberal project (something which is missing, for instance, from a variety of capitalism literature, see Hall and Soskice 2001, and from global value chain approaches; for a Marxist critique of this see Starosta 2010). The diversity invites us to find out how similar processes induced by neo-liberalism (for instance, labour flexibility, outsourcing, subcontracting, privatisation of public services and reforms of the welfare state) are linked and connected across the world.

One of these linkages is clearly represented by the parallel process of de-industrialisation/de-localisation and its consequences on working conditions and workers' quality of life. The disappearance of industrial districts and factories in large areas of the industrialised world has destroyed once homogeneous class communities, has atomised and dispersed workers in the ever increasing service sector, has led to a decrease in unionisation and an overall individualisation of employment. Meanwhile, within the new international division of labour, processes of de-localisation and outsourcing of services and manufacturing in emerging economies and production based on global chains have completely transformed the world of work across the North/South divide. This has almost reverted previous assumptions about the formal and the informal, about protected and precarious work, and about the standard of work between the developing and developed world. The mobility of capital and the availability of new information technologies is creating new spaces of work in which differences are blurring. The structure of work and employment has changed so dramatically in recent years that it makes sense to talk about the emergence of a new class of workers: the precariat (Standing 2011). While the extent to which this is really a new class is highly debatable, partly because of the heterogeneity of work relations that have existed historically within capitalism (see Chapter 3), today, however, precariousness seems to be the unifying keyword. Unpaid stages and internships, indefinite renewal of temporary contracts, traditional wage relations camouflaged by consultancy projects to avoid the payment of social security obligations, self-employment, and a myriad of so-called 'atypical' forms of work co-exist today. In many parts of the world and in both the public and private sector, they exist alongside more traditional, regular forms of employment. Thus, while in the past precariousness was associated with the informality of the developing world urban labour markets, neo-liberal globalisation has transformed it into the key feature of capital accumulation in the urban economy of the world cities (Sassen 2001, Beck 2000). In this context and in addition to this 'informality within the formal economy', the use of illegal migrants and their discrimination in terms of wages and labour conditions has also been used to reduce overall labour standards and thus increase precariousness (Wills et al. 2010, Chapter 10 in this book).

While it is then possible to argue for a transnational and a transversal precariousness (across regions, sectors of the economy and typologies of employment), the extent to which neo-liberal globalisation has also produced an increase of people working directly within the informal economy should not be underestimated. While in certain realities the lack of extended industrialisation and the absence of more dynamic labour markets has always explained the existence of high level of informality, the liberalisation of the economy, processes of privatisation, the shrinking of state employment and other measures adopted by developing countries as part of the structural adjustment programmes promoted by international financial institutions, have increased the number of people in the informal sector. This can be noticed not just for countries in which informality has always been very high, like in the majority of the African world (Lindell 2010). In Argentina, where, on the contrary, formal employment has for decades been very high, the adoption of neo-liberal reforms during the 1990s has produced a major fracture between protected and unprotected workers which has remained, the recent economic expansion notwithstanding.

The overall increase of precarious/informal work at world level cannot, however, be understood just as the effect of states' free market oriented employment and income generation policies. While these policies, increasing unemployment and degrading work, have contributed to making a large and cheap labour force available for capital at local levels, other factors have also contributed to this. The emergence of China and South East Asia as the manufacturing hub of the world and the opening to the market of virtually all former socialist states has made available to capitalist expansion new masses of workers, expanding the labour market at a global level. This has, on the one hand, increased competition for capital investment among workers in different world regions and, on the other hand, by cheapening the cost of manufactured commodities, it has reduced salaries for workers in the industrialised world. These geo-political changes, the technological developments associated with globalisation and the interconnections of the world's economic activities have generated new cycles of growth and capital accumulation. This, however, has been relatively low, has been built since the beginning of neo-liberalism on financial speculation rather than on cycles of production and has thus been centred, according to Harvey (2010), on the renewal and acceleration of processes of primitive accumulation, making this a permanent rather than a historically transitory phenomenon. Various processes of what Harvey calls 'accumulation by dispossession' can be seen at play within the current capitalist dynamics. The destruction and exploitation of the environment to provide infrastructures and new opportunities for private capital expansion, the appropriation of new lands or the privatisation of previously common lands, while destroying the means through which entire communities had been used to guarantee their subsistence and survival, further increasing the 'reserve army' needed by capital in its endless expansion, has subsumed the lives of more and more people into market relations. Similarly, the privatisation of services that were previously guaranteed by the welfare state, such as health, education and social security, has re-commodified these services and made more costly the reproduction of workers. Finally, the financialisation of the economy, that has made people responsible for crisis, as the subprime mortgage crisis demonstrated, can be seen as another powerful vehicle to allow capital accumulation by dispossession.

Many of the dispossessions that Harvey identifies as permanent features of the current process of capitalist accumulation affect directly the possibility of workers' social reproduction. The reproduction of human beings, the satisfaction of their material as well as social needs, is a fundamental condition that allows the selling of labour power in the market. But despite its importance, this work has always remained invisible, not just to the political economy but also to the whole of society and this despite the feminist revolutions of the 1960s and 1970s (Picchio 1992). Women have historically borne the cost of social reproduction either by working for free at home for the well-being of the family or, with the full insertion of more women into the labour market, delegating domestic activities to other women. In both cases, however, the theoretical and practical invisibility of reproductive work has left untouched the gendered division of labour in society. Against a scenario of informality, precariousness, crisis and capital's continued processes of capital primitive accumulation, women have been, as Silvia Federici reminds us in Chapter 4, 'the shock absorbers of economic globalization, having had to compensate with their work for the deteriorating economic conditions produced by the liberalisation of the world economy and the states' increasing dis-investment in the reproduction of the workforce'.

In this brief overview of the changes imposed by neo-liberal globalisation on the world of work, a number of issues, which will be dealt in details in the following chapters, have been mentioned. The first concerns the transformations associated with the process of de-industrialisation/de-localisation. This process changes completely the landscape of work in both the de-industrialised and the newly industrialised realities, creating new jobs, new skills, new urban geographies, a diversification of wages and employment relations and, overall, shaping new working classes. This implies, in turn, the need to think about what this working class is, what kind of workers are composing it and to reflect upon what Silver calls in her chapter 'the making, unmaking and remaking' of the working classes in the history of capitalist dynamics (Chapter 2). The second concerns the issues of precariousness and informality. While this is emerging as the current trend in terms of type of employment at the global level there is still not enough information about what informal work is, what are workers' perceptions about it and the interaction between work and formal/informal social spaces, an argument that will be considered later by Mollona in Chapter 8. The third and last issue discussed refers to the need to insert social reproduction as a category in the understanding of work. This is today especially relevant not just because reproduction continues to fall on the shoulders of women and remains essential for the existence of wage workers. But also because reproduction itself is becoming a contested terrain of struggle, as the many movements fighting for the preservation of the environment, customary rights and common lands are showing.

RENEWING THE FIELD OF STUDY

The changes on the world of work produced by globalisation have been widespread and have completely revolutionised the traditional framework of analysis within the field of the sociology of work and labour relations, imposing a reflection on the validity of existing theoretical paradigms about work, centred fundamentally on studies of the social relations and regulation of work in the waged, protected and male dominated industrial factory. Research on work in the service sector (Korczynski and MacDonald 2009), on creative labour (Smith and McKinlay 2009), on migrants working conditions (Wills et al. 2010), on call centres (Taylor and Bain 2005), on the retail sector (Grugulis and Bozkurt 2011), on the variable forms of the so-called atypical work (De la Garza Toledo 2011) and studies of work organisation and workers' subjective experiences of work in the labour process tradition (Bolton and Houlihan 2009) are just a few examples of recent research streams adding to the field of employment relations. Other studies, particularly by social anthropologists have highlighted the interaction between work and formal/informal social spaces in urban contexts (Mollona 2009, Lazar 2012), have reflected on debates on the nature and origin of the informal sector of the economies (Fernandez-Kelly and Shefner 2006), have proposed interdisciplinary approaches to community-based workers' organisation (Mcbride and Greenwood 2009) and have focused on the relation between precariousness and citizenship (Barchiesi 2011). Finally, from a labour geography perspective, the relational concepts of space and mobility have been used to assess different levels of workers' militancy (Rainnie et al. 2010).

Within the renewal of the sociology of work, Miriam Glucksmann has recently questioned the validity and relevance of the concept of the division of labour (Glucksmann 2009). In her view, the original concept, which emphasised technical matters as an excuse to divert attention from managerial and class power, needs to be enlarged not just to give proper recognition to the gender discrimination implicit in what feminists called the 'peopled' division of labour, but also to include the multiple forms of work often co-existing in the same time/space dimension, arguing that work varies depending on the existence of different modes of socio-economic provisions (for instance, market/ non-market, public/private) and of work activity developed differently through the different phases of a whole economic cycle (production, distribution, exchange and consumption). For Glucksmann, the insertion of women in the labour market, the privatisation of services such as childcare and the increasing precariousness of workers are among the reasons why individuals are daily experiencing variations in their work: from paid to unpaid, from formal to informal, from voluntary to market-imposed. Thus the concept of the Total Social Organisation of Labour could be used to give sense to these interconnections of work. Similarly, though at a different level, the concept of Instituted Economic Processes of Labour is proposed to highlight the connections existing between the work done in the spheres of production, exchange, distribution and consumption, spheres that are seen as constituting a unity within the economy. The increasing inclusion of the consumer and thus of consumers' work as an integral part in the production process (assembly of furniture, home banking, call centres, etc.) justifies this new concept. Finally, the interconnections and interplay between the technical division of labour, work performed across different socio-economic modes and sphere of economic activity, would allow configuring the overall socio-economic formation of labour.

Glucksmann's framework is very sophisticated and certainly useful for studying empirical variations of work, particularly in a world that is increasingly interconnected and in which individuals can play simultaneously at different levels. However, on the one hand it downplays the role that profitability has in shaping the division of labour along gender or ethnic lines and, on the other hand, it seems to relegate the role of the increasing commodification and re-commodification of life imposed by the capitalist system through the renewal of processes of primitive accumulation. The private/public and market/non-market modes identified by Glucksmann, expressions of what she calls a 'multi modal capitalism' (Glucksmann 2009, p. 887), remain inserted within a capitalist logic and this needs to be explained at the outset. In this sense, the privatisation of public services, the retreat of the welfare state and, more generally, the cut in workers' economic and social rights introduced with neo-liberalism, has had a considerable effect on work, not just producing new articulations between different spheres and modes of work but also, by putting the logic of the market back into important spheres of life, conditioning the way in which work has to be performed; not any longer to provide a social service but, instead, to provide a market product.

While the developments in the field mentioned above and Glucksmann's work seem to suggest that previous paradigms have been updated to include recent changes in the structure of work, once we direct the focus of our attention specifically to the literature on the organisation and representation of workers, we have to notice that there is still a tendency to concentrate on institutions, formal regulations and strategies for inclusion, almost replicating the 'old' scheme of union representation and collective bargaining which was so centred on the post-war development of the industrialised countries, and this, paradoxically, even when the object of analysis is precarious/informal sector workers (Schurman and Eaton 2012). More generally, progressive research about workers, either when discussing organisational strategy (Simms, Holgate and Heery 2012), social movement unionism and renewal (Fairbrother 2008), labour internationalism (Bieler, Lindberg and Pillay 2008) or mobilisation theory (Kelly 1998), at least in the Anglo-Saxon world, it is rarely disconnected from the presence or reference to a union actor. Overall this tendency to concentrate on institutions (unions, but to the same extent also NGOs or advocacy groups) has, on the one hand, set apart the study of workers' self-activity in collective organising and, on the other hand, has often reduced the subject of study to work relations in formal employment contexts.

Particularly for those interested to explain workers' resistance and organisation, workers matter in explaining the social processes conducive to collective action only as far as they are represented by a trade union that engages in a formal struggle with a formal employer in an environment regulated by legislation (Atzeni 2010). While research on the role of these institutions and their organising strategies remains fundamental in perspective to improve the daily reality of workers, especially in the informal/precarious sector of the economy, where almost by definition workers are unorganised and need to build from scratch, workers' self-activity rather than institutions matters in building their resistance and mobilisation, generating alternative forms of organisation and representation of workers' interests and/or renewing the class- and movement-based side of trade unionism (see the chapers by Cohen and Darlington in Part 2).

Workers' self-activity is, however, conditioned by the combination of multiple structural factors. The type of labour process can foster co-operation and enlarge the scope for the establishment of solidarity among workers or, on the contrary, can increase their level of atomisation; the strategic location of the economic activity can give workers more chances to make their complaints visible and legitimise their organisation or, on the contrary, make any forms of organisation risky; the kind of remuneration workers receive and the employer for whom they are working (private, the state, or both) is another of the factors shaping possibilities for action. The political context and the institutional framework can favour strategic alliances with other social movements, and promote wider mobilisation by framing the grievances of specific groups of workers within more general political claims for change.

All these factors limit and often hide from view the role of workers' self-activity in resisting alienation and exploitation but, empirically, examples of spontaneous collective action have abounded. At crucial moments in history, when crises produce unemployment, falling wages, poverty, when there are situations threatening their lives but also when they struggle for better wages, workers have autonomously reacted, reversing unfavourable working and economic conditions. Historically all workers, quite independently from the kind of labour relations under which their work was performed (waged/unwaged, formal/informal, free/un-free) rebelled and often in spontaneous ways (van der Linden 2008).

But apart from the examples that can be provided, can we make a case for the theoretical relevance of workers' self-activity?

According to Fox Piven (2008), neo-liberal globalisation rather than reducing opportunities, is offering new possibilities for the exercise of what she calls 'power from below'. For many decades in many countries, the prospects for social change depended on the exercise of electoral democracy and on the institutional strength of the labour movement, and this contributed to the idea that possibilities for change were directly proportional to the material resources available to institutions to defend people's rights and claims for more equal societies. In the current scenario of precariousness, flexibility and the mobility of capital, the role of trade unions and labour parties as organisations defending labour power has diminished and democracy has been jeopardised by the power of multi-national corporations and international finance. While this context makes it now more difficult to build social change by accumulating resources in representing institutions, Fox Piven argues that globalisation, through the interconnectedness and increasingly complex web of producing relations on which it is based, is also providing increasing opportunities for the exercise of power by ordinary people. But a new conceptualisation of power from below is required, that of 'inter-dependent' power, which would certainly be not based on resources but on the co-operative nature of social relations in the workplaces and in societies. Social life is cooperative life and, in principle, all people who make contributions to these systems of cooperation have potential power over others who depend on them (Fox Piven 2008, p. 5). Moreover, this power, which can be said to be the expression of societies' structural conditions, is also a manifestation of the need to break institutional rules as these 'reflect the power inequalities in our societies and because they do, they can suppress the actualization of interdependent power from below' (p. 12).

More generally, different conceptualisations of power, which cannot be discussed here at great length, are supportive of the idea that those who are dominated generate resistance to domination, though this can be in more open or hidden forms and lead to more or less stable collective organisations (Scott 1990, Lukes 1995, Moore 1978).

Moving to the Marxist field, workers' self-activity or self-determination has long been within the tradition of autonomous Marxism. This is a stream that originated in Italy during the 1960s with the work of Panzieri and Tronti and was later consolidated internationally with Negri's re-reading of Marx's Grundrisse (Negri 1992). Autonomists argued that technological changes and the development of capitalism had to be seen not exclusively from the point of view of capital. Workers had an autonomous power in shaping the way work was divided in the factory. Thus, cycles of struggle deriving from this antagonism could be expected. These conceptualisations were later extended to the whole of society (the social factory) during the struggles of the students and housewives. These groups, rather than the reserve army of labour, were seen as an active part of the working class.

Recently, John Holloway (2010), talking about 'cracks' as a way of producing radical change, has refreshed this idea of an autonomous power of working people, by arguing that countless spaces of self-activity, of rejection of work as imposed by the logic of capital, are constantly appearing and producing 'cracks' or revolts against this logic. Rehabilitating Marx's distinction of the twofold character of labour, as abstract and useful labour (the first an activity abstracted from its specificities and producing value, the second based on creative and productive human activity), Holloway argues for the existence of two different kinds of antagonisms. The first is generated by capital's constant effort to discipline our time and life so as to convert useful labour – our 'doing' or our creative activity – into value-producing labour. This attempt produces struggles against abstract, capitalist labour. The second antagonism is against exploitation, once our 'doing' has been transformed into labour. While both are struggles against capital, the struggle of workers against abstract labour is the one that has historically dominated. Here the role of trade unions has been important as they have basically always fought for wage labour as wage labour, taking for granted and accepting the institutional and structural context in which their action was taking place. In the current global scenario, while the struggle against abstract labour has lost part of its strength due to the decline of trade unionism and the crisis of social democracy, the relentless and increasing (for the speed of technological development) attempts by capital to commodify our entire life and to force us into labour is producing insubordination, refusal and cracks.

INTERDISCIPLINARY PERSPECTIVES ON LABOUR AND WORKERS' RESISTANCE

For all those approaching the study of labour and labour relations for the first time it would probably be extremely difficult to understand the theoretical and empirical limits of the field of study and the connections existing between the economic and social dimension of human labour. Similarly, the monetary rewards associated with the use of labour in the organisation of production and distribution hide from view the complexity of the social processes underlining what, superficially, might appear to be a relatively straightforward economic transaction. Labour is, in many ways, at the centre of social life, it affects workers individually, in their collective relations, in their workplace, at home and in their neighbourhoods. The patterns of domination associated to the use of labour affect the overall structure of societies. These in turn adapt and respond to similar developments in different ways and forms, expressing different values, regulations and social arrangements as to the role of labour and workers in the evolution of societies.

Beside this 'natural' complexity, as has been clear from the arguments presented in the previous sections, an understanding of labour and labour relations in the global world requires a broader view of the subject. First, while the study of the workplace remains fundamental to an understanding of the relations between labour and capital at a micro level, there is a need to take into account how precariousness and informality have de-contextualised and de-structured traditional workplaces and employers/employees relations. This is particularly important when the focus of our analysis is on forms of representation and resistance. Trade unions are and will remain powerful machines to organise workers collectively but workers' own self-activity remains the *conditio sine qua non* and the root of any more stable organisation. Second, workplace analysis needs to be integrated in a clearer and better-defined approach what to global capitalism is, to understand its historical dynamics and patterns of accumulation and to link these to local developments. Third, given the centrality and interconnectedness of labour to many of the human life's spheres, there is a need to enlarge our understanding of labour in general, adding knowledge that comes from overlapping disciplines in the social sciences and including non-mainstream, yet fundamental, topics (such as social reproduction). Fourth, and probably most importantly, there is a need to look at labour studies from a radical and coherent theoretical perspective. While various theoretical approaches can be valid, the different strands of contemporary Marxism offer valid support for the analysis of labour.

The chapters in this book try to address the points made above. From this 'broadening' of the view, it becomes clear, however, not just how complex are the social relations in which workers are inserted but also how this complexity provides workers with opportunities for resistance. Capitalist societies constantly provide structural conditions for the emergence of workers' resistance and organisation. This is hopefully the most important message that the chapters in this book can offer to the readers.

The book's first part, 'Theoretical Issues: Explaining the Centrality of Labour', is opened by a chapter written by David Spencer on Marx and Marxist views on work and the capitalist labour process. Marx's writings on work remain a fundamental reference point for all those approaching the study of labour as these writings offer insights on specific aspects of work organisation and workplace relations by inserting them into the broader political economy of capitalism. The development of capitalism as a system and the discovery of its mechanisms of reproduction are the pivotal points to understanding how a purposeful and creative human activity is transformed and appropriated by capital in the form of 'labour' and how, as a consequence, work is organised through a specifically capitalist labour process. David Spencer in this chapter drives us initially through some more philosophical aspects of Marx's vision of work by highlighting, on the one hand, the importance he gives to work, considered as a constitutive element of human life and thus with an intrinsically positive value and, on the other hand, by underlining how the process of transformation of work into labour and the pressure of valorisation, constraining the full development of work as a fulfilling human activity, generates in turn alienation and exploitation. In the second part of the chapter the focus shifts towards the analysis of the work of Braverman on the capitalist labour process and on the so-called labour process debate that followed from the publication of Braverman's book in 1974. Braverman's contribution has been fundamental to re-install at the level of the labour process Marx's dialectical approach. Criticising the approaches existing in the sociology of work, Braverman argued that analysis of work relations needed to be inserted in the broader historical dynamics of the capitalist labour process and that changes within this were to be interpreted as the result of changing patterns of capital accumulation. Applying this view to the US in the 1970s he saw that technology automation was used by capitalists to constantly undermine the skilfulness of the workers and thus that a tendency of de-skilling could be identified within the historical development of capitalism. In the final part of the chapter space is given to the debates that followed the work of Braverman. These were initially critical readings and interpretations of his work but have evolved through the decades into a stand-alone subject that, though now disconnected from its origin in Marxist political economy, continues to offer key insights to understand issues of control and co-operation at work.

In the second chapter Beverly Silver powerfully argues against the view, dominant in academic and political discourse during the last three decades, of the disappearance of labour and the labour movement from the social landscape. An historical analysis of the different phases of capitalist development in different geographical areas of the world shows, rather than univocal trends, the cyclical recurrence of similar patterns of interaction between labour and capital, with mutual influences. This interaction is articulated around two main axes. The first is the existence of a structural and endemic resistance of workers to the commodification of their labour, resistance which can occur, following Marx's and Polanyi insights, both at the level of the workplace and the society. The second is based on the perpetual changes imposed by capitalist competition. This latter, imposing rapid technological development produces not just changes in the organisation of production but also, with the creation of new products and industries, in the dominant cultural and consumption models. These evolving trends in the development of historical capitalism, affect the type, form and location of workers' struggles against commodification. These struggles, however, shape in turn the patterns of capitalist accumulation dominating within a particular geographical and historical context. Thus, for Silver working classes are constantly and alternatively made, unmade and re-made following the interactions between capital and labour. While not necessarily revolutionary nor on the brink of extinction, labour movements across time and space have been fundamental actors in shaping the dynamics of global capitalism and, as Silver's argument shows, will probably continue to do so.

In the third chapter Marcel van der Linden explores from an historical perspective the contemporary relevance of the concept of the working class. Which categories of workers have constituted (and constitute today) the working class? How valid are previous conceptualisations of it? These questions are all the more important if we consider the forms and methods of labour exploitation used currently by global capitalism. Processes of outsourcing and de-localisation, increasing precariousness, have indeed left room for the growth of forms of forced, indentured employment which barely resemble the free wage labourer identified by Marx as the prototype of the working man and of a potentially revolutionary class which has 'nothing to lose than its

chains'. Van der Linden's chapter shows us how the different historical requirements of capitalism and the different geographical areas to which the system
had to adapt itself have produced, very often, hybrid and transitional forms
of employment, rather than a standardisation towards free wage labour. While
this form has tended to dominate others, becoming the second most prevalent
form of work after work performed at home, within the field of employment
relations analyses of the wage relation, and particularly that formalised by
a contract, has led to the virtual disappearance of all other forms of labour
exploitation and subsumption by capital. In parallel with this standardisation,
collective action has been basically intended and studied in the form of strike,
ignoring, on the one hand how social reality has often presented us with cases
of workers' rebellions using different methods of struggle (riots, occupations,
roadblocks), depending on the resources available to them; on the other hand,
how these same methods have been used alternatively by different categories of
workers. Van der Linden's chapter, enlarging the concept of the working class
to all sorts of subaltern employment relations, helps, in summary, to think
about the world of work in the global era in a broader and interconnected way.

Following in the book's aim to broaden and update the sphere of analysis of work within global capitalism, in the fourth chapter Silvia Federici
focuses on what is undoubtedly the biggest category of forgotten workers,
domestic workers, reflecting on the reproductive nature of their work and
on the importance it has within today's division of work. Drawing on the
work of Marxist feminists in the 1960s and 1970s, Federici raises a critique to
Marx and Marxists for the theoretical invisibility to which reproductive work
has always been relegated. Considering the work involved in the reproduction of the commodity labour economically relevant has led not just to the
perpetuation of huge gender differences in terms of employment conditions
and opportunities, but it has also hidden from view the strict dependency
existing between house/domestic work and changes in the patterns of global
accumulation. In this sense, processes of reduction of the welfare state, privatisation or the austerity measures currently adopted by governments to control
the crisis, have all impacted the work of reproduction, transferring to the
'non-economic' and 'invisible' sphere of the home the costs of economic transformations to re-establish capital profitability on a larger scale. What are the
prospects for emancipation for the millions of women who still represent the
bulk of domestic workers? The fight to include domestic work into the waged
sector has proven to be limited since it has never been accompanied by a full
social re-evaluation of the economic importance of the work done privately.
The full entry of women into the productive workforce, while it has opened up
new spaces and opportunities for some of them, it has basically displaced the

problem of reproductive work to other women to whom the care of children and of the house has been delegated. In the light of this and of the risks existing in the commercialisation of reproductive work, in terms of health or emotions, Federici argues that we collectively need to have a say about the way our reproduction is organised, aiming for the recovery of spaces of co-operation in the re-organisation of reproductive work and the re-appropriation of the commons.

The fifth chapter by Ralph Darlington, which opens part two of the book 'Classical Issues: Explaining Workers' Resistance and Organisation', signals a shift in the book's focus and a return to the 'traditional' wage workers and to their preferred form of organisation: the trade unions. From a theoretical and historical perspective, Darlington argues that the function played by trade unions in building workers' organisation remains fundamental and this not just to defend workers' immediate interests at the workplace but also as a way of opposing capitalist power at a society level. Historically, trade unions have always alternated between these spheres of action, appearing often contemporaneously as organisations representative of workers as a class, as a sector and as a group and/or as a political/electoral force. These different identities have never been fixed and have changed depending on a number of external circumstances and possibilities but are also a reflection of the double nature of trade unionism. On the one hand, trade unions are an expression of the inherent conflict of interests existing within capitalism between workers and employers, the first interested in keeping the value of their wages high and the second, driven by the profit imperative, interested in keeping the cost of labour as low as possible. On the other hand, trade unions exist also as organisations whose function is fundamentally that of negotiating the value of labour power, thus mediating between workers' and employers' conflicting interests. This double nature of trade unions makes their actions often contradictory, installing conflicting internal dynamics between base and leadership of the organisation. Despite these limits, however, trade unions continue to represent, as Darlington argues, the basic defence organisation of the workers, their collective reaction to the inequalities and exploitative conditions generated by work relations under capitalism.

In the sixth chapter by Sheila Cohen, we delve deep into the dynamics leading workers to organise into trade unions. The chapter makes use of current and historical examples and of ongoing discussions about strategies for trade unions' renewal to vividly show how 'spontaneous resistance' and workplace activists are often at the roots of trade unionism. This emphasis on the 'movement' as compared to the 'institutional' side of workers' organising through trade unions is particularly important when thinking about processes of globalisation and of the possibility of workers' collective action. The precariousness to which we referred earlier in this chapter, as the common denominator of both the old manufacturing and the new service/knowledge jobs across the globe, while taking millions of workers out of the possibility of representation through a trade union, is nevertheless constantly renewing the basis and creating the conditions for workers' own collective self-organising. Indeed, it is this activity that is the necessary precondition for the consolidation of trade unions as institutions. Cohen's and Darlington's chapters, though the latter is from a more general perspective, help to ground workers' self-activity theoretically and empirically and contribute to a fresh look at the field of study on workers' collective action by firmly inserting this within a clear class perspective.

In Chapter 7 Maurizio Atzeni deals with the issue of workers'control, workers' democratic decision-making power on production, and administration. While discussions and empirical studies on employee participation and involvement have represented an important stream of research in the field of the sociology of labour and industrial relations, the theoretical issues raised by the more radical experiences of workers' control have rarely found an audience, and this not just in the academic but also in the trade unions' sphere. Thus, as with other of the issues treated in this book, workers' control has for a long time been a forgotten theme of research despite its theoretical relevance and the historical recurrence of cases of workers' control. The drive for profitability, structuring the labour process in a hierarchical and segmented way, represents a material and ideologically powerful obstacle to the concrete manifestation of cases of workers' control. Cases of productive units run by workers cannot avoid the influence of the market in their decision-making processes. But the empirical manifestation of workers' control tells us also of the great transformative potential that workers' self-activity has in envisaging a more democratic and truly empowering working environment and, together with this, it tells us how workers' control might represent the seed for an alternative political economy, a political economy of the working class.

Chapter 8 starts the last part of the book, 'Contemporary Issues: Workers' Organising in the Global World'. In the chapter Massimiliano Mollona explores, from a social anthropology perspective, how different historical and geographical shifts in the capitalist pattern of production and different working classes' opposition to these shifts have changed our conceptualisation and understanding of what informal labour is and of the relation of this to wage work. The chapter is divided into three main sections. In the first is considered the emergence of informal labour in the context of the industrialisation of post-colonial Africa. In the second, the spread of informality in both the North and South is seen within the context of the flexible production model which started to develop worldwide in coincidence with the shift to neo-liberalism in the 1980s. In the third, recent changes in terms of patterns of development in the BRIC countries and their influence on the formal/informal composition of the workforce are analysed. Making use of social anthropologists in-depth ethnographic studies, Mollona's chapter evidences all the nuances and grey areas often existing between formal and informal, how they are mutually inter-related and how these interrelations, while responding to a specific model of capital accumulation and profitability are also built and reinforced by moral values and discourses associated to the different ways in which human labour is deployed.

In Chapter 9 Gregor Gall attempts to reflect on the extent to which labour conflict has been shaped by the emergence of new forms of collective action. The strike has been used traditionally by workers across the world, since it has always represented the most powerful tool in the hands of workers and trade unions to put pressure on governments and employers. While strikes remain today relevant in any analysis of forms of collective action, these have never been the only form taken by labour conflict. Occupations, industrial actions short of a strike, the use of non-disruptive methods to raise pub-lic awareness of workers' complaints, individual acts as part of a collective strategy, roadblocks and general strikes have also been used by workers. The ongoing economic and financial crisis, threatening employment and work-ing conditions, has increased the number of less traditional forms of labour conflict. Similarly, the changing landscape of global capitalism, with its new methods of flexible production and work organisation and the introduction of new communication technologies, displacing and separating workers, has reduced the role of the workplace as the site of action and forced workers to experiment with new forms of labour conflict. Against this background, in the transnational overview offered in the chapter, Gall argues, however, that completely new forms of labour conflict are rare and thus that the focus of attention should be not just on the innovative character of the form of labour conflict per se but also on the changing context surrounding workers. In this sense the use of a similar type of action can produce radically different out-comes depending on which group of workers is using it and on the existing cultural and social milieu.

In the last chapter, Immanuel Ness looks at the relations existing between governments' policies on migration, business strategies to reduce the cost of recruiting migrants, and workers' and trade unions' organising efforts to resist these strategies. The focus of the chapter is primarily on the US since this country's labour market has historically heavily relied on migrant workers.

But trends emerging there can be considered to a large extent common to other migration-receiving regions of the rich world. This can be said particularly for the reality emerging from the contradictions existing between political discourses emphasising the problems migration can generate on social cohesion and native workers' employability and more pragmatic business strategies of using migration to reduce production costs. Governments' policies on migration reflect these contradictions, resulting in practice in worsened salary and working conditions for both migrants and local workers. In the US, successive governments have, on the one hand, favoured the legal entry under certain conditions of selected categories of migrants, under the scheme of the guest workers programmes and, on the other hand, by toughening policies on illegal migration, have created a de facto new class of over-exploited, undocumented workers. While both categories of workers increase the reserve army of labour, guaranteeing capital interest of reducing costs by eroding wages and working conditions, guest workers are in a more precarious condition and are often reduced, by the very specific nature of their contracts, which include confinement to one employer, almost to the condition of indentured labourers, an increasingly important form of wage labour within global capitalism. The conditions of precariousness that affect both guest and undocumented migrants have produced, very often, spontaneous, unorganised forms of resistance with partial victories for workers who have gained a voice also through trade unions representation but, as Ness argues in the chapter, a further extension of the guest workers programme will jeopardise these efforts as it will legally allow employers to downgrade decent jobs in entire sectors of production. Indeed, globalisation has speeded up the restructuring of production not only by de-localisation to newly industrialising countries but also by using workers' increasing opportunities for cross border mobility.

REFERENCES

Amin, S. (2008), 'Foreword: rebuilding the unity of the labour front', in Bieler, A., Lindberg, I. and Devan, P., *Labour and the Challenges of Globalization. What Prospects for Transnational Solidarity?* London: Pluto Press.

Atzeni, M., Durán-Palma, F. and Ghigliani, P. (2011), 'Employment relations in Chile and Argentina', in A. Wilkinson and M. Barry, M. (eds), *Handbook of Comparative Employment Relations*, Cheltenham:Edward Elgar, pp. 129–52.

Atzeni, M. (2010), *Workplace Conflict*, Basingstoke: Palgrave Macmillan.

Barchiesi, F. (2011), *Precarious Liberation, Workers, the State, and Contested Social Citizenship in Postapartheid South Africa*, New York: SUNY Press.

Beck, U. (2000), *The Brave New World of Work*, Cambridge: Polity Press.

Bieler, A., Lindberg, I. and Pillay, D. (2008), *Labour and the Challenges of Globalization. What Prospects for Transnational Solidarity?* London: Pluto Press.

Bolton, S. and Houlihan, M. (2009), *Work Matters: Critical Reflections on Contemporary Work*, Basingstoke: Palgrave Macmillan.

De la Garza Toledo, E. (2011), *Trabajo no clásico, organización, y acción colectiva*, Mexico City, Mexico: UNAM.

Fairbrother, P. (2008) 'Social movement unionism or trade unions as social movements', *Employee Responsibilities and Rights Journal*, vol. 20, no. 2: 213–20.

Fernandez-Kelly, P. and Shefner, J. (2006), *Out of the Shadow. The Informal Economy in Latin America*, University Park, PA: Pennsylvania State University Press.

Fox Piven, F. (2008), 'Can power from below change the world?', *American Sociological Review*, vol. 73, no. 1, 1–14.

Glucksmann, M. (2009), 'Formations, connections and divisions of labour', *Sociology*, vol. 43, no. 5, 878–95.

Grugulis, I. and Bozkurt, O. (eds) (2011), *Retail Work*, Basingstoke: Palgrave Macmillan.

Hall, P. A. and Soskice, D. (eds) (2001), *Varieties of Capitalism: The Institutional Foundations of Comparative Advantage*, New York: Oxford University Press.

Harvey, D. (2005), *A Brief History of Neo-liberalism*, Oxford: Oxford University Press.

Harvey, D. (2010), *The Enigma of Capital and the Crises of Capitalism*, London: Profile Books.

Holloway, J. (2010), *Crack Capitalism*, London: Pluto Press.

Kelly, J. (1998), *Rethinking Industrial Relations*. London: LSE/Routledge.

Korczynski, M. and MacDonald, C.L. (2009), *Service Work: Critical Perspectives*, London: Routledge.

Lazar, S. (2012), 'A desire to formalize work? Comparing trade union strategies in Bolivia and Argentina', *Anthropology of Work Review*, vol. 33, no. 1, 15–24.

Lindell, I. (ed.) (2010) *Africa's Informal workers: Collective Agency, Alliances and Transnational Organizing in Urban Africa*. London: Zed Books.

Lukes, S. (1995), *Power. A Radical View*, 2nd edn, Basingstoke: Palgrave Macmillan.

McBride, J. and Greenwood, I. (2009), *Community Unionism*, Basingstoke: Palgrave Macmillan.

Mollona, M. (2009), *Made in Sheffield: An Ethnography of Industrial Work,* Oxford: Berghanh.

Moore, B., Jr., (1978), *Injustice. The Social Bases of Obedience and Revolt*, New York: M.E. Sharp.

Negri, A. (1992), Marx beyond Marx: Lessons on the Grundrisse, London/New York: Autonomedia/Pluto Press.

Picchio, A. (1992), *The Political Economy of the Labour Market,* Cambridge: Cambridge University Press.

Rainnie, A., McGrath-Champ, S. and Herod, A. (2010), 'Making space for geography in labour process theory', in P. Thompson and C. Smith, C. (eds), *Working Life. Renewing Labour Process Analysis*, Basingstoke: Palgrave Macmillan, pp. 219–313.

Sassen, S. (2001), *The Global City: New York, London, Tokyo*, New York: Princeton University Press.

Schurman, S. And Eaton, A. (2012), 'Trade union organizing in the informal economy: A review of the literature on organizing in Africa, Asia, Latin America, North America and Western, Central and Eastern Europe', Report to the Solidarity Centre. Available at: http://smlr.rutgers.edu/news-events/review-of-trade-union-organizing-in-informal-economy (accessed 23 July 2013).

Scott, J. C. (1990), *Domination and the Arts of Resistance: Hidden Transcripts*, New Haven: Yale University Press.

Simms, M., Holgate, J. and Heery, E. (2012), *Union Voices – Tactics and Tensions in UK Organizing*. Ithaca, New York: Cornell University Press.

Smith, C. and McKinlay, A. (2009), *Creative Labour*, Basingstoke: Palgrave Macmillan.

Standing, G. (2011), *The Precariat: The New Dangerous Class,* London and New York: Bloomsbury Academic.

Starosta, G. (2010), 'Global commodity chains and the Marxian law of value', *Antipode*, vol. 42, no. 2, 433–65.

Taylor, P. and Bain, P. (2005), 'India calling to the far away towns: The call centre labour process and globalization', *Work Employment and Society*, vol. 19, no. 2, 261–82.

Van der Linden, M. (2008), *Workers of the World: Essays Toward a Global Labour History*, Leiden: Brill.

Wills, J. et al. (2010), *Global Cities at Work: New Migrant Divisions of Labour*, London: Pluto Press.

part 1

THEORETICAL ISSUES: EXPLAINING THE CENTRALITY OF LABOUR WITHIN CAPITALISM

Part II

THEORETICAL ISSUES: EXPLAINING THE CENTRALITY OF LABOUR WITHIN CAPITALISM

1

MARX AND MARXIST VIEWS ON WORK AND THE CAPITALIST LABOUR PROCESS

David A. Spencer

INTRODUCTION

The writings of Karl Marx and the Marxist tradition offer a profound analysis of work. Marx combined an analysis of work as a vital human activity, with a critique of the form of work under capitalism. Work, in Marx's view, remained 'alienating' under capitalist conditions; however, it retained the potential to become a life-enhancing activity in a future communist society. The alienation of the worker from his or her work could not be overcome, according to Marx, without the abolition of capitalism, and the move to communism. Marx's analysis of work has remained, and continues to remain, a source of inspiration for critical work researchers as well as political activists.

Marxist analysis of work was renewed and reinvigorated in the 1970s. The pioneering work of Harry Braverman (1974) and others brought about a fresh debate about the application of Marx's original ideas to the study of the capitalist labour process. This debate has continued in the years that have followed (see Thompson and Newsome 2004). One of its fruits has been the development and promotion of 'labour process theory'. The latter, while still incorporating Marxist concepts and language, has forged its own path and has become progressively more open to different perspectives and approaches.

Labour process theory remains a prominent influence on critical scholarship on work in the sociology of work, industrial relations, and organisation theory (Thompson and Newsome, 2004; Thompson, 2010). It remains a matter of debate whether and in what ways the Marxist tradition can enrich the analysis of the capitalist labour process.

This chapter considers the contribution of Marx and some aspects of the Marxist tradition to the analysis of work. A few words of clarification need to be made at the outset. First, the writings of Marx on the topic of work are voluminous and cannot be fully considered in a single chapter. Readers interested in a fuller treatment of Marx's writings on work should consult other more detailed sources (see, for example, Sayers 2011). They could also consider reading some of the original work-related writings of Marx. Second, the Marxist literature on work is large and is impossible to summarise here. For example, although not covered below, there is a literature associated with the autonomist or workerist tradition in Marxism that deals with issues relating to the capitalist labour process, the bifurcation between work and labour, and struggles over and against labouring activity under capitalism (Cleaver, 2000; Holloway, 2010). Readers could follow up discussion presented below with further reading that draws on literatures such as those just highlighted. For the purposes of this chapter, particular attention will be given to the labour process debate. Although the latter was initially based in the UK, it has become much more international in scope and contributors. In addition, the issues it discusses, such as the nature of conflict between labour and capital in the workplace and the transformation of work under the imperative of capital accumulation, have wide relevance and apply to many different national contexts.

The organisation of the chapter is as follows. The next section identifies the importance of work as an activity within Marx's writings. The following section discusses Marx's key concept of alienation. The section after that considers Marx's discussion of exploitation and the organisation of work under capitalism. The subsequent section examines Marx's vision of work in a future communist society. The next two sections address (i) the contribution of Braverman, and (ii) Labour process theory as a prominent example of modern critical scholarship on work. The final section provides a conclusion.

THE IMPORTANCE OF WORK IN HUMAN LIFE

The activity of work occupies a central place in Marx's writings. Work is defined as an activity through which people engage with and transform nature in order to meet their material needs. It is necessary for people to produce things they need to live, and work has remained and will continue to remain a necessity. But work is so much more than just a route to consumption. As Marx emphasised, people are shaped and changed by the activity of work (Marx 1976: 283).

At one level, work is a social and communal activity. People forge important social connections via work and these have wider ramifications for the nature of society as a whole (Marx 1968: 80). Marx referred to the way that societies can be distinguished by the social organisation of work. How work is organised and how producers relate to one another has a direct bearing on the character of society. Marx's attempt to define societies on the basis of the form or mode of work that predominates in those societies forms a central part of his materialist approach to the study of history.[1]

At another level, work affects the development and overall well-being of people. Who people are and able to become is influenced by the work they do. Marx referred to the way that people realise and develop their capabilities and identities through the activity of work. Work is not just a chore to be endured; it is also a potentially liberating activity that can improve the life experiences of people.

To see this last point, consider the below quote from the *Grundrisse*, in which Marx challenges Adam Smith's depiction of work as 'toil and trouble'. Smith had maintained that people would want to avoid work because its performance would deprive them of their freedom. He also maintained that the experience of work would be negative: people would prefer to spend their time doing activities other than work (see Smith 1976: vol. 1, 47).[2] Marx responded to Smith in the following way:

> It seems quite far from Smith's mind that the individual, 'in his normal state of health, strength, activity, skill, facility', also needs a normal portion of work, and of the suspension of tranquillity. Certainly, labour obtains its measure from the outside, through the aim to be attained and the obstacles to be overcome in attaining it. But Smith has no inkling whatever that this overcoming of obstacles is in itself a liberating activity – and that, further, the external aims become stripped of the semblance of merely external natural urgencies, and become posited as aims which the individual himself posits – hence as self-realisation, objectification of the subject, hence real freedom, whose action is, precisely, labour.
>
> (Marx 1973: 610)

Several aspects of the above quote can be commented upon. One aspect concerns the stress that is placed on work as a positive undertaking. The 'overcoming of obstacles' as a part of work is seen as a potentially 'liberating activity'. Indeed, work can become so absorbing and interesting that it is pursued for its own sake, rather than just for the sake of its 'external ends'. Marx was clear that work could be a means for 'self-realisation' and 'real freedom' and he disputed the attempt made by Adam Smith and other classical economists to draw a direct association between work and unhappiness. To be sure, as will be shown below, Marx recognised that work would be resisted by workers; however, he sought to link this resistance to the form of work evident under capitalism. The mistake of classical political economy was to miss the historical origins of work resistance and to omit consideration of possible ways to overcome the costs of work by the transcendence of capitalism.

To emphasise the importance of work even further, Marx categorised work as a part of the 'species being' of mankind. Through work, people could affirm and realise their humanity. Humans are not sloth-like, but rather are productive and creative beings, with an urge to shape and change nature. In Marx's words: 'the productive life is the life of the species. It is life-engendering life. The whole character of a species – its species-character – is contained in the character of its life activity; and free, conscious activity is man's species-character' (Marx 1977: 68).

To summarise, Marx stressed the positive sides of work. He dismissed arguments that work is universally a 'bad thing', and instead pointed to the way that society creates and reproduces an aversion to work. Work could be and indeed ought to be a fulfilling and satisfying activity (see Sayers, 2005). In Marx's view, as argued below, the prime impediment to the achievement of work as a positive and fulfilling activity is the capitalist system of work.

WORK AND THE ALIENATION OF THE WORKER

Marx's writings on work incorporated the idea of 'alienation'. Marx first introduced this idea in the *Economic and Philosophical Manuscripts*, written in the early 1840s. It continued to figure in Marx's later writings. Alienation, in essence, refers to the inability of people to exercise control over the work they do. While Marx argued that alienation had existed in slave and feudal societies, he felt it took on a particular form under capitalism. In capitalist society, the means of production are owned by the capitalist class, and the working class as the majority class must offer their labour services for hire in order to survive. The lack of control exercised by workers over the way that work is organised and conducted, Marx argued, has a profound negative influence on the quality of work life.

Marx identified four different dimensions of alienation under capitalism. First, workers are alienated from the product of their own labour because it is owned by the capitalists who hire them for a specified period of time. They are unable to use the things that they produce to sustain life, since these things are the property of capitalists. Marx stressed that the workers' alienation would grow in proportion to the amount of commodities they create in production. Under normal circumstances, it would be expected that greater production would advance the welfare of workers, by enlarging the goods available to them. Yet, in capitalism, the reverse is the case. By adding to the volume of produced commodities, workers only increase the 'hostile and alien' force that dominates their lives (Marx 1977: 64). For Marx, increased production leads necessarily to the impoverishment of the working class:

> It is true that labour produces wonderful things for the rich – but for the worker it produces privation. It produces palaces – but for the worker, hovels. It produces beauty – but for the worker, deformity. It replaces labour by machines, but it throws one section of the workers back to a barbarous type of labour, and it turns the other section into a machine. It produces intelligence – but for the worker, stupidity, and cretinism.
>
> (Marx 1977: 65)

Second, it is argued that workers are alienated from the activity of work itself. In working for capitalists, workers relinquish control over the direction of their own labour within production. What and how work is done is decided upon by capitalists, not workers. Marx stressed that this loss of control over the labour process would mean that work itself would no longer exist as a creative force; rather it would be viewed by workers as a purely functional activity that is performed to earn wages. Marx indicated, too, that the power of capitalists in production would be used to the disadvantage of workers; under the pressure to make profit, capitalists would find it in their own interests to lengthen work time, and to intensify work (see below). In these ways, the alienation of workers from work itself would grow even more severe.

The third dimension of alienation is the estrangement of workers from their 'species being'. As pointed out above, Marx viewed the ability to participate in creative work as an essential part of human nature. The fact that under capitalism workers are unable to exercise any direct control over the product and process of labour means that they are effectively denied the opportunity to work creatively. Work, instead of being the source of self-realisation, becomes a simple means to income and is associated with endless toil and drudgery.

Finally, Marx referred to the alienation of workers from their fellow human beings. Workers confront their own estrangement from their 'species being' in the lives of other workers who are equally degraded and dehumanised by the experience of work. Self-estrangement forms the basis for the 'estrangement of man from man' (Marx 1977: 69). Further, workers are alienated from one another by the fragmentation of tasks which undermines co-operation, by the imposition of a hierarchical work structure which pits workers against one another, and by the lack of any form of collective decision-making over the organisation and control of work.

Marx argued that alienation ultimately is the source of great misery to the working class as a whole and is the cause of opposition to the activity of work itself. According to Marx, under capitalism:

> The worker...only feels himself outside his work, and in his work feels outside himself. He feels at home when he is not working, and when he is working he does not feel at home. His labour is therefore not voluntary but coerced; it is *forced labour*. It is therefore not the satisfaction of a need; it is merely a *means* to satisfy needs external to it. Its alien character emerges clearly in the fact that as soon as no physical or other compulsion exists, labour is shunned like the plague.
>
> (Marx 1977: 66; emphasis in original)

Here we can note that Marx stresses the historical roots of the temporal divide between work and leisure, and argues that instrumental attitudes towards work, instead of being a ubiquitous feature of reality, are in fact the product of capitalism. Workers possess a positive preference for leisure and a negative preference for work, not because of their natural proclivity for idleness, but instead because of their 'alienation' in capitalist production. Marx argued that the commonsense view of work as an unpleasant necessity is symptomatic of the alienated experience of work under capitalism (see Sayers 2005). Indeed, such a view plays a vital role in justifying the suffering of the working class by denying that anything can be done to resolve the costs of work.

Marx contended that alienation would not just affect the working class; it would also impact on the capitalist class as well. Capitalists have no way of realising their true humanity, since their own needs are subordinated to those of capital accumulation. All members of capitalist society effectively are enslaved by the structures and processes of capitalism: their lives are governed by conditions that appear to exist independently of them, and over which they have no control. While commodities express definite social relations between people, as Marx (1976: 165) put it, these relations assume 'the fantastic form of a relation between things'. Capital, value, money and so on command power over the lives of people and restrict the opportunity for free creative activity (see Fromm 1961: 49).

In *The Holy Family*, Marx and Engels indicated that while capitalists are alienated under capitalism they have material interests in not overcoming this situation:

> The propertied class and the class of the proletariat present the same human self-estrangement. But the former class feels at ease and strengthened in this self-alienation, it recognises estrangement *as its own power* and has in it the *semblance* of a human existence. The latter feels annihilated in estrangement; it sees in it its own powerlessness and the reality of an inhuman existence.
> (Marx and Engels 1975: 36; emphasis in original)

In spite of their alienation, capitalists would defend capitalism in order to ensure that their own material advantage over the working class is preserved. In contrast, Marx envisaged that the working class would come to develop an awareness of its own alienation under capitalism and would seek to negate the power of capitalists. Marx saw proletariat revolution as a necessary and inevitable consequence of the development of capitalist society. Such a revolution would bring about the negation of alienation and the restoration of work as a freely creative activity. Marx's vision of work under a future communist society is considered later under the heading 'Achieving a non-alienating form of work'. In the next section, we examine Marx's views on exploitation under capitalism and on the nature and development of capitalist work relations.

EXPLOITATION AND THE ORGANISATION OF WORK

Marx explained how workers are exploited under capitalism. Workers appear to receive wages that represent full payment for the time they work in production when, in fact, their wages cover only the 'necessary labour time' that is required to meet their own needs. During 'surplus' or 'unpaid' labour time, workers produce 'surplus value' that enables the capitalists who hire them to make a profit (see Fine and Saad-Filho 2003). Marx stressed how exploitation is an endemic aspect of capitalism and how it could not be removed by any kind of reform of the labour market or work organisation. Exploitation, he argued, could only be resolved by the removal of capitalism.

In the pursuit of increases in surplus value production, capitalists would adopt various different methods. One method would be to increase the number of hours worked by workers. Longer work hours would directly benefit capitalists by increasing the length of unpaid labour time. However, extensions in work time ran the risk of undermining the productivity and health of workers. Marx suggested that, while in the early stages of capitalism, capitalists would look to increase work hours in order to increase surplus value production, in later stages they would adopt more subtle and ingenious methods. Such methods essentially consisted in efforts to reduce the length of necessary labour time. The latter could be achieved by technological improvements that result in a cheapening in the commodities consumed by workers. Marx's view was that capitalists would use technology to increase unpaid labour time relative to paid labour time:

> The objective of the development of the productivity of labour within the context of capitalist production is the shortening of that part of the working day in which the worker must work for himself, and the lengthening, thereby, of the other part of that day, in which he is free to work for nothing for the capitalist.

> (Marx 1976: 438)

The technological and organisational changes occurring within capitalist production, while enabling capitalists to increase surplus value, bring only misery to workers. On the one hand, workers face having to perform more simple tasks in production and are reduced to mere executors of tasks prescribed by capitalists. On the other hand, they confront the prospect of performing work more intensively and with fewer opportunities for discretion and control. In vivid prose, Marx set out what he saw as the negative consequences of factory work on the lives and well-being of workers:

> Factory work exhausts the nervous system to the uttermost; at the same time, it does away with the many-sided play of the muscles, and confiscates every atom of freedom, both in bodily and intellectual activity. Even the lightening of the labour becomes an instrument of torture, since the machine does not free the worker from work, but rather deprives the work itself of all content. Every kind of capitalist production, in so far as it is not only a labour process but also capital's process of valorisation, has this in common, but it is not the worker who employs the conditions of his work, but rather the reverse, the conditions of work employ the worker.

> (Marx 1976: 548)

What had the potential to liberate workers from common drudgery, machinery, thus had become under capitalism a mechanism to control and exploit them. In the capitalist workplace:

> all means for the development of production undergo a dialectical inversion so that they become means of domination and exploitation of the producers; they distort

the worker into a fragment of man, they degrade him to the level of an appendage of a machine, they destroy the actual content of his labour by turning it into a torment.

(Marx 1976: 799)

There are, though, inherent contradictions in the development of capital- ist production. While the use of technology gives to capital the ability to increase surplus value, it also brings forth a tendency for the rate of profit to fall. Marx believed that a reduction in the profit rate would come about through the effects of labour saving technical change (see Fine and Saad-Filho 2004). Further, he argued that political struggle against capitalist exploitation would grow over time as workers come to realise the opposition between their own interests and those of capital. Notwithstanding the controlling force of technology and the existence of unemployment caused by technical change, workers would come to acquire the collective strength and organisation to challenge the power of capital. As Marx wrote, while the constant revolution of the labour process:

> creates the real conditions for the domination of labour by capital, perfecting the process and providing it with the appropriate framework . . . by evolving conditions of production and communication and productive forces of labour antagonistic to the workers involved in them, this revolution creates the real premises of a new mode of production, one that abolishes the contradictory form of capitalism. It thereby creates the material basis of a newly shaped social process and hence of a new social formation.

(Marx 1976: 1065)

In effect, the very processes which augment capitalist domination would also tend towards its demise. Marx claimed that capitalism would ultimately founder under its own internal contradictions. As we will see below, in the move to communism, Marx believed that work would become a fulfilling activity.

ACHIEVING A NON-ALIENATING FORM OF WORK

Marx was dismissive of policy and political agendas that sought to reform cap- italism. Higher wages advocated by trade unions, for example, were viewed as 'nothing but *better payment for the slave*', for they 'would not win either for the worker or for labour their human status and dignity' (Marx 1977: 72–3; emphasis in original).[3] Work could not be rendered as non-exploitative and non-alienating without the abolition of capitalism itself.

Marx did not have that much to say about the nature of a future communist society. What he did say, however, gave some useful insights into Marx's thinking about the potential benefits of communism as a rival to capitalism. Marx thought that in the move to communism a general transformation in work would occur. On the one hand, technology would be used to create additional free time for people to perform activities of their own choosing. Under capitalism, as suggested above, technology is used to create profit for capitalists. Under communism, it would be used to enlarge the 'realm of freedom' in which people can develop their own individualities (Marx 1992: 959). Marx's view was that communism would re-harness the technology of capitalism in order to increase time for creative activities. On the other hand, communism would enable people to experience fulfilment in work. With technology used to eliminate drudgery and with work carried out for the collective good, people would come to realise in work their innate creative capacities (see Sayers 2003; 2011). As Marx wrote:

> It is self-evident that if labour-time is reduced to a normal length and, furthermore, labour is no longer performed for someone else, but for myself, and, at the same time, the social contradictions between master and men, etc., being abolished, it acquires a quite different, a free character, it becomes real social labour, and finally the basis of *disposable time* – the *labour* of a man who has also disposable time, must be of a much higher quality than that of the beast of burden.
>
> (Marx 1972: 257; emphasis in original)

Marx indicated how the 'free character' of work under communism would produce not just improvements in the quality of work but also gains in the output of workers. Capitalism places artificial constraints on productivity via the hierarchal and coercive nature of the capital–labour relation. Communism, by contrast, would help to raise the attractiveness of work by providing work opportunities that draw upon the capabilities of workers and that aim to meet the needs of the community. Under communism, people would have greater opportunities both inside and outside work to realise their talents and this would pave the way for further improvements to technology, adding to the potential for greater free time.

Marx referred directly to what he saw as the positive transformation that would occur in the character of work under conditions where people 'carried out production as human beings':

> Let us suppose that we had carried out production as human beings. Each of us would have in two ways affirmed himself and the other person. 1) In my production I would have objectified my individuality, its specific character, and therefore

enjoyed not only an individual manifestation of my life during the activity, but also when looking at the object I would have the individual pleasure of knowing my personality to be objective, visible to the senses and hence a power beyond all doubt. 2) In your enjoyment or use of my product I would have the direct enjoyment both of being conscious of having satisfied a human need by my work, that is, of having objectified man's essential nature, and of having thus created an object corresponding to the need of another man's essential nature. 3) I would have been for you the mediator between you and the species, and therefore would become recognised and felt by you yourself as a completion of your own essential nature and as a necessary part of yourself, and consequently would know myself to be confirmed both in your thought and your love. 4) In the individual expression of my life I would have directly created your expression of your life, and therefore in my individual activity I would have directly confirmed and realised my true nature, my human nature, my communal nature.

Our products would be so many mirrors in which we saw reflected our essential nature.

This relationship would moreover be reciprocal; what occurs on my side has also to occur on yours.

(Marx 1975: 227–8)

This emotive passage conveys Marx's thinking about the way in which work would become a life-affirming activity under communism. People, in short, would gain enjoyment from producing things that not only realise their own creative needs but also meet real social needs. The gains from work both for workers and society as a whole are to be contrasted with the state of affairs under capitalism. Within capitalist society, workers suffer alienation in work and work is carried out for the sake of making a profit for the capitalist class. Under communism, however, workers would come to experience work as 'a *free manifestation of life*, hence an *enjoyment of life*' (Marx 1975: 228; emphasis in original) and work would be pursed for the benefit of all in society.

In order to enhance individual capabilities under communism, Marx saw it as important that individual workers be given the opportunity to vary their work tasks. In contrast to writers like Adam Smith, Marx did not see any necessary or permanent role for the division of labour as a means to increase labour productivity. Rather, in a future communist society, each person would be able 'to do one thing today another tomorrow, to hunt in the morning, fish in the afternoon, rear cattle in the evening, criticise after dinner ... without ever becoming hunter, fisherman, shepherd or critic' (Marx and Engels 1976: 53). The point is that under communism no one individual would be confined to the same task for the rest of their days and there would be opportunities for people to move between different tasks. The fact that people had collective ownership over production and some say over what work they do would help to strengthen incentives to work and to raise labour productivity.

Marx's discussion of communism emphasised the idea that work is not irredeemably irksome; rather its character as a scourge on human life is peculiar to capitalism and is resolvable by the creation of a communist society. It was emphasised that for people to find intrinsic benefit in work they first had to be given the freedom to develop their creative capacities in as many activities as possible and this requires of necessity a reduction in the length of the working day. Working under communal conditions and free to pursue activities for their own ends, Marx contended, people would come to develop an interest in performing work for its own sake.

Critics may point out that Marx's outline of communism is impressionistic and utopian. They might also argue that real world experiments in 'communism' have failed. But this is perhaps unfair on Marx. Marx thought that the character of communism could not be fully worked out until capitalism had been eliminated. Our collective imagination of alternatives would not be truly realised until the demise of capitalism. Further, the systems of work evident under some previous communist regimes resembled those present under capitalism: the much-maligned practices of 'scientific management', for example, were implemented in the Soviet Union (Charlie Chaplin's bleak representation of working life in his film *Modern Times* (1936) was as much a challenge to communist Russia as capitalist America). There is also the point that communism has not yet developed, as Marx envisaged, through the full development of capitalism. Previous experiments in 'communism' largely took place under circumstances where capitalism had not fully developed and they cannot be interpreted as true 'tests' of the veracity of Marx's arguments in favour of a communist system. That said, there are many questions that Marx's discussion of communism leave unanswered and there is still much to be worked out in assessing the nature and viability of a communist society. Even for non-Marxists, however, Marx's writings offer useful lessons about the possibility and necessity for building a system of work that is compatible with human creative as well as material needs.

BRAVERMAN AND THE REVIVAL OF MARXIAN SCHOLARSHIP ON THE CAPITALIST LABOUR PROCESS

The publication in 1974 of Braverman's *Labour and Monopoly Capital* brought about a revival of Marxist scholarship on the capitalist labour process. This seminal work attempted to interpret the transformation of work during the twentieth century through the lens of Marx's original analysis of work. Braverman argued that the ideas of Marx and Marxist political economy could be used to identify and understand the degradation of work that had occurred and was continuing to occur in the era of 'monopoly capitalism'. He showed how science and technology are not neutral forces, but instead they are harnessed by capitalists to exploit and alienate workers. Politically, Braverman contributed to the critique of capitalism by showing the limits to human progress imposed by developments within the capitalist labour process. As we shall see below, while Braverman became the inspiration for the subsequent 'labour process debate', his influence on the analysis of the labour process under capitalism has waned over time.

Braverman, like Marx, sought to relate changes in the capitalist labour process to the broader process of capital accumulation. Under the pressure to accumulate capital, capitalists must constantly adapt and overhaul production. Braverman focused, in particular, on the tendency for capitalists to reduce the skilfulness of work. Reductions in the skilfulness of work enable capitalists to increase their power over workers. By increasing their power, capitalists are able to achieve their broader aim of securing an increase in surplus value. A key contribution of Braverman was to identify and explain a tendency towards de-skilling and to show how this tendency is born of a drive by capitalists to subordinate workers within production. He gave special attention to the process of scientific management as a mechanism that assisted capitalists in turning workers into more pliant and reliable inputs into production.

Now, Braverman was aware that his work contained some limitations. For example, it neglected the subjective element of the labour process and instead concentrated on the system-wide forces acting upon and transforming the capitalist labour process (see Braverman 1974: 27). Braverman wrote that while it was important to focus on subjects and subjectivity it was also essential to consider the broader economic and political context in which work relations are situated. This point was made in part because of what Braverman saw as weaknesses in established sociological research on work. Sociologists of work, he argued, had tended to focus on the particularities of work and workplaces and had not properly considered the systematic nature and dynamic of the capitalist labour process. Braverman, by contrast, wanted to capture the big picture and to develop an integrative account and critique of work and work relations under capitalism.

The approach that Braverman proposed was in no way deterministic. To the contrary, he drew insight from Marx's dialectical approach to comprehend what he saw as the complex determination of science and technology in society

(Braverman 1974: 21). He emphasised how the development of society in general is itself highly complex and does not conform to some fixed pattern. 'Social determinacy', wrote Braverman,

> does not have the fixity of a chemical reaction, but is a *historic process*. The concrete and determinate forms of society are indeed 'determined' rather than accidental, but this is the determinacy of the thread-by-thread weaving of the fabric of history, not the imposition of external formulas.
>
> (Braverman 1974: 21; emphasis in original)

Turning to the transformation of the capitalist labour process, Braverman again stressed the role of historical and social mediation. He stated, on the one hand, how '[t]he subjective factor of the labour process is removed to a place among its inanimate objective factors' (Braverman 1974: 171). Yet, on the other hand, he stressed how this is only 'the ideal towards which management tends', one which can be 'realised by capital only within definite limits, and unevenly among industries' (Braverman 1974: 171–2). The attempt made by capitalists to separate mental and manual labour 'is itself restrained in its application by the nature of the various specific and determinate processes of production. Moreover, its very application brings into being new crafts and skills and technical specialities that are at first the province of labour rather than management' (Braverman 1974: 172). Not only do contingencies in the workplace produce counter-pressures against de-skilling forces, but also scientific management itself requires, if only for a temporary period, the creation of new skills and competencies (Armstrong 1987: 146). In Braverman's account, workers are not relinquished of skills in a straightforward and inexorable fashion. Instead, the process is presented as altogether more complex, involving frequent shifts, setbacks and transformations.

Braverman's so-called 'de-skilling thesis', in short, represents no more than a tendency inherent within capitalism that can never be realised in some complete and all-conquering form. The contradictions and counter-pressures created by the separation of mental and manual labour do not refute the 'law of de-skilling' as such, but rather indicate its actual causal movement and dynamic. Those who doubt the subtlety of Braverman's analysis need to consider his important comment that:

> the shape of our society, the shape of any given society, is not an instantaneous creation of 'laws' which generate that society on the spot and before our eyes. Every society is a moment in the historical process, and can be grasped only as part of that process.
>
> (Braverman 1974: 21)

Although Braverman identified de-skilling as an important systematic tendency under capitalism, he neither posited nor sought an invariant law of de-skilling. He emphasised that de-skilling would only be actualised where conditions allowed it to develop. At a minimum, this demonstrated the possibility and opportunity for collective opposition to the degradation of work.

There are, nonetheless, some weak points in Braverman's work. His emphasis upon the disciplinary role of science and technology in the workplace can be seen to be partial and one-sided. Braverman tended to see capitalists as engaged in a constant struggle to subordinate and control workers. Two points can be made here. The first point is that the controlling influence of capitalists over workers is limited. Even with traditional production line technology, workers are still able to disrupt production and capitalists must rely on some element of consent from workers to achieve their goals. The second point is that capitalists have interests in eliciting the consent of workers, in addition to directly controlling them. Without such consent, indeed, there would be little opportunity for capitalists to utilise the creativity and ingenuity of their workforce. Braverman's neglect of the creation and management of consent at work can be seen as a key missing element in his work. An important contribution of modern research on the labour process, as we shall see below, has been to demonstrate the co-determination of control and consent in the management of labour, going beyond Braverman's account of the way in which capitalists manage the labour process.

MODERN DEBATES ON THE CAPITALIST LABOUR PROCESS

The work of Braverman along with other Marxist research on the capitalist labour process (CSE 1976; Friedman 1977; Burawoy 1979) provided the basis for the labour process debate. One outcome of this debate has been the development of labour process theory that has become more variegated and more accommodating of different viewpoints over time. It, for example, took a postmodern turn in the 1990s. Nonetheless, there have been continued efforts to sustain and promote a 'core' labour process theory that retains roots in a radical (though not necessarily Marxist) political economy (see Thompson and Newsome 2004; Thompson 2010).

The labour process debate in its early stages was essentially a debate around the merits and demerits of Braverman's *Labour and Monopoly Capitalism* (1974). While most researchers welcomed and praised the contribution of Braverman, they also signalled the need to extend, revise, and even reject the approach taken by Braverman. The common criticism then as now is that Braverman painted a too narrow and restrictive picture of developments in the workplace. His depiction of workers as being overwhelmed by capitalist control strategies and his identification of a de-skilling tendency derived from the capital accumulation process are seen to have overlooked important detail as to how work relations are conducted and governed in the real world. Much early research in labour process theory sought to fill some gaps left by Braverman. Friedman (1977), for example, explained how workers are managed in the workplace via strategies of direct control and responsible autonomy. Burawoy (1979), from a different perspective, focused on the importance of workers' consent to work. Based on ethnographic research, he showed how consent is manufactured in the workplace through the formal and informal practices and activities of the workplaces. Burawoy's important and highly insightful contribution inherited from Braverman an understanding of surplus value production; however, he looked to develop a more detailed analysis of the processes that led to the extraction as well as obfuscation of surplus value within production.

While authors such as Burawoy retained some of the core aspects of Braverman's work, other subsequent contributions to the labour process debate looked to take their own path that ultimately led away from Braverman and also Marx. In the 1980s, attention increasingly turned to concrete issues of skill and managerial control and this had the effect of reducing the scope of labour process research. One casualty of this turn was the neglect of 'the larger political economy picture' (Thompson 2010: 8): labour process research became more focused on the minutiae of individual workplaces and the broader processes of capital accumulation and competition were relatively neglected (see also Nichols 1999: 115). Subsequent research only worsened this trend. The embrace of postmodernism in the 1990s pushed labour process research in the direction of protracted discussion around the issue of subjectivity (O'Doherty and Willmott 2001). The analysis of the subjective side of work was not without merit, but the focus on issues relating to the individual and self-identity tended to dominate discourse, to the exclusion of wider concerns concerning capital accumulation and exploitation. To be sure, there remained discussion about capital–labour conflict and even emancipation, but this discussion retained no clear root in either Marxism or a radical political economy. This disconnect led to criticism that labour process theory was losing its theoretical and political focus as well as distinctiveness (see Nichols 1999; Spencer 2000).

Rejecting both postmodernism and the focus on contingent relations at the level of the workplace, some leading protagonists have called for a restatement of the 'core' principles of labour process theory. This move is in part a reaction against a perceived loss of direction in the labour process debate itself. But it is also an effort to renew the contribution of labour process theory as a lens through which to understand the transformation of work in contemporary capitalism. Thompson (2010) has stressed that at its heart labour process theory is concerned with the way that labour power as a commodity is converted into labour under the exigencies of capital accumulation. Following this, four core principles of labour process theory have been identified (see Thompson and Newsome 2004: 134–5; Thompson 2010: 10). First, the labour process is essential to economic as well as human reproduction, and, as such, emphasis must be given to the role of labour and the capital–labour relationship. Second, there is a 'logic of accumulation' that puts pressure on capital to continually transform the production process. Here there is recognition of the economic imperatives that impact on the nature and transformation of work under capitalism. Third, there is a 'control imperative' that leads capital to reduce the 'indeterminacy gap' between labour power and labour. Capitalists face the problem of converting workers' potential to work (labour power) into actual work done (labour) and their success in addressing this problem depends on their ability to exert some control over workers. Fourth, there is a 'structured antagonism' between capital and labour that in turns produces conflicting processes of conflict and co-operation in the workplace. At a basic (class) level, the interests of workers and capitalists are in opposition; however, in concrete terms, workers have interests in complying at work if only to stay in their jobs while capitalists have interests in gaining the consent of workers in order to realise the creativity contained in labour power.

The above four principles are inspired either directly or indirectly by insights taken from Marxist political economy. While they are undoubtedly useful as a starting point for an analysis of the capitalist labour process, they also require some development if they are to be applied successfully. For example, the appeal to capital accumulation requires consideration of the wider context in which work relations are situated. That is, it requires going beyond the labour process as such. The 'connectivity problem' as Thompson and Newsome (2004: 133) term it, is resolvable only by developing a more integrative approach to labour process research that consists in an awareness of how the labour process connects with the broader processes and tendencies of capital accumulation.

It should be mentioned that 'core' labour process theory represents a departure from Marx in some key respects: see, in particular, Thompson and Newsome (2004: 137) who refer to labour process theory as 'post-Marxist'. It rejects, for example, the labour theory of value and thereby the theory of exploitation as originally developed by Marx (Thompson 2010: 11–12). It also dispenses with Marx's so-called 'gravedigger' thesis that implies that capitalism will give way to communism by a revolution led by the working class. Some criticism of Marx's certainty on revolution is doubtless in order (see Hyman 2006: 48). The shift away from value theory is more debatable, however. For if properly understood, value theory can offer help to the understanding of how the labour process interconnects with the broader system of production under capitalism (see Spencer 2000).[4] There are certainly some who would contend that labour process theory would be well-served by re-examining its relationship with the Marxist tradition (see Nichols, 1999).[5]

Thompson (2010: 13) has argued for a renewed focus on 'the connections between the capitalist political economy and the labour process'.[6] Similar sentiments have been expressed by Nichols (1999) and Spencer (2000). Indeed, it is important that the capitalist labour process be located in a political economy framework. Often research on work can become focused on the particularities of individual workplaces and can lose sight of how these individual workplaces fit into the political economy of capitalism. Future research on the labour process under capitalism, it can be argued, will only succeed in grasping the 'bigger picture' if it integrates material from different disciplines. A renewed political economy of the labour process, in short, requires a renewed political economy tradition. Here the continued fragmentation of the social sciences can be seen as an impediment to a revival of a political economy approach to the study of the capitalist labour process. But with Thompson and Nichols it is to be hoped that despite the obstacles such an approach can be forged and promoted as a part of wider theorisation and critique of capitalist production relations. Here one can argue that Marxist political economy can offer real help in integrating material from across the social sciences and in providing a focal point for opposition to the structures and imperatives of the capitalist labour process.

CONCLUSION

This chapter has shown how work is a central aspect of the writings of Marx as well as a key theme in the Marxist tradition. Marx regarded work as a vital human activity. Human beings are seen to realise their essential being in work. Unlike many rival conceptualisations of work, Marx did not consider that work is universally and inevitably irksome. Quite to the contrary, he maintained that humans are animated and uplifted by the work they do. Given the right conditions, work can be a source of fulfilment and pleasure for workers.

However, Marx pointed out that under capitalism workers suffer alienation. The fact that workers cannot control the work they do and the fact that work is orientated to profit creation reduces the creative and intrinsic benefits of work. Work, in effect, becomes for workers a means to an end: a source of drudgery and pain that is routinely 'shunned like the plague'. Marx's theory of alienation offers a powerful demonstration of the human costs of work under capitalism. But this theory is so much more than just a critique of work as it exists in capitalist society. It is also a demonstration of the possibility of creating a different and superior form of work. Marx argued that capitalism would give way to communism and that the move to communism would lead to the realisation of a form of non-alienating work. In a future communist society, people would work under relations of mutual recognition and would be afforded the free time to develop their own capacities in activities that they themselves chose to undertake. Such conditions, Marx argued, would enable workers to experience their work as fulfilling.

Interest in Marx's ideas on work has been sustained to some extent through the labour process debate. The latter has produced much valuable research on the nature and outcomes of the labour process under capitalism. One significant insight concerns the complex balance between consent and conflict at the heart of the capitalist employment relationship. Yet, it is also clear that the labour process debate is in need of development and revision. Even leading proponents of labour process theory have suggested that labour process theory needs to develop an understanding of the place of the labour process in the system of capitalism as a whole. The argument here would be that research on the capitalist labour process can still learn lessons from the Marxist tradition and that attempts to develop a 'post-Marxist' approach to the capitalist labour process are liable to present more problems than they solve. In arguing this point, one does not mean to suggest that the Marxist tradition offers answers to all questions. But it does suggest the need to engage with Marxist concepts and theories to forge a distinctive and critical analysis of the capitalist labour process. Beyond theory, such an analysis would also like Marx seek to agitate for change and to press for a form of work that fits with rather than subverts humanity.

NOTES

1. The emphasis given by Marx to work in the formation of people and society is well illustrated in the following quote: 'The way in which men produce their means of subsistence depends first of all on the nature of the means of subsistence they actually find in existence and have to reproduce. This mode of production must not be considered

simply as being the production of the physical existence of the individuals. Rather it is a definite form of activity of these individuals, a definite form of expressing their life, a definite *mode of life* on their part. As individuals express their life, so they are. What they are, therefore, coincides with their production, both with *what* they produce and with *how* they produce. Hence what individuals are depends on the material conditions of their production. (Marx and Engels 1976: 37; emphasis in original.)

2. A negative conceptualisation of work has been a dominant feature of economics discourse (see Spencer 2009).

3. Marx suggested that trade unions could play a role in organising and mobilising the working class; However, they had to progress beyond a merely reformist agenda and promote the ultimate goal of revolution.

4. For a restatement of Marx's value theory, see Brown (2008). For a discussion of its relevance to the study of labour (market) issues, see Fine (1998).

5. As Nichols (1999: 115) puts it, 'looking to the future, it would be a welcome step forward were it to be accepted that "labour process" is not a sexy phrase for "work organisation", and that the study of the labour process should be related to that of a valorisation process (or what we might simply term a surplus producing process)'.

6. Thompson has also advocated the incorporation of critical realism into labour process research (see Thompson and Vincent 2010).

REFERENCES

Armstrong, P. (1987) 'Labour and monopoly capital', in R. Hyman and W. Streeck (eds) *New Technology and Industrial Relations*, Oxford: Basil Blackwell, pp. 143–60.

Braverman, H. (1974) *Labour and Monopoly Capital*, New York: Monthly Review.

Brown, A. (2008) 'A Materialist Development of Some Recent Contributions to the Labour Theory of Value', *Cambridge Journal of Economics*, vol. 32, 125–46.

Burawoy, M. (1979) *Manufacturing Consent: Changes in the Labour Process Under Monopoly Capitalism*, Chicago: University of Chicago.

Cleaver, H. (2000) *Reading Capital Politically*, Oakland: AK Press.

CSE (Conference of Socialist Economics) (1976) *The Labour Process and Class Strategies.* Pamphlet, no.1, London: Stage 1.

Fine, B. (1998) *Labour Market Theory: A Constructive Reassessment*, London: Routledge.

Fine, B. and Saad-Filho A. (2003) *Marx's 'Capital'*, 4th edn, London: Pluto Press.

Friedman, A. (1977) 'Responsible autonomy and direct control', *Capital and Class*, vol. 1, 43–57.

Fromm, E. (1961) *Marx's Concept of Man*, New York: Ungar.

Holloway, J. (2010) *Crack Capitalism*, London: Pluto Press.

Hyman, R. (2006) 'Marxist thought and the analysis of work', in M. Korczynski, R. Hodson, and P. Edwards (eds), *Social Theory at Work*, Oxford: Oxford University Press, pp. 26–55.

Marx, K. (1968) 'Wage labour and capital', in *Marx/Engels. Selected Works in One Volume*, London: Lawrence and Wishart, pp. 71–93.

Marx, K. (1972) *Theories of Surplus Value*, part 3, London: Lawrence and Wishart.

Marx, K. (1973) *Grundrisse*, Harmondsworth: Penguin.

Marx, K. (1975) 'Comments on James Mill', in *Marx and Engels: Collected Works*, vol. 3, London: Lawrence and Wishart, pp. 211–28.

Marx, K. (1976) *Capital*, vol. 1, trans. Ben Fowkes, London: Penguin.

Marx, K. (1977) *Economic and Philosophic Manuscripts*, London: Lawrence and Wishart.

Marx, K, and Engels, F. (1975) *The Holy Family*, in *Marx and Engels: Collected Works*, vol. 4, London: Lawrence and Wishart, pp. 5–211.

Marx, K. and Engels, F. (1976) *The German Ideology*, Moscow: Progress Publishers.

Nichols, T. (1999) 'Industrial sociology and the labour process', in H. Beynon and P. Glavanis (eds), *Patterns of Social Inequality*, London: Longman, pp. 109–19.

O'Doherty D and Willmott, H. (2001) 'Debating labour process theory: The issue of subjectivity and the relevance of poststructuralism', *Sociology*, vol. 35, 457–76.

Sayers, S. (2003) 'Creative activity and alienation in Hegel and Marx', *Historical Materialism*, vol. 11, no. 1, 107–28.

Sayers, S. (2005) 'Why Work? Marxism and human nature', *Science and Society*, vol. 69, no. 4, 606–16.

Sayers, S. (2011) *Marx and Alienation: Essays on Hegelian Themes*, Basingstoke: Palgrave Macmillan.

Smith, A. (1976) *An Inquiry into the Nature and Causes of the Wealth of Nations*, R.H. Campbell and A.S. Skinner (eds), Oxford: Clarendon Press.

Spencer, D.A. (2000) 'Braverman and the contribution of labour process analysis to a critique of capitalist production – 25 years on', *Work, Employment and Society*, vol. 14, 223–43.

Spencer, D.A. (2009) *The Political Economy of Work*, London: Routledge.

Thompson, P. (2010) 'The capitalist labour process: Concepts and connections', *Capital and Class*, vol. 34, 7–14.

Thompson, P. and Newsome, K. (2004) 'Labour process theory, work and the employment relation' in B.E. Kaufman (ed.) *Theoretical Perspectives on Work and the Employment Relationship*, Cornell: Cornell University Press.

Thompson, P. and Vincent, S. (2010) 'Beyond the boundary: Labour process theory and critical realism', in P. Thompson and C. Smith (eds) *Working Life: Renewing Labour Process Analysis*, Basingstoke: Palgrave Macmillan.

2

THEORISING THE WORKING CLASS IN TWENTY-FIRST-CENTURY GLOBAL CAPITALISM

Beverly Silver

Since the 1990s it has been commonplace for scholars and political commentators around the world to speak of the death of labour and class-based movements. In 2010, however, the world's major newspapers were suddenly filled with reports of labour unrest around the world. In the first half of 2010 there were a series of front page articles on widespread labour unrest in Chinese factories following strikes at major automakers such as Honda and Toyota; intense protests by Bangladeshi garment workers including violent clashes with police that forced the shutdown of the country's busiest export processing zone; reports on escalating labour unrest in India including worker occupations at Hyundai and go-slows at the German car parts supplier Bosch; mass demonstrations against austerity from Greece, Portugal and Italy to Spain, France and the UK. In August and September, there were reports of widespread labour unrest in Egypt, riots against rising food prices in Mozambique, and a general strike of public sector and mineworkers in South Africa. In late December there were reports of mass protests against unemployment and rising food prices in Tunisia – the start of what would be called the 'Arab Spring'.[1]

The United States – the world hegemonic power of the twentieth century – was notably absent from the list of countries making it into the international press reports of labour unrest in 2010. By 2011, however, with mass protests against the elimination of collective bargaining rights for public sector workers in the state of Wisconsin (February 2011) and the launching of the Occupy movement in New York City (September 2011), labour unrest in the United States was also front-page news in the international press. It is no coincidence that by this time it also became increasingly common to hear scholars and pundits alike suggest that we were in the midst of a historically significant worldwide wave of class-based protest and labour unrest.[2]

The dominant approach in the social sciences since the 1980s had been to assume that labour and class-based mobilisations are a relic of the past. 'Globalisation', it was argued, had unleashed an intense competition among workers worldwide, and was resulting in a relentless downward spiral in workers' power and welfare. This came to be referred to as the 'race-to-the-bottom' thesis. Most social scientists were focused on explaining the weakness of labour and the absence/impossibility of autonomous labour militancy, and thus found themselves flat-footed in marshalling the analytical frameworks needed to make sense of the recent upsurge of labour unrest.

This chapter lays out the conceptual and theoretical components for an alternative world-historical approach to the study of working-class formation; one that emphasises the recurrent making and *remaking* of working classes *across time and space* with the evolution of historical capitalism. Seen from this perspective, workers and workers' movements were central actors not only in the evolution of global capitalism in the twentieth century; they will continue to play a central role in twenty-first-century global capitalism.[3]

THE COMMODIFICATION OF LABOUR AND THE ENDEMIC NATURE OF WORKERS' RESISTANCE IN HISTORICAL CAPITALISM

Both Karl Marx (1867) and Karl Polanyi (1944) contended that one of the historical specificities of capitalism as a social system is the commodification of labour. Moreover, both argued that labour is a 'fictitious commodity' and that treating human beings as commodities like any other would necessarily lead to deeply felt grievances and resistance. From this perspective, labour unrest is a fundamental aspect of the labour–capital relationship and should be expected anytime and anywhere we find the commodification of labour.

In Marx's analysis in volume 1 of *Capital*, labour–capital conflict is to be found first and foremost in the 'hidden abode of production'. The commodity 'labour power' (which he assumes is purchased on the labour market for its full cost – i.e., for the costs of its reproduction) is embodied in human beings who complain and resist if they are made to work too long, too hard or too fast. Yet, capitalists, under competitive pressure from other capitalists (and without countervailing restraints imposed by workers themselves), inevitably tend to push workers too long, too hard or too fast. Struggles over the extent and intensity of exploitation in the workplace, thus, are endemic to the labour–capital relation.

For Polanyi, in contrast, the fundamental focus of struggles is the labour market. Since the commodity labour is 'no other than the human beings themselves of which every society exists', to 'include them in the market mechanism means to subordinate the substance of society itself to the laws of the market' (Polanyi, 1944: 71). Each extension or deepening of unregulated labour markets has necessarily been countered by a movement toward the 'self-protection of society' through a variety of mechanisms including social legislation, factory laws, unemployment insurance and trade unions (Polanyi, 1944: 130, 176–7). This is especially so when the 'laws of the market' result in mass unemployment or the payment of below-subsistence wages.

In sum, from both a Marxian and a Polanyian perspective, labour unrest is an endemic feature of historical capitalism. However, because historical capitalism is characterised by recurrent dramatic changes in the organisation of production and consumption, the shape of labour unrest, including the form that struggles take as well as their primary (geographical and industrial) location, has also undergone periodic dramatic transformations.

HISTORICAL CAPITALISM, CREATIVE-DESTRUCTION AND THE MAKING, UNMAKING AND REMAKING OF THE WORLD WORKING CLASS

The idea that capitalism is characterised by ceaseless change is captured by Joseph Schumpeter's (1954) concept of creative-destruction; and by Marx's and Engel's famous phrase in *The Manifesto*: 'all that is solid melts into air'. This process of ceaseless change has, in turn, resulted in the recurrent making, unmaking and *remaking* of working classes on a world scale. Those, who over the past several decades, have been confidently pronouncing the death of the working class and labour movements have tended to focus single-mindedly on the *unmaking* side of this process – most notably the unmaking of the industrial mass production working classes in much of the Global North. But if we work from the premise that the world's working classes and workers' movements are recurrently made, unmade and remade, then we have a powerful antidote against the common tendency to prematurely pronounce the death of the working class every time a historically specific working class is 'unmade'.

From this perspective, we are primed to be on the lookout for the outbreak of fresh struggles – both by new working-classes-in-formation and by old working classes being unmade; that is, struggles by those experiencing the 'creative' and 'destructive' sides of the process of capital accumulation, respectively. Indeed, as will be discussed below, today we see both of these types of workers' struggles, with the strike wave by China's new migrant working class most closely corresponding to the 'new working-class-in formation' type and the anti-austerity protests in Europe most closely corresponding to the 'old working classes being unmade' type.[4]

One of the key driving forces behind the tendency toward 'ceaseless change' is labour-capital conflict.[5] Historically, capitalists have responded to strong labour movements by pursuing various strategies designed to reduce labour costs and increase control at the point of production. Four key strategies stand out: what we have called (1) the 'spatial fix' or geographical relocation of capital in search of cheaper and more controllable labour; (2) the 'technological fix' or the reorganisation of the production process, including the introduction of labour-saving technologies; (3) the 'product fix' or the movement of capital out of established industries subject to intense competition and into new industries and product lines; and (4) the 'financial fix' or the movement of capital completely out of trade and production and into finance and speculation.

Each of these strategies has uneven effects, systematically making and unmaking working classes, and strengthening/weakening workers' bargaining power, across industries and geographical space. These 'fixes' are attempts by capital to resolve crises of profitability and control, but they only succeed in 'rescheduling' the crises in time and space. In other words, they are only temporary and/or local solutions to capitalist crises.[6] We focus on the spatial and technological fixes in the next two sections of this chapter, and on the product and financial fixes in the penultimate sections.

THE SPATIAL FIX

The geographical relocation of production to lower-wage regions has been widely seen as having unleashed an intense competition among workers worldwide, undermining workers' bargaining power and resulting in a relentless downward spiral in wages and working conditions. But the historical evidence supports a fundamentally different thesis that can be summed up in the phrase: *where capital goes, labour-capital conflict shortly follows.* Over the course of the twentieth century we can see a déjà vu pattern whereby manufacturing capital recurrently pursued spatial fixes – that is, moved into new geographical locations in search of cheaper/more docile labour – but rather than creating a straightforward race to the bottom, the result was the creation of new working classes and strong new labour movements within a generation in each new favoured site of production. Put differently, the 'creative' side of the creative-destructive process associated with the spatial fix not only creates production in new sites; it also creates new working classes and workers' movements.

This pattern can be seen clearly in the world automobile industry,[7] which spread across the globe in successive spurts, from its origins in the United States in the 1910s and 1920s (where capital was attracted to the cheap and repressed labour of the time in the Detroit area) to the big expansion of Fordist mass production of automobiles in Western Europe in the 1950s; to the 'manufacturing miracles' in Brazil and South Africa in the 1960s and South Korea in the 1970s; and finally to China, with the massive expansion of the automobile industry from the late 1990s to the present.

Although a significant part of the motivation behind the move to each new location was the availability of cheap and disciplined labour, strong and effective labour movements emerged in each site within a generation. This happened in the United States with the 1936–7 automobile sit-down strikes that set off a nationwide strike wave leading to the institutionalisation of unions in mass production industries by the mid-1940s. And it happened again with the 'resurgence of class conflict' in Western Europe in the 1960s and 1970s; and with the emergence of militant independent workers' movements in the face of authoritarian and labour-repressive regimes in Brazil, South Africa and South Korea in the 1970s and 1980s.

The recent wave of strikes in China is among the latest affirmations of the postulate that 'where capital goes, labour-capital conflict follows' (Silver and Zhang 2009). The case of China is particularly instructive. Almost all observers thought that the migrant workers who flocked to the booming export-oriented factories in the coastal areas in the late 1990s were part of a virtually inexhaustible supply of cheap labour in China's rural areas. As such, most argued that it would be a long time (if ever) before they would openly protest their wages and working conditions. To be sure, there was a significant amount of labour unrest in China in the mid- and late-1990s, but it was almost entirely in the form of protests by workers being laid off from state-owned enterprises as part of the 'economic reform' process. These were protests by the working class that had originally been 'made' during the Mao era, but were now being 'unmade' as enterprise restructuring and market reforms led to mass lay-offs. Put differently, these were the workers suffering the 'destructive' consequences of the capitalist process of creative-destruction.[8]

However, starting around 2004, a wave of strikes hit factories in China's Pearl River Delta, followed by a more massive wave of strikes beginning in 2010, including major strikes in the automobile industry in the summer of 2010. The latter touched off a nationwide wave of strikes, most of which were successful in bringing about rising wages and the recognition of trade union representatives chosen by the workers themselves. The movement of capital into China had created a new and increasingly militant working class – the outcome of the 'creative' side of the creative-destructive process.

One response of capitalists to the wave of labour unrest in China has been the same response that we have seen for a century or more – the relocation of production in search of cheaper and more docile labour. There are widespread reports of factories moving from the coastal areas of China to interior provinces within China and to poorer countries elsewhere in Asia such as Vietnam, Cambodia and Bangladesh. But almost immediately, the thesis that 'where capital goes, conflict follows' received fresh confirmation with reports of strikes hitting foreign-owned businesses in each of these countries as well as in the interior provinces within China.[9] By the end of 2012, commentators were noting that there was 'nowhere left to run for factory owners in Asia... Manufacturers are slowly beginning to understand that wherever they go in the search for cheap and compliant labour, workers will not remain cheap and compliant for very long.'[10]

THE TECHNOLOGICAL FIX

The social science literature on labour movements over the past several decades has also tended to work from a perspective that one-sidedly emphasises the *weakening* effects of transformations in the organisation of production and the labour process on workers' power. However, as is the case for the spatial fix, so technological fixes have had a contradictory effect on workers' power.

Let's take the historical example of the take-off of mass production industrialisation in the United States in the early twentieth century. The introduction of the assembly line and associated technological/organisational transformations led to a clear weakening of the *labour market* bargaining power of the established working class as the skills of many craft-workers were made obsolete. Moreover, capitalists were suddenly able to draw on vast pools of newly minted unskilled and semi-skilled factory workers, including immigrants from around the world; they were able to lower labour costs dramatically and increase their control over the labour process. Notwithstanding all these factors that weakened workers' power in the labour market vis-a-vis capital, mass production workers spearheaded a major and highly successful strike wave in the 1930s and 1940s in the United States (with the first major successful strikes taking place in 1936–7; that is, during a period of mass unemployment in the midst of the Great Depression).

The success of these strikes relied heavily on *workplace bargaining power* – that is, workers' ability to cause costly disruptions via direct action at the point of production. Indeed, the very same transformations that had weakened labour's marketplace bargaining power in the early twentieth century simultaneously strengthened labour's workplace bargaining power. The assembly line allows a relatively small number of strategically placed activists to disrupt the output of an entire plant. And with the increasing integration of production among plants within a corporation, a strike in a plant producing a key input can bring all downstream factories, even an entire corporation, to a standstill. Moreover, with the increasing concentration and centralisation of production, the economic losses a work stoppage imposes on capital (and sometimes on whole national economies) also increases in scale (Edwards 1979; Arrighi and Silver 1984).

Strong workplace bargaining power was on display when workers occupied the General Motors factory that produced the bulk of Chevrolet's engines in December 1936. Production at all assembly plants across General Motors was quickly brought to a virtual halt and the corporation was forced to abandon its uncompromisingly anti-union stance and negotiate with the United Autoworkers Union. The power to cause costly disruptions in production with relatively small-scale stoppages was also seen in autoworker strike waves in Western Europe in the late-1960s and 1970s, in South Africa and Brazil in the 1970s and 1980s and South Korea in the 1980s and 1990s (Silver, 2003: chapter 2).

Workplace bargaining power was also on full display in May 2010 when a strike at a single factory that produced 80 per cent of the automatic gear boxes for Honda's four final assembly operations quickly shut down Honda's entire operations in China. And it was on display in June when another strike, this time at an exhaust components supplier, forced Honda to shut down all assembly operations in China again. Both strikes resulted in significant victories for workers.[11]

The wave of strikes by workers in China beginning in 2010 was not only a reminder of the significant disruptive power of workers under Fordism, but also evidence that the transformations associated with 'globalisation' and 'post-Fordism' have not had a straightforward weakening impact on workers' bargaining power as has been widely assumed. It is not a coincidence that the highly effective strikes by Chinese autoworkers mentioned above originated in parts factories (engine and exhaust) involved in 'just-in- time' (JIT) production. JIT production – pioneered by Japanese auto assemblers, and widely adopted since the 1980s – involves keeping on hand little or no inventory of parts for assembly in order to save money by eliminating the redundancies that were built into Fordism. Parts are delivered 'just-in-time' from supplier to assembly factories. But with the elimination of the buffer supply of parts, a strike that stops production in one key parts factory can bring assembly operations throughout the corporation to a halt within a matter of days or less.

Another example of how technological/organisational change associated with globalisation has strengthened workers' power at the point of production is the vulnerability of the tightly integrated supply chain that has emerged with the global outsourcing of production. A recent example is the April 2011 strike by truck drivers serving the port at Shanghai, during which the strong workplace bargaining power of transportation workers involved in the global supply chain was on clear display. After only a few days, the financial press began reporting mounting concerns that the strike could cause significant disruptions not only to Chinese exports but to the entire global supply chain.[12]

Among the responses of capitalists to the strong workplace bargaining power of labour has been the further introduction of new technologies aimed at automating production and decreasing the reliance of capital on human labour – that is, further technological fixes. Let's take the example of the Taiwanese company FoxConn (Hon Hai Electronics), which is a major subcontractor for Apple and other big electronic firms. When faced with a wave of labour unrest in its Guangdong plants starting in 2009, FoxConn responded, in part, by relocating some of its factories to interior provinces within China (that is, with a spatial fix). As we would expect, based on the analysis in the previous section, FoxConn's geographical relocation did not resolve its problems with labour control. Labour unrest emerged almost immediately in the company's newly established factories in interior provinces in China.[13]

FoxConn also responded with a technological fix. In 2011 the company's chairman announced plans to install robotic arms in its Chinese plants, where over one million workers were employed. The announced target of installing one million robots by 2014 was a bit of hyperbole. Indeed, in June 2012 FoxConn's chairman admitted that achieving that target would take significantly longer than he had initially proclaimed. Nevertheless, a push forward with automation has been visible. At the company's Shenzhen Longhua plant, for example, workers reported that robotic arms were replacing labour: 'There were about 20 to 30 people on the line before. But after they added the robots [in 2012] it went down to five people who just pushed buttons and ran the machines.'[14]

So far, in this section we have argued that the effect of the introduction of labour-saving technology on workers' power has been twofold. On the one hand, it increases the 'workplace bargaining power' of those who still have jobs, as the greater integration and capital intensity of production heightens the vulnerability of capital to disruptions at the point of production, including small-scale and localised stoppages. On the other hand, to the extent that the overall demand for labour decreases and/or existing scarce skills are made obsolete, the bargaining power of workers in the labour market is weakened. Understanding the combined impact of these two countervailing trends on workers' power is a key for understanding the future of the working-class in twenty-first-century global capitalism.

Let's deal first with the impact of technological change on the labour market bargaining power of workers, especially the global balance of labour supply and demand. On the one hand, the commonly heard prediction that we are moving towards a world without workers is not credible. FoxConn, for example, scaled back its automation program, in part because it realised that it is not efficient and/or practical to automate all tasks: in product lines that change rapidly, a huge capital investment in specialised robots would not pay off in time, and many activities in manufacturing (not to mention in personal services) still require a 'human touch'.[15]

On the other hand, even optimists about the benefits of technological change have expressed alarm about the speed with which jobs are being eliminated by advances in artificial intelligence, and the paucity of compensating new jobs being created. Tasks previously thought to be impervious to automation are now said to be next in line, ranging from 'self-driving vehicles that will eventually put taxi and truck drivers out of work' to automated systems that have already 'demonstrated that they can do approximately what legal researchers, pharmacists and biology researchers do' (Lanier, 2013; Krugman, 2013). Indeed, automation and the use of artificial intelligence to replace workers appears to have replaced geographical relocation of production as the most prominent explanation in the literature to account for the recent explosion in the ranks of the unemployed and under-employed in the Global North and the phenomenon of 'jobless growth'.

THE INSTITUTIONAL CONTEXT

But technological advances in themselves are not the root cause of 'jobless growth'. Rather the root cause is the *political decisions about how the economic gains from technological advances will be distributed*. A comparison of the late nineteenth/early twentieth century with the mid-twentieth century will help clarify this point. Like today, the last decade of the nineteenth century and the first decades of the twentieth century were a time of rapid technological change *and growing class inequality*. The benefits from increases in labour productivity accrued disproportionately to the wealthiest (that is, the rich got much richer). In the US, for example, the share of disposable income accruing to the top 1 per cent rose during the first three decades of the twentieth century, hitting a peak of 23 per cent in 1929 (Wade 2009). Technological change and labour weakness seemed to go hand in hand.

But, then, for the next half-century (from the 1930s through the 1970s) the trend went in reverse; that is, although technological change continued at a rapid pace, the distribution of income became more equal. The share of the top 1 per cent fell almost continuously until it reached only 9 per cent in the late 1970s, while the share going to those in the middle expanded substantially (Wade 2009). What accounts for the trend toward greater inter-class income *equality* in this period notwithstanding the fact that labour-saving technologies continued to be introduced at a rapid pace within the US and worldwide? It is the political–institutional context that fundamentally sets this period apart.

More specifically, the trend towards greater equality in this period was fostered by the institutional reforms at the factory, nation state, and international levels that were implemented in the post-Second World War era – that is, the Keynesian (mass consumption/production) social compact with labour in the Global North and the development project in the Global South.[16] Indeed, one central element of the post-Second World War mass consumption/production social compact was a compromise between labour and capital over the question of technological change. In this compromise, workers accepted management's right to make autonomous decisions about the organisation of production, *including the unfettered right to introduce labour-saving technologies*; however, in exchange, management was expected (or contractually obliged) to increase real wages in step with increases in labour productivity. As a result, *during the decades when the labour–capital social compact was in effect, economic gains reaped from the introduction of labour-saving technologies were far more evenly distributed.*

The trend toward a more equal and broad-based sharing of the benefits from technological change at the factory-level was reinforced at the national level by the active role that states played in job creation. Moreover, international monetary and trade institutions were re-designed to mesh with the pursuit of Keynesian policies, explicitly recognising the right and duty of nation states to protect their citizens from the ravages of unregulated world-market forces. Thus, for example, the post-Second World War (Bretton Woods) international monetary system was based on the premise that governments would (indeed, should) use the macroeconomic tools at their disposal to promote high levels of employment. As a result, job losses from technological change were offset by job expansion in both the private and public sectors, including the expansion of state employment financed via more-or-less progressive taxation (Ruggie, 1982; Maier, 1987: 121–52; Burley 1993).

But what accounts for the emergence of a more 'labour-friendly' institutional context in the mid-twentieth century? The post-Second World War social contracts were fundamentally a reformist response by the world's elites to decades of revolutionary challenges from below. The first half of the twentieth century had been characterised by wars and economic depression, but also by widespread and escalating anti-capitalist challenges from labour, socialist and national liberation movements. With the victory of the Soviet Revolution in the midst of the First World War followed by the victory of the Chinese Revolution in the aftermath of the Second World War, those in power in the capitalist world became convinced that serious institutional change was necessary if capitalism was to be saved. Keynesianism was seen as supplying an attractive third way between the Soviet model of centralised planning (which had gained in power and prestige in the 1930s and 1940s) and traditional laissez-faire policies (which had lost all credibility in the course of the Great Depression and the related social-political catastrophes of the era). US economic advisers fanned 'out to the far corners of the U.S.-controlled portion of the globe' preaching the Keynesian gospel (Hirschman, 1989). The promise held out by US world leadership was to universalise US consumption norms and make possible the 'American dream' for all.

But this promise was fraudulent in the context of historical capitalism. To generalise the labour–capital social compacts of the post-war era on a global scale would bring about an intense squeeze on profits, given their strong redistributional effects. Moreover, the production and consumption model associated with the 'American way of life' could only function as long as the vast majority of the world's population were excluded from full participation. Any serious effort to generalise this extremely resource-intensive and wasteful form of production was not only ecologically unsustainable, it would also touch off intense competition over finite natural resource inputs – something that would first become clear with the oil price shocks of the 1970s. Indeed, by the late 1960s and 1970s capitalism was facing a serious worldwide crisis of profitability – together with an environmental crisis – as workers' movements in both the First and Third World mobilised to demand what, in essence, was a quicker fulfilment of the explicit and implicit promises of US hegemony.[17]

In response to the crisis of the 1970s, economic and political elites abandoned the mass consumption social contract and the development project, and launched the neo-liberal counter-revolution. Starting in the 1980s (with the Reagan/Thatcher era) and accelerating in the 1990s (following the collapse of the Soviet Union), the post-war social compacts broke down at the factory, the national and the international level. The international monetary institutions established at Bretton Woods after the Second World War (especially the International Monetary Fund) shifted from promoting high levels of employment to imposing austerity (Arrighi, Silver and Brewer, 2003).

By the end of the twentieth century the gains from technological change were once again flowing to those at the top of the income and wealth hierarchy. This was a global phenomenon with the rise and spread of the neo-liberal project, but the United States led the pack. After decades of declining inequality, the share of income going to the top 1 per cent in the US began to rise in the 1980s, it ballooned in the 1990s, and by 2006 the share of the top 1 per cent reached 23 per cent, the same as in 1929 (Wade 2009). The pendulum had swung back.

In sum, throughout the twentieth century, spatial and technological fixes proceeded apace; however, for approximately four decades following the Second World War – the so-called Golden Age of Keynesianism and Development – these fixes went hand in hand with a trend toward the redistribution of income in favour of labour. During these decades the institutional arrangements at the factory, national and international levels were what we might call 'labour friendly', promoting rising real wages and low levels of unemployment. These institutional arrangements, in turn, were a reformist response to escalating labour militancy and social revolutionary challenges on a world scale in the first half of the twentieth century.

These labour-friendly institutional arrangements brought under control the revolutionary challenge facing the world capitalist system in the first half of the twentieth century. However, by the 1970s, these reforms had brought about a deep crisis of profitability for the world capitalist system. If the post-Second World War response was reformist, then the post-1980s response to the crisis of profitability was counter-revolutionary. In the subsequent decades, the labour-friendly institutional arrangements at the factory, national and international levels were dismantled in favour of neo-liberal polices. The outcome was geographically uneven, but the trend was clear: declining real wages, skyrocketing unemployment and redistribution of income from labour to capital. The gains from technological fixes and other economic advances were again flowing overwhelmingly to capital.

THE PENDULUM SWING FROM CRISIS OF PROFITABILITY TO CRISIS OF LEGITIMACY

Underlying this twentieth-century pendulum swing from greater inequality to greater equality and back again is a fundamental contradiction of historical capitalism – that is, an inherent tension between profitability and legitimacy. As argued at the outset of this chapter, labour unrest is an endemic aspect of historical capitalism as workers resist being treated as a commodity on the labour market and in the workplace. However, capitalist production cannot proceed smoothly or effectively without a minimum level of co-operation from workers. Efforts to control labour through pure repression are not sustainable *over the entire space-time* of capitalism since capitalist development tends to recurrently create strong new workers' movements. Moreover, as argued in the previous two sections, spatial and technological fixes designed to undermine and/or bypass militant workers' movements have unintended consequences, at best 'rescheduling' the time and place of mass labour unrest rather than eliminating it.

At the same time, however, making significant concessions (including redistributing economic gains from capital to labour) – as was promised with the post-Second World War mass consumption/mass production social compact – is not sustainable *over the entire space-time* of the capitalist system. Profits can be made only as long as a small minority of the world's workers are paid at (or near) their full costs for the reproduction of their labour power. However, extending the mass consumption/production social contract to the majority of the world's workers – as was the promise inherent in the post-Second World War development project – necessarily brought about a deep crisis of profitability for capitalism. At the same time, the failure to make good on the promise to universalise the American way of life was engendering a deep crisis of legitimacy for capitalism.

Thus, one type of crisis (profitability/legitimacy) can only be resolved by measures that eventually bring about the other type of crisis. The result has been an oscillation between historical phases characterised by the establishment of new social compacts that partially de-commodify labour and produce growing inter-class equality (e.g., the 1930s–80s) and histor-ical phases characterised by the breakdown of established social compacts, the re-commodification of labour and growing inter-class inequality (e.g., the 1980s to the present). Put differently, the result has been a pendu-lum swing between world-systemic crises of profitability (1870s, 1970s) and world-systemic crises of legitimacy (1930s and today).[18]

A NEW SWING OF THE PENDULUM?

What are the implications of the foregoing analysis for theorising the world working class in the early twenty-first century? One implied hypothesis is that we are in the midst of another deep crisis of legitimacy for capitalism, and that the 2010–11 global wave of labour unrest (with which we began this chapter) is a prelude to a growing wave of anti-capitalist movements; and that this wave of unrest will push the world's elites away from neo-liberalism towards a new set of labour-friendly social and developmental compacts analogous to the mid-twentieth century compacts; resulting, in turn, in a swing of the pen-dulum back toward a phase of growing inter-class equality in which the share of economic gains going toward labour once again rises.

How plausible is this hypothesis? The remainder of this chapter will lay out several reasons why it is plausible to hypothesise that we have reached the end of the neo-liberal pendulum swing, but also several reasons to suspect that a simple swing back to the mid-twentieth century labour and developmental social compacts is not possible.

One characteristic of the early twentieth-century upsurge of labour and social revolutionary struggles was that it was a combination of unrest rooted in the *creative* and the *destructive* sides of capitalist development. In other words, it was a combination of protests by new working classes being made in the industrial and geographical sites where capitalist production was growing quickly (especially in mass production and mining) and protests by estab-lished working classes being unmade (especially in craft-based industries). Moreover, this unrest clustered in time, creating simultaneous world-scale explosions of protest, in particular on the eve and aftermath of the First and Second World Wars.

While there were major outbursts of labour unrest throughout the decades of the mass consumption/production social contract, these unrest waves at the local and national level did not cluster in time. The reformed political–institutional context of the post-war decades had taken much (albeit not all) of the steam out of revolutionary challenges. Moreover, successive spatial fixes played out in a way that produced a geographically uneven strengthening/weakening of labour as well as a lack of solidarity between the (strengthened) working-classes-in-formation and (weakened) working classes in the process of being unmade. The latter tended to see the former as competitive threats rather than comrades.[19]

Does the 2010–11 wave suggest that we are on the cusp of a return to a period in which major waves of labour unrest (rooted in both the creative and destructive sides of capitalist development) cluster in time, creating world-scale explosions of labour unrest? There is some evidence that this may be the case. First, there was a geographical simultaneity to the labour protest – spanning every continent in 2010–11 – that we have not seen since the end of the Second World War. Second, the protests were an outcome of both the creative and destructive impacts of capitalist development on the world working class. On the one side, there was the widespread and militant labour unrest in sites of rapid industrial expansion such as China, Vietnam, Bangladesh and India; on the other side, the widespread protests against austerity and the breakdown of the welfare state, most notably in Eurozone countries.

Last but not least, the world's elites show no signs of being willing and/or able to implement a reformist response that might overcome the widening and deepening crisis of legitimacy facing the world capitalist system. Indeed, since the 2008 financial meltdown – the deepest crisis to hit the core countries since 1929 – the world's elites have followed a strategy of doubling-down on neo-liberalism; that is, tightening the austerity noose in the Eurozone and elsewhere, while continuing to channel the gains from technological change to the wealthiest. (Indeed, by 2011 the share of income going to the top 1 per cent in the United States had reached the highest level on record, surpassing the 1929 and 2006 record highs.) Under these conditions, there are good reasons to believe that the wave of unrest in 2010–11 was no mere flash in the pan; but rather a sign that the steam is building up toward a long period of growing, worldwide and explosive anti-capitalist challenges from below.[20]

To be sure, there have been some signs of a counter-movement. In China, for example, the government has attempted to diffuse the mass wave of labour unrest through a labour law reform that is in many ways analogous to the US government response to labour unrest in the 1930s. Both the 1935 National Labour Relations Act (the Wagner Act) in the United States and the 2008 Labour Contract Law in China were responses to the threat of social instability posed by mounting social unrest, on the one hand, and the threat of economic instability due to insufficient demand (as wages stagnated in the face of rapidly rising labour productivity), on the other hand. Both the 1935 US law and the 2008 Chinese law sought to specify and expand workers' rights and improve wages and working conditions, while channeling unrest into formal legal (routine) grievance procedures.[21]

In the US, the passage of the Wagner Act (and the strike waves that preceded and followed it) led to a durable social contract that was openly ruptured only in the 1980s. However, because of a fundamental difference in the global competitive environment, a simple repeat of the US mass production/ consumption social contract in China is not possible today. In order to clarify this point, we need to introduce the concept of the product cycle and our third 'fix' – the product fix.

THE PRODUCT CYCLE

In the previous sections we put forward the argument that the geographical relocation of capital in mass production industries over the course of the twentieth century – that is, successive 'spatial fixes' – has created new militant working classes everywhere capital has gone. In mass production industries, especially the automobile industry, we can see a clear cyclical pattern where capital is attracted to new sites of production in search of cheap and controllable labour, but strong labour movements emerge in each new site of production – from the US to Western Europe to Brazil, South Africa and South Korea and most recently to China.

However, this recurrent cycle of labour militancy and capital relocation is not a simple repetition. Rather, each recurrence unfolded in a fundamentally different competitive environment as mass production manufacturing spread across the globe. Raymond Vernon's (1966) product cycle theory, which distinguishes three phases in the lifecycle of all products – innovation, maturity, standardisation – is helpful for explaining this process. In the innovation phase the number of competitors is low and profits are high; however, as products reach the stage of maturity and finally standardisation, the number of actual and potential competitors grows, as does the pressure to cut costs.

This has important implications for the *outcome* of major waves of labour unrest – especially for the kind of labour–capital accord that labour movements can achieve and the degree of durability for the gains secured. Whereas the strike wave in the US automobile industry in the 1930s and 1940s took place during the innovation phase of the mass production automobile industry, when containing costs was relatively unimportant for ensuring capitalist profits, the recent strike wave in China is taking place during the standardisation phase of the product lifecycle, when the mass production of automobiles and other manufacturing activities is subject to intense international competition, and profit margins are extremely thin. Thus, while US autoworkers were able to translate their strong workplace bargaining power into several decades of rising wages and expanding benefits, it is unclear that Chinese autoworkers will be able to do the same, despite some initial short-term successes. As long as production in China is concentrated in economic activities that are subject to intense competitive pressures, it is not clear how Chinese workers can translate their strong workplace bargaining power into a long-term stable social contract.

To be sure, the Chinese government is making efforts to jump up in the global value-added hierarchy, which might in turn, open the door to a longer-term stable labour-capital compact. It is an open question whether these efforts will be successful. Historically, innovations in capitalist production have clustered in high income countries, whereas China is, at most, a middle-income country. Moreover, historically, new leading industries have emerged in the rising world hegemonic power – for example, the mass production of textiles in the United Kingdom in the nineteenth century and the mass production of automobiles in the United States in the twentieth century.

Last but not least, there is an adding up problem. By definition, only one or a handful of locations can reap the high profits that come with being the innovator. Thus, one country's success in jumping up the value-added hierarchy (and thereby obtaining an important precondition for a stable labour–capital accord) necessarily presumes the failure of other countries to obtain the same objective. Put differently, high profits in capitalism historically have been derived not only from *exploitation* but also from *exclusion* (Arrighi, Silver and Brewer 2003). The monopoly windfall profits that have underwritten mass consumption social contracts are not generalisable to the world as a whole.

THE PRODUCT FIX

Nevertheless, the rise and fall of leading industries has important implications for the spatial-temporal patterning of working-class formation and labour unrest on a world-scale. In the nineteenth century the textile industry became a key site of world working-class formation and world labour unrest; in the twentieth century, the automobile industry became a key site of world working-class formation and world labour unrest. For just as the main geographical sites of labour unrest shift from place to place along with each spatial fix, so the main industrial sites of working-class formation and protest have shifted from industry to industry together with the rise/decline of leading sectors of capitalist development (Silver, 2003: chapter 3).

This brings us to our third fix – that is, the *product fix* or the movement of capital out of industries and economic activities subject to intense competition (i.e., economic activities where Vernon's standardisation phase has been reached) and into new (innovative) spheres with few competitors and high profit margins. Each product fix – like each spatial and technological fix – sets off a process of creative-destruction in which existing working classes are weakened or unmade and new working classes are formed. A critical next task, from this perspective, is to identify the likely successor(s) of the automobile complex as the leading industry of world capitalism and to explore the nature of workers' bargaining power therein.

It is difficult to identify a single product that plays a role equivalent to that played historically by the textile complex in the nineteenth century or the automobile complex in the twentieth century. Various candidates have been proposed from semiconductors and education to advanced robotics and renewable energy; while some argue that no single product will have the same impact as textiles had in the nineteenth century and automobiles in the twentieth century (Manyika et al, 2013; see also Silver, 2003, chapter 3).

This is a big and important question. Here we will only focus on a partial but key symbolic snapshot. In 1955 General Motors was the number 1 ranked company on the US Fortune 500 list of largest companies in terms of revenues and held the number 1 position virtually every year for the remainder of the twentieth century. By 2002, however, Walmart Stores moved into the number 1 position and was still number 1 in 2013. Likewise, Walmart held the top spot on the Global Fortune 500 list virtually every year since the list began in 2005. Equally, if not more important, Walmart Stores is far-and-away the Fortune 500 corporation with the most employees – 2,200,000 employees in 2013 – and is the largest employer in the United States apart from the federal government. Finally, five of the six largest employers on the Fortune 500 list are in the retail sector (Walmart, McDonalds, Target, Kroger, Home Depot).[22]

Thus, the retail sector has been one of the key sites of new working-class formation; and if our thesis that 'where capital goes, conflict follows' is also valid with regard to the product fix, then we should expect the retail sector to emerge as a key site of labour militancy. Indeed, 2012–13 witnessed an unprecedented upsurge of strikes in the fast food industry in the United States and growing protest activity by Walmart workers.[23] Whether this labour unrest is a 'flash in the pan' or the harbinger of a more fundamental transformation remains to be seen. But the theoretical framework outlined in this chapter so far gives us reason to think that these actions might be a first step in a process that transforms today's precarious workers into tomorrow's stable working class.

To be sure, the workplace bargaining power of retail workers appears to be far weaker than the workplace bargaining power of automobile workers. Nevertheless, it is important to bear in mind that most early twentieth-century observers of Fordism were convinced that the transformations associated with the spread of industrial mass production had created a fundamentally weak working class with little chance of winning autonomous struggles. It was only post-facto – with the success of mass production unionisation in the 1930s and 1940s and the attendant transformation of precarious autoworkers into a stable working class – that Fordism came to be seen as inherently labour strengthening rather than labour weakening. Indeed, based on the theoretical framework put forward in this chapter, it is plausible that we find ourselves on the eve of an analogous post-facto shift in perspective in which assumptions about the inherent weakness of today's precarious workers are upended.

THE FINANCIAL FIX

The fourth *fix* is what we have called the *financial fix*. The financial fix can be conceptualised as the continuation of the product cycle by other means. With the intensification of competitive pressures in production, capitalists sometimes seek to move into less crowded and more profitable lines of production (the product fix), but they also sometimes choose to pull their capital out of trade and production entirely and reinvest in financial deals and speculation. This latter is the financial fix.

For the past several decades (more or less since the 1980s) we have been living through a period in which the financial fix has become a dominant strategy for restoring capitalist profits. The end of the nineteenth century and first two decades of the twentieth century was another such period (Arrighi, 1994; Silver and Arrighi, 2011; see also Krippner 2011). The latest financialisation of capitalism gathered steam in the late twentieth century as it became increasingly clear that spatial, technological and product fixes were at best only temporary and local solutions to crises of profitability and labour control (as discussed above).

Understanding the financial fix is crucial for theorising the working class in twenty-first-century global capitalism. However, the impact of the financial fix on labour is different from the other fixes discussed so far. For the spatial, technological and product fixes we emphasised their contradictory impact on working-class formation and labour movement strength. We showed the dual nature of all three; that is, how they both unmade and made working classes; both weakened and strengthened labour's bargaining power.

An analysis based on these three fixes alone would lead us to the conclusion that, although there may be working classes that are weakened locally and temporally, the main effect of the process of capitalist development is to increase the size and strength of the world working class. Put differently, our analysis of the first three fixes leaves us without an explanation for the deep crisis of labour movements worldwide since the 1990s.

In the section above on 'The Institutional Context' we argued that the crisis of labour movements, and the dramatic increase in inequality, could not be traced to spatial or technological fixes. Instead it was traceable to a political decision by the world's elites to abandon the mass consumption and developmentalist social compacts. The financial fix gives us an additional explanation. Financial expansions are associated with the unmaking of established working classes, but unlike spatial and product fixes, they do not create significant new working classes in their place. Put differently, the destructive side of the process of creative-destruction process is predominant as capital flows out of trade and production rather than from one geographical/industrial location to another (Silver, 2003: chapter 4).

The financial fix, together with the abandonment from above of the mass consumption and developmentalist social compacts, provides us with an explanation for how labour movements were undermined and how the deep crisis of capitalist profitability in the 1970s was eventually resolved. But as with all 'solutions' for capitalist crises, it was only partial and temporary. The crisis of profitability was resolved through measures that have brought about a new deep crisis of legitimacy for capitalism.

A RADICAL RETHINKING OF EVERYTHING

The pendulum is poised to swing back. But from the analysis put forward in this chapter it should also be clear that a simple swing of the pendulum back to the Keynesian mass production/mass consumption social contracts of the mid-twentieth century is neither possible nor desirable. While these social compacts resolved the crisis of legitimacy of capitalism at the system level, they were profitable and ecologically sustainable only so long as the vast majority of the world's population were excluded from their benefits.

If we are to imagine a world in which profits are subordinated to livelihood *for all*, then we have to imagine a world that moves beyond the resource-intensive western model of capitalist development. In short, it requires us to radically rethink everything.

NOTES

1. Taking the *Financial Times* (London) as an illustration, we find among the many prominent articles on labour unrest around the world in 2010: 'Austerity plans spark protests in Eurozone' (24 February), 'Bosch locks out staff amid India unrest' (12 March), 'Police break up Hyundai strike in Chennai' (9 June), 'Workers' rage' (9 June, on anti-austerity protests in Europe), 'Chinese workers' protests spread' (10 June), 'Fears grow over China labour unrest' (11 June), 'Bangladesh doubles wages in clothes industry to stem unrest' (30 July), 'Strike hobbles South Africa public services' (19 August), 'Seven die in Mozambique food rioting' (3 September), and 'Tunisian unemployment sparks unrest' (28 December).

2. Simon Schama's suggestively titled commentary published in the *Financial Times* (22 May 2010) – 'The world teeters on the brink of a new age of rage' – actually only referred to European anti-austerity protests, but by 2011 the European ferment was widely seen to be part of a global upsurge of labour and class-based social protest.

3. These arguments are developed at greater length (and with extensive citations to the literature) in Silver (2003).

4. In *Forces of Labour* (2003: 20), I labelled these two types of struggles 'Marx-type labour unrest' (that is the struggles of newly emerging working classes born out of the material expansions of capitalism) and 'Polanyi type labour unrest' (that is, the struggles by established working classes to defend ways of life and livelihood that are in the process of being 'unmade' including resistances by workers who had benefited from established social compacts with capital and states to their being abandoned from above). This conceptual distinction *partly* parallels David Harvey's (2003) 'struggles against accumulation in production' and 'struggles against accumulation by dispossession'.

5. Another key driving force behind the tendency towards ceaseless change is competition among capitalists, which in turn, is both influenced by and influences the dynamics of labour-capital conflict.

6. David Harvey (1989: 196), building on Marx's theorisation of the dynamics of capital accumulation, introduced the concept of the 'spatial fix'. I take off from this starting point in *Forces of Labour* in order to conceptualise the spatial, technological, product and financial fixes as strategies for the containment of capitalist crisis, especially crises of labour control.

7. See Silver (2003; chapter 2) for a detailed discussion of this déjà vu pattern for the twentieth- century world automobile industry.

8. See the chapters on the 'rustbelt' protests in C.K. Lee (2007).

9. For example: 'Cambodian workers threaten mass strike', *Fibre 2 Fashion*, 31 December 2012. Available at: http://www.fibre2fashion.com/news/apparel-news/newsdetails. aspx?news_id=119475; 'Export powerhouse [Bangladesh] feels pang of labour strife', *New York Times*, 23 August 2012. Available at: http://www.nytimes.com/2012/08/24/ world/asia/as-bangladesh-becomes-export-powerhouse-labour-strife-erupts.html); 'Bangladesh doubles wages in clothes industry to stem unrest', *The Financial Times*, 30 July 2010; 'Strike explosion in Vietnam', *Lianhe News* (Taipei, Taiwan), 28 April 2008; 'Vietnam's factories grapple with growing unrest', *Financial Times*, 19 January 2012. Available at: http://www.ft.com/intl/cms/s/0/67380b5c-427e-11e1-97b1-00144feab49a.html#axzz2UPmtbIvA); 'Worker dispute halts production at Chinese electronics plant' [on Compal factory strike in Chengdu, Sichuan Province],

Wall Street Journal, 25 October 2012. Available at: http://online.wsj.com/article/ SB10001424052970203937004578078472126687996.html.

10. 'Nowhere left to run for factory owners in Asia', *China Labour Bulletin*, 15 January 2013. Available at: http://www.clb.org.hk/en/node/110196

11. 'Honda forced by strikes to halt China operations', *Financial Times*, 28 May 2010; 'Strike force', *Financial Times*, 11 June 2010.

12. 'Third day of strike threatens China's exports', Reuters News Service (US), 22 April 2011; On the late twentieth and early twenty-first-century logistics revolution in global transportation and its potential for strengthening labour's power, see Bonacich and Wilson (2008).

13. See for example, 'Foxconn plant [in Taiyuan, Shanxi Province] closed after riot, company says' *New York Times*, 24 September 2012. Available at: http://www.nytimes.com/ 2012/09/25/technology/foxconn-plant-in-china-closed-after-worker-riot.html and 'Foxconn factory workers riot in [Chengdu, Sichuan Province] China', *CNN*, 8 June 2012. Available at: http://www.cnn.com/2012/06/07/world/asia/foxconn-workers-riot.

14. 'Hon Hai [FoxConn] hits obstacles in push to use robots', *Wall Street Journal*, 11 December 2012. Available at: http://online.wsj.com/article/SB100014241278873240 24004578172022369346936.html.

15. In some cases, the required 'human touch' has been achieved by pushing tasks that were formerly performed by wage workers onto consumers themselves – among the most visible examples are self-check-out lines at supermarkets and purchasing airline tickets on the Internet. The enlistment of the labour of consumers themselves, in turn, points to the importance of theorising the nature of the relationship between workers and consumers as a central part of our efforts to theorise the working class in twenty-first-century global capitalism.

16. The argument briefly outlined in this and the following paragraphs on the rise and demise of the mass consumption and development social contracts (and its relationship to the mass labour and social revolutionary movements of the first half of the twentieth century) is more fully developed in Silver (2003: chapter 4) and Arrighi and Silver (1999: chapter 3). On the rise and fall of the development project see also McMichael (2012) and Arrighi, Silver and Brewer (2003).

17. On the non-generalisability of the mass production-consumption development model, see Arrighi, Silver and Brewer (2003).

18. For an early effort to distinguish among different types of capitalist crises, see Arrighi (1978); for further elabouration of the above argument, see Silver (2003: chapters 1 and 4); also Arrighi and Silver (1999: chapter 3).

19. On the contrast between the patterning of labour unrest in the first half of the twentieth century versus the second half of the twentieth century, see Silver (2003: chapter 4). On the lack of solidarity see Silver and Arrighi (2000).

20. Whether the protests by these differently located working classes will converge in solidarity or split along racial, ethnic and citizenship divides will be critical in determining how the global wave of labour unrest will unfold.

21. See the opening paragraphs of the National Labour Relations Act. For the text of the law, see www.nlrb.gov/about_us/overview/national_labour_relations_act.aspx. On the Chinese Labour Contract Law see Kahn and Barboza, "China Passes A Sweeping New Labour Law"; see also Zhang (forthcoming: chapters 3 and 7). For a comparison of the New Deal period in the US and the current situation in China, see Silver and Zhang (2009).

22. For 2013 Fortune 500 list, see http://money.cnn.com/magazines/fortune/fortune500/ 2013/full_list/; for historical archive see http://money.cnn.com/magazines/fortune/ fortune500_archive/full/1955/401.html.

23. Saki Knafo, "Seattle's Fast-Food Workers Strike as National Movement Begins to Claim Small Victories", *The Huffington Post*, 30 May 2013. Available at: http://www.

huffingtonpost.com/2013/05/30/seattle-fast-food-workers-strike_n_3361608.html;
Josh Eidelson, 'Walmart workers launch first-ever "prolonged strikes" today', *The Nation*, 28 May 2013. Available at: http://www.thenation.com/blog/174551/walmart-workers-launch-first-ever-prolonged-strikes-today#axzz2WLOcLmH8.

REFERENCES

Arrighi, Giovanni. 1978. 'Towards a theory of capitalist crisis', *New Left Review*, vol. 111, September–October, 4–24.

Arrighi, Giovanni. 1994. *The Long Twentieth Century: Money, Power and the Origins of Our Times*, New York: Verso (2nd edition, 2010).

Arrighi, Giovanni and Beverly J. Silver. 1984. 'Labour movements and capital relocation: The US and Western Europe in world-historical perspective', in C. Bergquist, ed., *Labour in the Capitalist World Economy*, pp. 183–216. Beverly Hills, CA: Sage.

Arrighi, Giovanni and Beverly J. Silver. 1999. *Chaos and Governance in the Modern World System.* Minneapolis: University of Minnesota Press.

Arrighi, Giovanni, Beverly J. Silver and Ben Brewer. (2003) 'Industrial convergence and the persistence of the North-South divide', *Studies in Comparative International Development*, Spring 2003, vol. 38, no. 1, 3–31.

Bonacich, Edna and Jake Wilson. 2008. *Getting the Goods: Ports, Labour and the Logistics Revolution.* Ithaca: Cornell University Press.

Burley, Anne-Marie. 1993. 'Regulating the world: Multilateralism, international law, and the projection of the New Deal regulatory state', in J.G. Ruggie, ed., *Multilateralism Matters: The Theory and Praxis of an Institutional Form*, pp. 125–56. New York: Columbia University Press.

Claude, Jr., Inis. 1956. *Swords into Plowshares: The Problems and Progress of International Organization*, New York: Random House.

Edwards, Richard. 1979. *Contested Terrain: The Transformation of the Workplace in the Twentieth Century*, New York: Basic Books.

Gordon, David M., Richard Edwards and Michael Reich. 1982. *Segmented Work, Divided Workers: The Historical Transformation of Labour in the United States.* Cambridge: Cambridge University Press.

Harvey, David. 1989. *The Condition of Postmodernity: An Enquiry into the Origins of Cultural Change.* Oxford: Basil Blackwell.

Harvey, David. 2003. *The New Imperialism.* New York: Oxford University Press.

Hirschman, Albert O. 1989. 'How the Keynesian Revolution was exported from the United States, and other comments', in Peter A. Hall, ed., *The Political Power of Economic Ideas: Keynesianism Across Nations*, pp. 347–59. Princeton, NJ: Princeton University Press.

Kahn, Joseph and David Barboza. 2007. 'China passes sweeping new labour law', *New York Times*, 30 June. Available at: http://www.nytimes.com/2007/06/30/business/worldbusiness/30chlabour.html?pagewanted=all&_r=0.

Krippner, Greta. 2011. *Capitalizing on Crisis: The Political Origins of the Rise of Finance*, Cambridge, MA: Harvard University Press.

Krugman, Paul. 2013. 'Sympathy for the Luddites', *New York Times*, 13 June.

Lanier, Jaron. 2013. 'The online utopia doesn't exist: We need to reboot', *Wired*, 5 April. Available at: http://www.wired.co.uk/magazine/archive/2013/04/ideas-bank/the-online-utopia-doesnt-exist.

Lee, Ching Kwan. 2007. *Against the Law*, Los Angeles: University of California Press.

Maier, Charles. 1987. *In Search of Stability: Explorations in Historical Political Economy*, Cambridge: Cambridge University Press.

Manyika, James, Michael Chui, Jacques Bughin, Richard Dobbs, Peter Bisson, and Alex Marrs. 2013. *Disruptive Technologies: Advances That Will Transform Life, Business and The Global Economy,* McKinsey Global Institute. Available at: http://www.mckinsey.com/insights/business_technology/disruptive_technologies.

Marx, Karl. 1959. *Capital, volume 1.* Moscow: Foreign Languages Publishing House.

McMichael, Phillip. 2012. *Development and Social Change: A Global Perspective.* Los Angeles: Sage.

Polanyi, Karl. [1944] 1957. *The Great Transformation.* Boston: Beacon.

Ruggie, John G. 1982. 'International regimes, transactions and change: Embedded liberalism in the postwar economic order', *International Organization*, vol. 36, no. 2, 379–415.

Schumpeter, Joseph. 1954. *Capitalism, Socialism and Democracy.* London: Allen & Unwin.

Silver, Beverly. 2003. *Forces of Labour: Workers' Movements and Globalization since 1870,* New York: Cambridge University Press.

Silver, Beverly and Giovanni Arrighi. 2000. 'Workers north and south', in Leo Panitch and Colin Leys, eds, *Socialist Register 2001* (Theme: Working Classes: Global Realities), London: Merlin Press, 53–76.

Silver, Beverly and Giovanni Arrighi. 2011. 'End of the long twentieth century', in Craig Calhoun and Georgi Derluguian, eds, *Business as Usual: The Roots of the Global Financial Meltdown,* New York: NYU Press, pp. 53–68.

Silver, Beverly and Lu Zhang. 2009. 'China as emerging epicenter of world labour unrest', in Ho-fung Hung, ed., *China and the Transformation of Global Capitalism,* Baltimore: The Johns Hopkins University Press, pp. 174–87.

Standing, Guy. 2011. *The Precariat: The New Dangerous Class.* New York: Bloomsbury Academic.

Vernon, Raymond. 1966. 'International investment and international trade in the product cycle', *Quarterly Journal of Economics,* vol. 80, no. 2, 190–207.

Wade, Robert. 2009. 'The global slump: Deeper causes and harder lessons', *Challenge,* vol. 52, no. 5, September/October, 5–24.

Zhang, Lu. (forthcoming). *From Detroit to Shanghai? Globalization, Market Reform, and the Politics of Labour in the Chinese Automobile Industry,* Cambridge University Press.

3

WHO IS THE WORKING CLASS? WAGE EARNERS AND OTHER LABOURERS

Marcel van der Linden

INTRODUCTION

The concept 'working class' emerged in Western Europe towards the end of the eighteenth century, and was at first used especially in the plural form. The 'working classes' comprised all those people employed to work for wages in manual occupations. Probably the term came into use when, because of the rise of industrial capitalism and the concurrent growth of manufactures and factories, new groups of wage earners became visible who could be counted neither among domestic servants, nor among day labourers or journeymen.

The precise meaning of the term 'working class' is disputed. While some emphasise manual labour, broader interpretations are also advanced. Not infrequently, lower-level white-collar employees are also included in the working class, and sometimes the position is defended that *all* wage earners belong to the working class, except for higher managers. Nevertheless, until recently, all definitions of the working class being used had three aspects in common. First, they assumed that members of the working class share at least one characteristic, namely that they are *dependent on a wage* for their survival, while other sources of income are either lacking or much less important. Second, they involved the (often implicit) assumption that workers are part of *families* who in principle also belong to the working class.

Sometimes it is assumed that there is a male breadwinner who earns the income of the whole household, while other members of the family perform at most subsistence labour; sometimes the possibility is recognised that other family members can also contribute to household income. Third, all definitions assumed that the working class is next to, or counterposed to, *other social classes*, in particular the employers ('capitalists'), the self-employed, the un-free, and so-called 'lumpenproletarians' (beggars, thieves, etc.). In recent years elements of these assumptions have been questioned. An increasing number of scholars argues, that workers can earn 'hidden' wages, as in sharecropping where a peasant family supplies labour and the landowner the land and means of production, while the revenues are shared between them according to some formula; or self-employed workers, who are formally employers without staff, but in reality are often dependent on one specific client who is therefore their de facto employer. In addition, the boundaries between 'un-free' and 'free' workers are not as clearcut as is often assumed.

All these descriptions emphasise structural, social-economic characteristics. But the working class also has a subjective side, as shown by its culture, mentality and collective action. The influential British historian E.P. Thompson accordingly considered 'class' as an outcome of experience, emerging out of those socio-economic characteristics. 'Class', he argued, 'happens when some men, as a result of common experiences (inherited or shared), feel and articulate the identity of their interests as between themselves, and as against other men whose interests are different from (and usually opposed to) theirs' (Thompson 1963: 8–9). The ways in which 'class happens' can diverge strongly, and are unpredictable: 'We can see a *logic* in the responses of similar occupational groups undergoing similar experiences, but we cannot predicate any *law*. Consciousness of class arises in the same way in different times and places, but never in just the same way' (Thompson 1963: 9).

The present chapter will discuss some of the newer insights into processes of working-class formation and resistance.

FORMATION

In the early twenty-first century, wage labour has probably become the second most prevalent form of work (after domestic subsistence labour). But wage labour is not a phenomenon of recent vintage. Wage labour has been performed more or less sporadically for thousands of years. Originally it concerned work activities without a permanent character, such as the work of itinerant artisans, the service of military recruits or help with the harvest. The New Testament provides a good example of casual wage labour with the parable about the 'householder who went out early in the morning to hire labourers for his vineyard' (Matthew 20).

What is special about modern wage labour is not only that it has become a socially dominant phenomenon, but also that a relatively large part of the wage workers have longer-term jobs which often last for years, or sometimes even a lifetime. This historical change has occurred gradually or more rapidly from the fifteenth century, beginning in the North Atlantic region and then spreading to other parts of the world. Background causes of this development were, among others, the rise of capitalist production and distribution, growing state apparatuses which intervened more powerfully in economic and social life, and growing populations. These processes contributed to the emergence of regional, national and international labour markets, and new forms of social inequality.

These trends did not always lead to a growing number of wage workers (in the seventeenth and eighteenth centuries they were accompanied by an intensification of slavery), but in the long term they meant that more and more families depended on a wage for their survival. This 'proletarianisation' made a growing part of the world population dependent on one kind of income and, therefore, socially vulnerable:

> The opportunities or risks for such workers are determined by markets and market changes. They do not possess the tools they use, the raw materials they process, or the products they produce. Their work is determined by those who possess all of this in the form of capital and who, on this basis, employ and direct them (often through managers, supervisors, or other types of middlemen). The relation between wage workers and employers is based on a contract of exchange (work for wages), terminable by both sides, and not by extra-economic compulsion or tradition.
>
> (Kocka 1986: 282)

Parts of the large group of wage workers so emerging develop collective identities, based on shared interests, experiences, opinions, fears and expectations. They articulate these collective identities in all kinds of ways, through sociability, religious rituals, or organisations for mutual aid. Not infrequently the new identity is also the expression of a beginning class awareness, based on the consciousness that the interests of workers are different and often counterposed to those of the employers. Whether such consciousness emerges, and what exact forms it will have, always depends on the circumstances, and cannot be predicted in advance.

In some circumstances, class awareness becomes more militant, because groups of workers try to defend their perceived common interests against the state or the employers through economic or political action. In support of this struggle for their interests, they can form diverse kinds of organisations, such as trade unions, political parties or sometimes even paramilitary units. Here again it is true that this can happen in all kinds of different ways, and that the content of a conflict of interest can show great variations. Only rarely do such interest groups strive to unite all workers; more often they exclude segments of the class because of reasons of gender, ethnicity, nationality, education, etc.

'PERIPHERAL' WORKING CLASSES

In recent decades, more and more voices argue for a broad and inclusive interpretation of the working class. The distinctions between 'classical' wage earners and some other subordinate groups are very fine indeed. There exist, as we have seen, all kinds of forms of 'hidden' wage labour. This relativisation of the boundaries of the working class has recently motivated historians to redefine the working class, such that slaves and other un-free workers can also be included, just like ostensibly 'independent' self-employed operators (van der Linden 2008). The historians Peter Linebaugh and Marcus Rediker, for example, revealed how in the early-modern North Atlantic region a multi-form proletariat of 'hewers of wood and drawers of water' developed, with various sites of struggle: 'the commons, the plantation, the ship, and the factory'. They made it seem likely that slaves and maroons from Africa, indentured labourers from Europe, native Americans, and 'free' wage earners and artisans constituted a complex but also socially and culturally interconnected amorphous 'multitude', which was also regarded as one whole (a 'many-headed Hydra') by those in power. Linebaugh and Rediker referred to the 1791 rebellion of Haitian slaves as 'the first successful workers' revolt in modern history', thus explicitly considering the insurrectionary slaves as workers (Linebaugh and Rediker 2000: 319). They suggested that this revolution contributed to the segmentation of the rebellious 'multitude' in Europe and the Americas afterwards. 'Respectable' artisans and skilled workers now became afraid to be identified with the violent freedom fighters of African descent. *'What was left behind was national and partial: the English working class, the black Haitian, the Irish diaspora.'* The narrow nineteenth-century concept of the proletariat we find in Marx and others was, they suggest, a result of this segmentation.

We have to rethink the traditional notion of the working class. On the one hand, the experience of the *contemporary* world tells us, that the distinctions between 'classical' wage earners and some other subordinate groups are vague indeed. 'Pure' wage workers have been a minority in the labour force of many countries in the Global South; there, a process of class formation often did not develop until the very end. Most of these wage earners do not freely dispose of their own labour power – for example, because these workers are tied down by debts – or they do not have any formal (legally recognised) contractual relationship with their employers. In addition, wage labour in the South and often also in the North is carried out by households and families whose survival frequently remains partly dependent on subsistence labour as well – performed especially, but not exclusively, by women – and on independent production of commodities for the market, etc. The economic roles that different family members take on are often not fixed and permanent, but instead signify a transient social relationship, one that can be replaced rather quickly by other sources of income. That is one reason why the dividing line between workers and so-called *lumpenproletarians* (people who survive by means of begging, crime, prostitution, and so on) is not always easy to draw. Referring to Africa, Vic Allen concluded some forty years ago that

> In societies in which bare subsistence is the norm for a high proportion of all the working class, and where men, women, and children are compelled to seek alternative means of subsistence, as distinct from their traditional ones, the lumpenproletariat is barely distinguishable from much of the rest of the working class.
>
> (Allen 1972: 188)

In the Global North we see similar trends: the 'precariat' is growing quickly (Standing 2011), while self-employment as an alternative to joblessness is rising as well (Haynes 2011; Stern 2012).

On the other hand, *historical* studies reveal that in the past, the dividing line between chattel slaves, serfs, and other un-free subalterns taken together and 'free' wage earners was rather vague at best. On the African East Coast around 1900, for example, there lived quite a number of slaves who

> worked as self-employed artisans or skilled workers, some of whom had previously worked as day labourers but had learnt a more lucrative trade ... These self-employed slaves ... were respected for their knowledge and thus commanded exceedingly high prices in the market, but they were rarely for sale. With almost the same status as freed slaves, a number of them actually owned small garden plots, and occasionally even slaves.
>
> (Deutsch 2006: 71–2)

Especially Brazilian historians have pointed to the fluid dividing line between 'free' wage labour and chattel slavery, for example, in the case of the *ganhadores* (slaves for hire) who earned their own wage, part of which they had to hand over to their owners (Lara 1998; Reis 1997). In South Asia other ambivalences occur, for example, in the case of indentured labourers (*coolies*) who were employed in South Asia itself, but also in the Caribbean, Malaya, Natal, Fiji and elsewhere. Their situation is sometimes described as a 'new form of slavery', but at other times as 'nearly free' wage labour (Tinker 1974). In Australia, after lenghty hesitations, labour historians have no difficulty anymore in describing the numerous convict labourers originally settling in the country as 'working class' in the broad sense of the word, even though these workers performed forced labour (Roberts 2011). And for Europe, the new research reveals that many so-called 'free' workers were really *bonded* labourers, far into the nineteenth century. Master-and-servant laws, apprenticeship arrangements, etc., ensured that workers were tied to their employers, and had significantly fewer legal rights than the literature previously suggested. In this context, there has indeed been mention of 'industrial serfdom.' (McKinlay 1986; Steinfeld 1991; Hay and Craven 2004; Stanziani 2010). Contemporary analysts find that the relationship between a self-employed individual and his or her major customer is often hard to distinguish from the relationship between a wage earner and his or her employer (Form 1982; Steinmetz and Wright 1989).

CRITIQUING THE CLASSICS

These trends make it necessary to reconsider the connection between wage labour and capitalism. Classical thinkers like Max Weber and Karl Marx believed that capitalism and wage labour were two sides of the same coin. *Marx* reduced the working class to workers who as free individuals can dispose of their labour power as their own commodity, while they have no other commodity for sale (Marx 1976: 272). Capitalism is the mode of producion based on such workers. Other labour relations may also occur under capitalism, but they form 'an anomaly opposite the bourgeois system itself', which is 'possible at individual points within the bourgeois system of production", though "only because it does not exist at other points' (Marx 1973: 464). Other social groups like independent artisans and peasants have no real future and will decay and finally disappear in the face of Modern Industry' (Marx and Engels 1976: 494). Weber considered the 'formally purely voluntarist organization of labour' as the 'typical and dominant form for the satisfaction of the needs of the masses, with expropriation of the workers' means of production' (Weber 1921: 96).

But is there really such a privileged relationship between wage labour and capitalism? One could argue that Marx's distinction between chattel slave and 'free' wage earner was not correct. Marx engaged with issues related to slave labour in many passages of his work. He was more aware of the contrast between 'free' wage labour and slavery than most twenty-first- century scholars. As an expert on European antiquity (on which he wrote his doctoral thesis) and as a contemporary to the American Civil War, Marx was very much aware of the slavery problem (Backhaus 1974; de Sainte Croix 1975; Lekas 1988; Reichardt 2004). The first volume of *Capital* was published two years after the abolition of slavery in the United States in 1865 and 21 years before it was officially proclaimed in Brazil. Marx considered slavery a historically backward mode of exploitation that would soon be a thing of the past, as 'free' wage labour embodied the capitalist future. He compared the two labour forms in several writings. He certainly saw similarities between them – both produced a surplus product and 'the wage-labourer, just like the slave, must have a master to make him work and govern him' (Marx 1981: 510). At the same time, he distinguished some differences that overshadowed all the common experiences they shared. Let me offer some brief critical comments on them and indicate some doubts.

First: wage workers dispose of labour capacity, viz. 'the aggregate of those mental and physical capabilities existing in the physical form, the living personality, of a human being, capabilities which he sets in motion whenever he produces a use-value of any kind' (Marx 1976: 270) – and this labour capacity is the source of value; the capitalist purchases this labour capacity as a commodity, because he expects it to provide him with a 'specific service', namely the creation of 'more value than it has itself' (Marx 1976: 301). The same is not true of the slave's labour capacity. The slaveholder 'has paid cash for his slaves', and so 'the product of their labour represents the interest on the capital invested in their purchase' (Marx 1981: 762). But since interest is nothing but a form of surplus value, according to Marx it would seem that slaves would have to produce surplus value.[1] And it is a fact that the sugar plantations on which slave labour was employed yielded considerable profits, because the commodity – sugar – embodied more value than the capital invested by the plantation owner (ground rent, amortisation of the slaves, amortisation of the sugar cane press, etc.). So is it really the case that only the wage worker produces the equivalent of his/her own value plus 'an excess, a surplus-value' (Marx 1976: 317)? Or is the slave a 'source of value' as well?

Second: Marx states that labour power can

> appear on the market as a commodity only if, and in so far as, its possessor, the individual whose labour power it is, offers it for sale or sells it as a commodity. In order that its possessor may sell it as a commodity, he must have it at his disposal, he must be the free proprietor of his own labour capacity, hence of his person.
>
> (Marx 1976: 271)

The future wage worker and the money owner 'meet in the market, and enter into relations with each other on a footing of equality as owners of commodities, with the sole difference that one is a buyer, the other a seller; both are therefore equal in the eyes of the law' (Marx 1976: 271). In other words: labour power should be offered for sale by the person who is the carrier and possessor of this labour power and the person who sells the labour power offers it exclusively. Why should that be so? Why can the labour power not be sold by someone other than the carrier as, for example, in the case of children who are made to perform wage labour in a factory by their parents? Why can the person who offers (his or her own, or someone else's) labour power for sale not sell it conditionally, together with means of production? And why can someone who does not own his own labour power nevertheless sell this labour power, as in the case of rented slaves, whose owners provide them to someone else for a fee?[2]

Third: the wage worker embodies variable capital:

> It both reproduces the equivalent of its own value and produces an excess, a surplus value, which may itself vary, and be more or less according to circumstances. This part of capital is continually being transformed from a constant into a variable magnitude. I therefore call it the variable part of capital, or more briefly, variable capital.
>
> (Marx 1976: 317)

> It is only because labour is presupposed in the form of wage-labour, and the means of production in the form of capital (i.e. only as a result of this specific form of these two essential agents of production), that one part of the value (product) presents itself as surplus-value and this surplus-value presents itself as profit (rent), the gains of the capitalist, as additional available wealth belonging to him.
>
> (Marx 1981: 1021)[3]

To Marx, the slave is part of fixed capital and no different, economically, from livestock or machinery. 'The slave-owner buys his worker in the same way as he buys his horse' (Marx 1976: 377; the *Grundrisse* contain a similar passage: Marx 1973: 489–90). The slave's capital value is his purchasing price, and this capital value has to be amortised over time, just as with livestock and machinery (Marx 1981: 597). But how justified is Marx in defining only wage labour as variable capital, on the grounds that 'this part of capital' can 'be more or less' (Marx 1976: 317)? Is the same not true of commodity-producing slave labour?

Fourth: when the wage worker produces a commodity, this commodity is 'a unity formed of use-value and value', for which reason 'the process of production must be a unity, composed of the labour process and the process of creating value [*Wertbildungsprozess*]' (Marx 1976: 293). No one will doubt that slaves producing cane sugar, tobacco or indigo are producing commodities, just like wage workers. But if this is the case, then slaves also produce value. Marx denies this, since he considers slaves part of constant capital and holds that only variable capital creates value.

Fifth: the wage worker always divests himself of his labour power 'for a limited period only, for if he were to sell it in a lump, once and for all, he would be selling himself, converting himself from a free man into a slave, from an owner of a commodity into a commodity' (Marx 1976: 271). Normally, one would refer to such a transaction (the 'sale' of a commodity in instalments, without any change of owner) as a lease and not as a sale – an obvious idea that was already formulated much earlier.[4] The distinction between a lease and a sale may appear insignificant, but it is not. 'When a sales contract is closed, the substance of the commodity becomes the property of the other party, whereas when a lease contract is closed, the other party merely purchases the right to use the commodity; the seller only makes his commodity available temporarily, without relinquishing ownership of it', as Franz Oppenheimer (1912: 120) has rightly noted. When A sells B a commodity, B becomes the owner in lieu of A. But when A leases B a commodity, A remains the owner and B merely receives the right to use the commodity for a fixed term. The 'substance' of the commodity remains with A, whereas B receives its 'use and enjoyment'.[5] Thus, if wage labour is the leasing of labour power, the difference between a wage worker and a slave does not consist in the 'definite period of time' (Marx 1976: 271) for which labour power is made available, but in the fact that in one case, labour power is leased, while in the other it is sold. Why do we not find this consideration in Marx? Presumably because it makes the process of value creation appear in a different light. The substance of the value of labour power is retained by the worker rather than being yielded to the capitalist. Engels held that lease transactions are 'only a transfer of already *existing*, previously *produced* value, and the total sum of values possessed by the landlord and the tenant *together* remains the same after as it was before' (Engels 1988: 320). Thus if wage labour were a lease relation as well, it could not create surplus value.

Sixth: according to Marx, the rate of profit tends to decline because the social productivity of labour increases constantly:

Since the mass of living labour applied continuously declines in relation to the mass of objectified labour that sets it in motion, i.e. the productively consumed means of production, the part of this living labour that is unpaid and objectified in surplus-value must also stand in an ever-decreasing ratio to the value of the total capital applied.

(Marx 1981: 319)

The endpoint of this tendency would of course be a situation in which variable capital has been reduced to zero and total capital consists exclusively of constant capital. In such a situation, the collapse of capitalism would be a fact. But the odd thing is that there already existed such a terminal phase prior to the industrial revolution, namely on the plantations of the seventeenth and eighteenth centuries. These plantations employed slave labour, so that according to Marx's premises, total capital consisted exclusively of constant capital. How are we to account for the economic dynamism of the plantations on this basis?

The example of slave labour shows Marx did not provide a consistent justification for the privileged position productive wage labour is given within his theory of value. There is much to suggest that slaves and wage workers are structurally more similar than Marx and traditional Marxism suspected. The historical reality of capitalism has featured many hybrid and transitional forms between slavery and 'free' wage labour. Moreover, slaves and wage workers have repeatedly performed the same work in the same business enterprise.[6] It is true, of course, that the slave's labour capacity is the permanent property of the capitalist, whereas the wage worker only makes his labour capacity available to the capitalist for a limited time, even if he does so repeatedly. It remains unclear, however, why slaves should create no surplus value while wage workers do. The time has come to expand the theory of value in such a way as to recognise the productive labour of slaves and other un-free workers as an essential component of the capitalist economy.

A NEW CONCEPT

The implications are far reaching. Apparently, there is a large class of people within capitalism, whose labour power is commodified in various ways. I would like to call this class the *extended or subaltern working class*. Its members make up a very varied group: it includes chattel slaves, sharecroppers, small artisans and wage earners. It is the historic dynamics of this 'multitude' that we should try to understand. We have to consider that in capitalism there *always* existed, and probably will continue to exist, several forms of commodified labour subsisting side by side.

In its long development, capitalism utilised many kinds of work relationships, some mainly based on economic compulsion, others with a strong non-economic component. Millions of slaves were brought by force from Africa to the Caribbean, to Brazil and in the southern states of the USA. Contract workers from India and China were shipped off to toil in South Africa, Malaysia or South America. 'Free' migrant workers left Europe for the New World, for Australia or the colonies. And today sharecroppers produce an important portion of world agricultural output. These and other work relationships are synchronous, even if there seems to be a secular trend towards 'free wage labour', a long-term decrease of 'un-free' labour, and a somewhat counter-cyclical development of self-employment (Linder 1983; Bögenhold and Staber 1991; Cowling 1997). Slavery still exists (see e.g. Bales 2012; estimates vary between 12 and 27 million people), and sharecropping is enjoying a comeback in some regions (e.g. in US agriculture, see Wells 1996). Capitalism could and can chose whatever form of commodified labour it thinks fit in a given historical context: one variant seems most profitable today, another tomorrow. If this argument is correct, then it behoves us to conceptualise the wage-earning class as one (important) kind of commodified labour among others. Consequently, so-called 'free' labour cannot be seen as the only form of exploitation suitable for modern capitalism but as one alternative among several.[7]

Against this theoretical and empirical background, a possible new definition of the working class could be: the ensemble of carriers of labour power whose labour power is sold or hired out to another person under economic or non-economic compulsions, regardless of whether the carrier of labour power is himself or herself selling or hiring it out and, regardless of whether the carrier himself or herself owns means of production. All aspects of this provisional definition will however require further reflection.

Such a reconceptualisation and broadening of the notion of the working class will help us to better understand the many forms of resistance that have been used by subaltern workers over time. The classical approach suggests, for example, that strikes are a form of collective action that is associated especially with free wage labourers. But if we look at the ways in which protest is expressed and pressure is exerted by the different groups of subaltern workers (including slaves, the self-employed, the lumpenproletarians and the 'free' wage labourers), these appear to overlap considerably. In the past, all kinds of subaltern workers went on strike. The sharecropping silver miners in Chihuahua protested as early as the 1730s against the termination of their work contracts by the owners of the mine. They entrenched themselves in the nearby hills:

There they built a makeshift stone parapet, unfurled a banner proclaiming their defiance, and vowed to storm the villa of San Felipe, kill [the mine owner] San Juan y Santa Cruz, and burn his house to the ground. For the next several weeks they refused to budge from their mountain redoubt, where they passed time by composing and singing songs of protest.

The miners returned only after mediation by a priest sent by the bishop (English Martin 1996: 51). Slaves regularly went on strike too. Serfs in Russia refused 'to recognize their owner's authority over them'; they stopped working for him and decided 'to go on strike' (Kolchin 1987: 258). On plantations in the British Caribbean in the early nineteenth century there were walkouts by slaves:

> The rebellions in Demerara in 1829 and Jamaica in 1831 both began as versions of the modern work strike, coupled with other acts of defiance, but not with killing. Only when the local militia retaliated with force, assuming that this was another armed uprising, did such an occurrence actually take place.
>
> (Craton 1982: 301; Schuler 1991: 382–3)

A broadened concept of the working class will enable us to rethink the strike phenomenon. By including slaves and indentured labourers, it becomes possible to see that the strike is a very important, but also a specific form of the collective refusal to work. So-called un-free workers have used other forms of collective refusal that deserve to be integrated in our analysis. We all know of the maroons, the slaves who fled the plantations in North America as well as the Caribbean and South America. But this kind of resistance is not confined to the New World. Already in the ninth century the *Zanj*, slaves of East African origin working in the salt marshes of South Iraq, left their masters as a group and constructed the city of Al Mukhtara, in a spot chosen for its inaccessibility. And at the mainland coast of Tanganyika in 1873, plantation slaves fled in huge numbers and founded the village of Makorora, 'hidden in a thicket of thorny bushes' and with 'heavy fortifications' (Popovic 1976; Glassman 1991: 308).

In 1921 coolies on tea plantations in the Chargola Valley in Assam protested when the authorities refused a wage increase. They deserted the plantations en masse:

> They resolved to go back to their home districts, chanting victory cries to Mahatma Gandhi and claiming to have served under his orders. Soon, the entire Chargola Valley looked deserted, with two gardens reported to have 'lost' virtually their entire labour force, and on an average, most gardens had suffered losses of around thirty to sixty per cent. The coolies of Chargola Valley marched right through Karimganj,

the subdivisional headquarters, continuing their onward journey either by train or on foot, and also by steamer they made their way back to their home districts.

(Varma 2007: 34)

Seen against this background, the strikes of so-called free wage earners constitute just *one* form of collective resistance against the exploitation of commodified labour. And we should also acknowledge that conversely free wage labourers have often used methods of struggle that are usually associated with other groups of subaltern workers, such as lynching, rioting, arson and bombing.

By broadening our view on commodified labour under capitalism, we will be better placed to write the history of all those anonymous individuals and families who, as the playwright and poet Bertolt Brecht, wrote, 'built Thebes of the seven gates', and so often 'cooked the feast for the victors'.

NOTES

1. 'Rent, interest, and industrial profit are only different names for different parts of the surplus value of the commodity, or the unpaid labour enclosed in it, and they are equally derived from this source and from this source alone' (Marx, 1985: 133).
2. Marx was quite aware of this practice of renting slaves, but he drew no theoretical conclusions from it. See for example: Marx 1981, p. 597: 'Under the slave system the worker does have a capital value, namely his purchase price. And if he is hired out, the hirer must first pay the interest on this purchase price and on top of this replace the capital's annual depreciation.'
3. This is why surplus labour appears in two very different forms in these two cases. In the case of wage labour, the wage form eradicates 'every trace of the division of the working day into necessary labour and surplus labour, into paid labour and unpaid labour' (Marx 1976: 680). By contrast, in the case of slave labour, 'even the part of the working day in which the slave is only replacing the value of his own means of subsistence, in which he therefore actually works for himself alone, appears as labour for his master. All his labour appears as unpaid labour' (Marx 1976: 680).
4. Marx himself referred repeatedly to the analogy between rent and wage labour. He did so most extensively in the *Theories of Surplus Value*, where he writes that the worker is paid for his commodity (his labour capacity) only after he has finished working: 'It can also be seen that here it is the worker, not the capitalist, who does the advancing, just as in the case of the renting of a house, it is not the tenant but the landlord who advances use-value' (Marx 1989: 302); see also Marx 1976, p. 279: 'The price of the labour-power is fixed by the contract, although it is not realized till later, like the rent of a house.' On this, see also Kuczynski, forthcoming.
5. Different from Oppenheimer's belief – 'only the labour capacity that is intended for sale (e.g. that of the work ox, the slave) is a commodity, not that intended merely for lease' (1912: 121) – a lease contract also operates according to the logic of the commodity; this is precisely why the leasing fee depends on the value of the leased commodity.
6. E.g. on the coffee plantations around São Paulo, or in a chemical factory in Baltimore (see Hall and Stolcke 1983; Whitman 1993).
7. A quantification of long-term trends is not yet possible, but a large database currently built at the International Institute of Social History in Amsterdam (the so-called

Global Collabouratory on the History of Labour Relations, 1500–2000) will soon make first estimates possible. See www.socialhistory.org/en/projects/history-labour-relations-1500-2000.

REFERENCES

Allen, V.L. (1972), 'The Meaning of the Working Class in Africa', *Journal of Modern African Studies*, vol. 10, no. 2, 169–89.

Backhaus, Wilhelm (1974), *Marx, Engels und die Sklaverei. Zur ökonomischen Problematik der Unfreiheit*. Düsseldorf: Schwann.

Bales, Kevin (2012), *Disposable People: New Slavery in the Global Economy*. updated with a new preface. Berkeley: University of California Press.

Bögenhold, Dieter and Udo Staber (1991), 'The decline and rise of self-employment', *Work, Employment and Society*, vol. 5, no. 2, 223–39.

Cowling, Marc and Peter Mitchell (1997), 'The evolution of U.K. self-employment: A study of government policy and the role of the macroeconomy', *The Manchester School*, vol. 65, no. 4, 427–42.

Craton, Michael (1982), *Testing the Chains. Resistance to Slavery in the British West Indies.* Ithaca, NJ: Cornell University Press.

De Sainte Croix, Geoffroy E.M. (1975), 'Karl Marx and the history of classical antiquity', *Arethusa*, vol. 8, 7–41.

Deutsch, Jan-Georg (2006), *Emancipation without Abolition in German East Africa c. 1884–1914*. Oxford: Currey.

Engels, Friedrich (1988), 'The Housing Question', in Karl Marx and Friedrich Engels, *Collected Works*, vol. 23. Moscow: Progress, 315–91.

English Martin, Cheryl (1996), *Governance and Society in Colonial Mexico: Chihuahua in the Eighteenth Century*. Stanford, CA: Stanford University Press.

Form, William (1982), 'Self-employed manual workers: Petty bourgeois or working class?', *Social Forces*, vol. 60, 1050–69.

Glassman, Jonathon (1991), 'The bondsman's new clothes: The contradictory consciousness of slave resistance on the Swahili coast', *Journal of African History*, vol. 32, no. 2, 277–312.

Hall, Michael and Verena Stolcke (1983), 'The introduction of free labour on São Paulo coffee plantations', *Journal of Peasant Studies*, vol. 10, no. 2/3, 170–200.

Hay, Douglas and Paul Craven (eds) (2004), *Masters, Servants, and Magistrates in Britain and the Empire, 1562–1955*. Chapel Hill: University of North Carolina Press.

Haynes, V. Dion (2011), 'High unemployment spurs rise in self-employed', *The Washington Post*, 24 April.

Kocka, Jürgen (1986), 'Problems of working-class formation: The early years, 1800–1875', in: Ira Katznelson and Aristide R. Zolberg (eds), *Working-Class Formation: Nineteenth-Century Patterns in Western Europe and the United States*. Princeton University Press 1986, pp. 279–350.

Kolchin, Peter (1987), *Unfree Labour. American Slavery and Russian Serfdom*. Cambridge, MA: Belknap.

Kuczynski, Thomas (forthcoming), 'What is sold on the labour market?' in: Marcel van der Linden and Karl Heinz Roth (eds), *Beyond Marx. Confronting Labour History and the Concept of Labour with the Global Labour Relations of the 21st Century*. Leiden and Boston: Brill.

Lara, Silvia Hunold (1998), 'Escravidão, cidadania e história do trabalho no Brasil', *Projeto História*, no. 16, 25–38.

Lekas, Padelis (1988), *Marx on Classical Antiquity. Problems of Historical Methodology*. New York: Wheatsheaf.

Linder, Marc (1983), 'Self-employment as a cyclical escape from unemployment', *Research in the Sociology of Work*, 2261–73.

Linebaugh, Peter and Marcus Rediker (2000), *The Many-Headed Hydra. Sailors, Slaves, Commoners, and the Hidden History of the Revolutionary Atlantic*. London: Verso.

Marx, Karl (1973), *Grundrisse. Foundations of the Critique of Political Economy (Rough Draft)*. Translated with a foreword by Martin Nicolaus. Harmondsworth: Penguin.

Marx, Karl (1976), *Capital*, vol. I. Trans. Ben Fowkes. Harmondsworth: Penguin.

Marx, Karl (1981), *Capital*, vol. III. Trans. David Fernbach. Harmondsworth: Penguin.

Marx, Karl (1985), 'Value, Price and Profit', in Karl Marx and Frederick Engels, *Collected Works*, vol. 20. Moscow: Progress, 101–49.

Marx, Karl (1989) 'Economic Manuscripts of 1861–63', in Karl Marx and Frederick Engels, *Collected Works*, vol. 32. Moscow: Progress.

Marx, Karl and Frederick Engels, 'Manifesto of the Communist Party', in Karl Marx and Frederick Engels, *Collected Works*, vol. 6. Moscow: Progress, 477–519.

McKinlay, Alan (1986), 'From industrial serf to wage-labourer: The 1937 apprentice revolt in Britain', *International Review of Social History*, vol. 31, no. 1 (April), 1–18.

Oppenheimer, Franz (1912), *Die soziale Frage und der Sozialismus. Eine kritische Auseinandersetzung mit der marxistischen Theorie*. Jena: Fischer.

Popovic, Alexandre (1976). *La révolte des esclaves en Iraq au IIIe, IXe siècle*. Paris: P. Geuthner.

Reichardt, Tobias (2004), 'Marx über die Gesellschaft der klassischenAntike', *Beiträgezur Marx-Engels-Forschung*, new series, 194–222.

Reis, João (1997), ' ' "The revolution of the Ganhadores": Urban labour, ethnicity and the African strike of 1857 in Bahia, Brazil', *Journal of Latin American Studies*, vol. 29, 355–93.

Roberts, David Andrew (2011), 'The "knotted hands that set us high": Labour history and the study of convict Australia', *Labour History* [Sydney], no. 100, 33–50.

Schuler, Monica (1991), 'Akan slave rebellions in the British Carribean', in: Hilary Beckles and Verene Shepherd (eds), *Caribbean Slave Society and Economy: A Student Reader*. Kingston and London, pp. 373–86.

Standing, Guy (2011), *The Precariat: The New Dangerous Class*. London: Bloomsbury.

Stanziani, Alessandro (ed.) (2010), *Le travail contraint en Asie et en Europe: XVII–XXe siècles*. Paris: Editions de la Maison des Sciences de l'Homme.

Steinfeld, Robert J. (1991), *The Invention of Free Labour. The Employment Relation in English and American Law and Culture, 1350–1870*. Chapel Hill: University of North Carolina Press.

Steinmetz, George and Erik Olin Wright (1989), 'The fall and rise of the petty bourgeoisie: Changing patterns of self-employment in the postwar United States', *American Journal of Sociology*, vol. 94 (March), 973–1018.

Stern, Melanie (2012), 'Self-employment: The rise of the "odd-jobbers" ', *The Guardian*, 2 March.

Thompson, E.P. (1963), *The Making of the English Working Class*. London: Gollancz.

Tinker, Hugh (1974), *A New System of Slavery: The Export of India Labour Overseas, 1830–1920*. London: Oxford University Press.

Van der Linden, Marcel (2008), *Workers of the World. Essays toward a Global Labour History*. Leiden and Boston: Brill.

Varma, Nitin (2007), 'Chargola exodus and collective action in the colonial tea plantatons of Assam', sephis e-magazine, 2 January. Available at: http://sephisemagazine.org/issues/vol._3_2.pdf, 2, 34–7.

Weber, Max (1921), *Wirtschaft und Gesellschaft*. Tübingen: Mohr.

Wells, Miriam J. (1996), *Strawberry Fields. Politics, Class, and Work in California Agriculture*. Ithaca, NJ: Cornell University Press.

Whitman, T. Stephen (1993), 'Industrial slavery at the margin: The Maryland chemical works', *Journal of Southern History*, vol. 59, no. 1, 31–62.

4

THE REPRODUCTION OF LABOUR POWER IN THE GLOBAL ECONOMY AND THE UNFINISHED FEMINIST REVOLUTION

Silvia Federici

INTRODUCTION

What follows is a political reading of the restructuring of the (re)production of labour power in the global economy, but it is also a feminist critique of Marx that, in different ways, has been developing since the 1970s.[1] At the centre of it is the argument that Marx's analysis of capitalism has been hampered by his inability to conceive of value-producing work other than in the form of commodity production and his consequent blindness to the significance of unpaid reproductive work, which is still mostly performed by women, in the process of capitalist accumulation. Ignoring this work has limited Marx's understanding of the true extent of the capitalist exploitation of labour, and the obstacles in way of the class struggle. It has also prevented him from realising that much of the work involved in the production of labour power is irreducible to mechanisation, and that a full-scale industrialisation of labour – presumably a condition, in his political theory, for the 'transition' to communism – is a practical impossibility, in addition to being a catastrophe for our environment.

85

What, then, are the prospects that Marxist theory may serve as a guide to 'revolution' in our time? I ask this question by analysing the restructuring of the reproduction of labour power in the global economy. My claim is that if Marxist theory is to speak to twenty-first-century anti-capitalist movements, it must rethink the question of 'reproduction' from a planetary perspective. Reflecting on the activities that reproduce our life reveals, in fact, the true extent of the capitalist exploitation of unpaid labour, and dispels the illusion that the automation of production may create the material conditions for a non-exploitative society. It shows that the obstacle to revolution is not the lack of technological know-how, but the divisions that capitalist development has produced in the working class, starting with the unequal power relations between women and men, through the organisation of the wage relation, and that the danger we face today is not the lack of technology but the prospect of a continuing industrialisation of the planet and corporate appropriation of its resources. From this viewpoint rethinking the question of reproduction helps us to consider how Marx's analysis and categories should be revised to fit the need of contemporary anti-capitalist struggle and the ongoing experimentation with and construction of alternative to capitalist relations.

MARX AND THE REPRODUCTION OF THE WORK FORCE

Surprisingly, given his theoretical sophistication, Marx ignored the existence of women's reproductive work. He acknowledged that, no less than every other commodity, labour power must be produced and, insofar as it has a monetary value, it represents 'a definite quantity of the average social labour objectified in it' (Marx, *Capital*: 274). But while he meticulously explored the dynamics of yarn production and capitalist valorisation, he was succinct when tackling the question of reproductive work, reducing it to the workers' consumption of the commodities their wages can buy and the work the production of these commodities requires. In other words, as in the neo-liberal scheme, in Marx's account too, all that is needed to (re)produce labour power is commodity production and the market. No other work intervenes to prepare the goods the workers consume or to restore physically and emotionally their capacity to work. No difference is made between commodity production and the production of the workforce. One assembly line produces both. Accordingly, the value of labour power is measured by the value of the commodities (food, clothing, housing) that have to be supplied to the worker, to 'the man, so that he can renew his life-process', that is, they are measured on the labour time socially necessary for their production (ibid.: 276–7).

Even when he discusses the reproduction of the workers on a generational basis, Marx is extremely brief. He tells us that wages must be sufficiently high to ensure 'the worker's replacements', his children, so that labour power may perpetuate its presence on the market (ibid.: 275). But, once again, the only relevant agents he recognises in this process are the male, self-reproducing workers, their wages and their means of subsistence. The production of workers is by means of commodities. Nothing is said about women, domestic labour, sexuality and procreation. In the few instances in which he refers to biological reproduction, he treats it as a natural phenomenon. He acknowledges that 'the maintenance and reproduction of the working class remains a necessary condition for the reproduction of capital', but he immediately adds: 'the capitalist may safely leave this to the worker's drives for self-preservation and propagation. All the capitalist cares for is to reduce the worker's individual consumption to the necessary minimum' (ibid.: 178). At no point does Marx imagine that procreation may be the terrain of a social stuggle, that women, for instance, may refuse it, and that this may affect the size of the work-force. In his account, only changes in the organization of production – such as leaps in technological know-how – can bring about changes in the size of the labor force, periodically creating, for instance, a surplus population of workers.

Why did Marx so persistently ignore women's reproductive work? Why, for instance, did he not ask what transformations the raw materials involved in the process of reproduction of labour power must undergo in order for their value to be transferred into their products (as he did in the case of other commodities)? I suggest that the conditions of the working class in England – Marx's and Engel's point of reference – partly account for this omission (Federici 2004). Marx described the condition of the industrial proletariat of his time as he saw it, and women's domestic labour was hardly part of it. Housework, as a specific branch of capitalist production, was under Marx's historic and political horizon at least in the industrial working class. Although from the first phase of capitalist development, and especially in the mercantilist period, reproductive work was formally subsumed to capitalist accumulation, it was only in the late nineteenth century that domestic work emerged as the key engine for the reproduction of the industrial workforce, organised by capital for capital, according to the requirements of factory production. Until the 1870s, consistently with a policy tending to the 'unlimited extension of the working day' and the utmost compression of the cost of labour power production, reproductive work was reduced to a minimum, resulting in the situation powerfully described in volume 1 of *Capital*, in the chapter on the Working Day, and in Engels' *The Condition of the Working Class in England* (1845): that is, the situation of a working class almost unable to reproduce itself, averaging a life expectancy of 20 years of age, dying in its youth of overwork (Marx, Capital: 347).

Only at the end of the nineteenth century did the capitalist class begin to invest in the reproduction of labour, in conjunction with a shift in the form of accumulation, from light to heavy industry, requiring a more intensive labour discipline and a less emaciated type of worker (Seccombe 1993: 71–80; Fortunati 1995, 170–1). In Marxian terms, we can say that the development of reproductive work and the consequent emergence of the full-time housewife were the products of the transition from 'absolute' to 'relative surplus' value extraction as a mode of exploitation of labour.

We can also presume that the difficulties posed by the classification of a form of labour not subject to monetary valuation further motivated Marx to remain silent on this matter. But there is a further reason, more indicative of the limits of Marxism as a political theory, that we must take into account, if we are to explain why not just Marx, but generations of Marxists, raised in epochs in which housework and domesticity were triumphant, have continued to be blind to this work.

I suggest that Marx ignored women's reproductive labour because he remained wedded to a technologistic concept of revolution, where freedom comes through the machine, where the increase in the productivity of labour is assumed to be the material foundation for communism, and where the capitalist organisation of work is viewed as the highest model of histori-cal rationality, held up for every other form of production, including the reproduction of the workforce. In other words, Marx failed to recognise the importance of reproductive work because he accepted the capitalist criteria for what constitutes work, and he believed that waged industrial work was the stage on which the battle for humanity's emancipation would be played.

With few exceptions, Marx's followers have reproduced the same assump-tions (witness the continuing love affair with the famous 'Fragment on Machines' in the *Grundrisse* (1857–8)), demonstrating that the idealisation of science and technology as liberating forces has continued to be an essen-tial component of the Marxian view of history and revolution to our day. Even Socialist Feminists, while acknowledging the existence of women's repro-ductive work in capitalism, have in the past tended to stress its presum-ably antiquated, backward, pre-capitalist character and imagined the socialist reconstruction of it in the form of a rationalisation process, raising its produc-tivity level to that achieved by the leading sectors of capitalist production.

One consequence of this blind spot in modern times has been that Marxist theorists have been unable to grasp the historic importance of the post-World War II women's revolt against reproductive work, as expressed in the Women's

Liberation Movement, and have ignored its practical redefinition of what constitutes work, who is the working class, and what is the nature of class struggle. Only when women deserted the organisations of the Left did Marxists recognise the political importance of the Women's Liberation Movement. To this day, many Marxists do not acknowledge the gendered character of much reproductive work, as it is the case of even an eco-Marxist like Paul Burkett, or pay lip service to it, as in Negri's and Hardt's conception of 'affective labour'. Indeed, Marxist theorists are generally more indifferent to the question of reproduction than Marx himself, who devoted pages to the conditions of factory children, whereas today it would be a challenge to find any reference to children in most Marxist texts.

I will return later to the limits of contemporary Marxism, to notice its inability to grasp the significance of the neo-liberal turn and the globalisation process. For the moment suffice it to say that by the 1960s, under the impact of the anti-colonial struggle and the struggle against apartheid in the United States, Marx's account of capitalism and class relations was subjected to a radical critique by Third Worldist political writers like Samir Amin (Amin 1970) and Andre Gunder Frank (Gunder Frank 1967, 1966) who criticised its Euro-centrism and his privileging the wage industrial proletariat as the main contributor to capitalist accumulation and revolutionary subject. However, it was the revolt of women against housework, in Europe and the US, and later the spread of feminist movements across the planet, in the 1980s and 1990s, that triggered the most radical rethinking of Marxism.

WOMEN'S REVOLT AGAINST HOUSEWORK AND THE FEMINIST REDEFINITION OF WORK, CLASS STRUGGLE, AND CAPITALIST CRISIS

It seems to be a social law that the value of labour is proven and perhaps created by its refusal Caffentzis 2013). This was certainly the case of housework, which remained invisible and unvalued until a movement of women emerged who refused to accept the work of reproduction as their natural destiny. It was women's revolt against this work in the 1960s and 70s that disclosed the centrality of unpaid domestic labour in capitalist economy, reconfiguring our image of society as an immense circuit of domestic plantations and assembly lines where the production of workers is articulated on a daily and generational basis.

Not only did feminists establish that the reproduction of labour power involves a far broader range of activities than the consumption of commodities, since food must be prepared, clothes have to be washed, bodies have to be stroked and cared for. Their recognition of the importance of reproduction and women's domestic labour for capital accumulation led to a rethinking of Marx's categories and a new understanding of the history and fundamentals of capitalist development and the class struggle. Starting in the early 1970s, first articulated in Mariarosa Dalla Costa "Women and the Subversion of the Community" (1971), a feminist theory took shape that radicalised the theoretical shift which the Third World-ist critiques of Marx had inaugurated, confirming that capitalism is not necessarily identifiable with waged, contractual work, arguing that, in essence, it is un-free labour, and revealing the umbilical connection between the devaluation of reproductive work and the devaluation of women's social position.

This paradigm shift also had political consequences. The most immediate was the refusal of the slogans of the Marxist left such as the ideas of the 'general strike' or 'refusal of work', both of which were never inclusive of house-workers. Over time, the realisation has grown that Marxism, filtered through Leninism and social-democracy, has expressed the interests of a limited sector of the world proletariat, that of white, adult, male workers, largely drawing their power from the fact that they worked in the leading sectors of capital industrial production at the highest levels of technological development.

On the positive side, the discovery of reproductive work has made it possible to understand that capitalist production relies on the production of a particular type of worker – and therefore a particular type of family, sexuality, procreation – and thus to redefine the private sphere as a sphere of relations of production and a terrain of anti-capitalist struggle. In this context, policies forbidding abortion could be decoded as devices for the regulation of the labour supply, the collapse of the birth rate and increase in the number of divorces could be read as instances of resistance to the capitalist discipline of work. The personal became political and capital and the state were found to have subsumed our lives and reproduction down to the bedroom.

On the basis of this analysis, by the mid-1970s – a crucial time in capitalist policy making, during which the first steps were taken towards a neo-liberal restructuring of the world economy – many feminists could see that the unfolding capitalist crisis was a response not only to factory struggles but to women's refusal of housework, as well as to the increasing resistance of new generations of African, Asians, Latin Americans, Caribbeans to the legacy of colonialism. In other words, they could see that *the capitalist crisis was essentially a crisis of the command over the process of social reproduction and in particular the reproduction of the workforce.* Key contributors to this perspective were activists in the Wages For Housework Movement, like Mariarosa Dalla Costa,

Selma James, Leopoldina Fortunati, who showed that women's invisible struggles against domestic discipline were subverting the model of reproduction that had been the pillar of the Fordist deal. Dalla Costa, for instance, in *Riproduzione e Emigrazione* (1974) pointed out that, since the end of World War II, women in Europe had been engaged in a silent strike against procreation, as evinced by the collapse of the birth rate and governments' promotion of immigration. Fortunati in *Brutto Ciao* (1976) examined the motivations behind Italian women's post-World War II exodus from the rural areas, their re-orientation of the family wage towards the reproduction of the new generations, and the connections between women's post-war quest for independence, their increased investment in their children, and the increased combativeness of the new generations of workers. Selma James in *Sex, Race and Class* (1975) showed that women's 'cultural' behavior and social 'roles' should be read as a 'response and rebellion against' the totality of their capitalist lives.

By the mid-1970s women's struggle were no longer 'invisible', but had become an open repudiation of the sexual division of labour, with all its corollaries: economic dependence on men, social subordination, confinement to an unpaid, naturalised form of labour, a state-controlled sexuality and procreation. Contrary to a widespread misconception, the crisis was not confined to white middle-class women. Rather, the first Women's Liberation Movement in the United States was arguably a movement formed primarily by black women. It was the Welfare Mothers Movement that, inspired by the Civil Rights Movement, led the first campaign for state-funded 'wages for housework' (under the guise of Aid to Dependent Children) that women have fought for in the country, asserting the economic value of women's reproductive work and declaring 'welfare' a women's right (Milwaukee County Welfare Rights Organization 1972).

Women were on the move also across Africa, Asia, Latin America, as the decision by the United Nations to intervene in the field of feminist politics as the sponsor of women's rights, starting with the Global Conference on Women, held in Mexico City in 1975, demonstrated. Elsewhere I have suggested that the United Nations played the same role, with respect to the spreading international women movements, that it had already played, in the 1960s, in relation to the anti-colonial struggle. (Federici 2000). As in the case of its (selective) sponsorship of 'decolonisation', The UN's self-appointment as the agency in charge of promoting women's rights enabled it to channel the politics of women's liberation within a frame compatible with the needs and plans of international capital and the developing neo-liberal agenda. Indeed, the Mexico City conference and those that followed stemmed in part from a realisation that women's struggles over reproduction were redirecting post-colonial economies towards increased investment in the domestic workforce and were the most important factor in the failure of the World Bank's development plans for the commercialisation of agriculture. In Africa, women had consistently refused to be recruited to work on their husbands' cash crops, and instead had defended subsistence-oriented agriculture, turning their villages from sites for the reproduction of cheap labour – as in the image of it proposed by Meillassoux[2] – into sites of resistance to exploitation. By the 1980s, this resistance was recognised as the main factor in the crisis of the World Bank's agricultural development projects, prompting a flood of articles on 'women's contribution to development', and later, initiatives aimed at integrating them into the money economy such as NGO-sponsored 'income generating projects' and micro-credit lending schemes. Given these events, it is not surprising that the restructuring produced by the globalisation of the world economy has led to a major reorganisation of reproduction, as well as a campaign against women in the name of 'population control'.

In what follows I outline the modalities of this restructuring, identify the main trends, its social consequences, and its impact on class relations. First, however, I should explain why I continue to use the concept of labour power, even though some feminists have criticised it as reductive, pointing out that women produce living individuals – children, relatives, friends – not labour power. The critique is well taken. Labour power is an abstraction. As Marx tells us, echoing Sismondi, labour power 'is nothing unless it is sold' and utilised (Marx, *Capital*: 277). I maintain this concept, however, for various reasons. First, I do so in order to highlight the fact that in capitalist society reproductive work is not the free reproduction of ourselves or others according to our and their desires. To the extent that, directly or indirectly, it is exchanged for a wage, reproduction work is, at all points, subject to the conditions imposed on it by the capitalist organisation of work and relations of production. In other words, housework is not a free activity. It is the production and reproduction of the capitalist most indispensable means of production: the worker (Dalla Costa 1971). As such, it is subject to all the constraints that derive from the fact that its product must satisfy the requirements of the labour market.

Second, highlighting the reproduction of 'labour power' reveals the dual character and the contradiction inherent in reproductive labour and, therefore, the unstable, potentially disruptive character of this work. To the extent that labour power can only exist in the living individual, its reproduction must be simultaneously a production and valorisation of desired human qualities and capacities, and an accommodation to the externally imposed standards of the labour market. As impossible as it is, then, to draw a line between the living individual and its labour power, it is equally impossible to draw a line between the two corresponding aspects of reproductive work. Nevertheless, maintaining the concept brings out the tension, the potential separation, and it suggests a world of conflicts, resistances, contradictions that have political significance. Among other things (an understanding that was crucial for the Women's Liberation Movement) it tells us that we can struggle against housework without having to fear that we will ruin our communities, for this work imprisons the producers as well as those reproduced by it.

I also want to defend the way in which I continue to maintain, against postmodern trends, the separation between production and reproduction. There is certainly one important sense in which the difference between the two has become blurred. The struggles of the 1960s in Europe and United States, especially the student and feminist movements, have taught the capitalist class that investing in the reproduction of the future generation of workers 'does not pay'. It is not a guarantee of an increase in the productivity of labour. Thus, not only has state investment in the workforce drastically declined, but reproductive activities have been reorganised as value-producing services that workers must purchase and pay for. In this way, the value that reproductive activities produce is immediately realised, rather than being made conditional on the performance of the workers they reproduce. But the expansion of the service sector has by no means eliminated home-based, unpaid reproductive work, nor has it abolished the sexual division of labour in which it is embedded, which still divides production and reproduction in terms of the subjects of these activities and the discriminating function of the wage and lack of it.

Lastly, I speak of 'reproductive', rather than 'affective' labour because in its dominant characterisation, the latter describes only a limited part of the work that the reproduction of human beings requires and erases the subversive potential of the feminist concept of reproductive work (Federici 2011). By highlighting its function in the production of labour power, and thus unveiling the contradictions inherent in this work, the concept of 'reproductive labour' recognises the possibility of crucial alliances and forms of co-operation between producers and the reproduced: mothers and children, teachers and students, nurses and patients.

Keeping this particular character of reproductive work in mind, let us ask then: how has economic globalisation restructured the reproduction of the workforce? And what have been the effects of this restructuring on workers and especially on women, traditionally the main subjects of reproductive work? Finally, what do we learn from this restructuring concerning capitalist development and the place of Marxist theory in the anti-capitalist struggles of our time? My answer to these questions is in two parts. First, I will discuss briefly the main changes that globalisation has produced in the general process of social reproduction and the class relation, and then I will discuss more extensively the restructuring of reproductive work.

NAMING OF THE INTOLERABLE: PRIMITIVE ACCUMULATION AND THE RESTRUCTURING OF REPRODUCTION

There are five major ways in which the restructuring of the world economy has responded to the cycle of struggles of the 1960s and 1970s and transformed the organisation of reproduction and class relations. First, there has been the expansion of the labour market. Globalisation has produced a historic leap in the size of the world proletariat, both through a global process of 'enclosures' that has separated millions from their lands, their jobs, their 'customary rights', and through the increased employment of women. Not surprisingly, globalisation has presented itself as a process of primitive accumulation, which has taken many forms. In the North, globalisation has taken the form of industrial de-concentration and relocation, as well as the flexibilisation and precarisation of work, and just-in-time (JIT) production. In the former socialist countries, there has been the de-statalisation of industry, the de-collectivisation of agriculture and privatisation of social wealth. In the South, we have witnessed the *maquilisation* of production, import liberalisation and land privatisation. The objective, however, has everywhere been the same.

By destroying subsistence economies, by separating producers from the means of subsistence and making millions dependent on monetary incomes, even when unable to access waged employment, the capitalist class has re-launched the accumulation process and cut the cost of labour production. Two billion people have been added to the world labour market demonstrating the fallacy of theories arguing that capitalism no longer requires massive amounts of living labour, because it presumably relies on the increasing automation of work.

Second, the de-territorialisation of capital and financialisation of economic activities, which the 'computer revolution' has made possible, have created the conditions whereby primitive accumulation has become a permanent process, through the almost instantaneous movement of capital across the world, breaking over and over the constraints placed on capital by workers' resistance to exploitation.

Third, we have witnessed the systematic disinvestment by the state in the reproduction of the work force, implemented through structural adjustment programs and the dismantling of the 'welfare state'. As already mentioned, the struggles of the 1960s have taught the capitalist class that investing in the reproduction of labour power does not necessarily translate into a higher productivity of work. As a result, a policy and an ideology have emerged that recast workers as micro-entrepreneurs, responsible for their self-investment, being presumably the exclusive beneficiaries of the reproductive activities expended on them. Accordingly a shift has occurred in the temporal fix between reproduction and accumulation. As subsidies to healthcare, education, pensions, and public transport have all been cut, as high fees have been placed upon them, and workers have been forced to take on the cost of their reproduction, every articulation of the reproduction of labour power has been turned into an immediate point of accumulation.

Fourth, the corporate appropriation and destruction of forests, oceans, waters, fisheries, coral reefs, animal and vegetable species has reached an historic peak. In country after country, from Africa to the Pacific Islands, immense tracts of crop lands, and coastal waters – home and sources of livelihood for large populations – have been privatised and made available for agribusiness, mineral extraction, or industrial fishing. Globalisation has so unmistakably revealed the cost of capitalist production and technology that it has become unconceivable to speak, as Marx did in the *Grundrisse*, of the 'civilizing influence of capital', issuing from its 'universal appropriation of nature' and 'its production of a stage of society [where] nature becomes simply':

> an object for mankind, purely a matter of utility, [where] it ceases to be recognized as a power in its own right; and the theoretical acknowledgement of its independent laws appears only as a stratagem designed to subdue it to human requirements, either as an object of consumption or a means of production.
>
> (Marx 1977: 363–4)

In 2011, after the BP spill and Fukushima – among other corporate-made disasters – as the oceans are dying, imprisoned by islands of trash, as space is becoming a junk yard as well as an army depot, such words can have for us only ominous reverberations.

In different degrees, these developments have affected all populations across the planet. Yet, the New World Order is best described as a process of re-colonisation. Far from flattening the world into a network of inter-dependent circuits, it has reconstructed it as a pyramidal structure, increasing inequalities and social/economic polarisation, and deepening the hierarchies that have historically characterised the sexual and international division of labour, which the anti-colonial and the women's liberation movements had undermined.

The strategic center of primitive accumulation has been the former colonial world, historically the underbelly of the capitalist system, the place of slavery and plantations. I call it the 'strategic center' because its restructuring has been the foundation and precondition for the global reorganisation of production and the world labour market.

It is here, in fact, that we have witnessed the first and most radical processes of expropriation and pauperisation and the most radical disinvestment by the state in the reproduction of the labour force. These processes are well documented (Mander and Goldsmith 1996; Yong Kim et al. 2000). Starting in the early 1980s, as a consequence of structural adjustment, unemployment in most 'Third World' countries has soared so high that the US Agency For International Development USAID could recruit workers offering nothing more than 'food for work'. Wages have fallen so low that women *maquila* workers have been reported buying milk by the glass and eggs or tomatoes one at a time. Entire populations have been demonetised, while their lands have been taken away for government projects or given to foreign investors. Presently, half the African continent is on emergency food aid. (Moyo and Yeros 2005: 1) In West Africa, from Niger, to Nigeria, to Ghana, the electricity has been turned off, national grids have been disabled, forcing those who can afford them to buy individual generators whose buzzing sound fills the nights, making it difficult for people to sleep. Governmental health and education budgets, subsidies to farmers, support for basic necessities, all have been gutted, slashed and axed. As a consequence, life expectancy is falling and phenomena have reappeared that capitalism's civilising influence was supposed to have erased from the face of the earth long ago: famines, starvation, recurrent epidemics, even witch-hunts. (Federici 2008) Where 'austerity' programs and land-grabbing could not reach, war has completed the task, opening new grounds for oil drilling and the harvesting of diamonds or coltan. As for the targets of these clearances, they have become the subjects of a new diaspora, siphoning millions of people from the land to the towns, which more and more resemble encampments. Mike Davis (2006) has used the phrase 'planet of slums' in referring to this situation, but a more correct and vivid description would speak of a planet of ghettos and a regime of global apartheid.

If we further consider that, through the debt crisis and structural adjustment, 'Third World' countries have been forced to divert food production from the domestic to the export market, to turn arable land from cultivation of edible crops to mineral extraction and bio-fuel production, to clear-cut their forests, and become dumping grounds for all kinds of waste, as well as grounds of predation for corporate gene hunters, then, we must conclude that, in international capital's plans there are now world regions destined to 'near-zero-reproduction'. Indeed, the destruction of life in all its forms is today as important as the productive force of biopower in the shaping of capitalist relations, as a means to acquire raw materials, dis-accumulate unwanted workers, blunt resistances, and cut the cost of labour production.

It is a measure of the degree to which the reproduction of the workforce has been underdeveloped that, worldwide, millions are facing untold hardships and the prospect of death and incarceration in order to migrate. Certainly migration is not just a necessity, but an exodus towards higher levels of struggle, a means to re-appropriate the stolen wealth, as argued by Yann Moulier Boutang and Dimitris Papadopoulos, Niamh Stephenson, Vassilis Tsianos among others (Moulier Boutang 1998; Papadopoulos et al. 2008). This is why migration has acquired an autonomous character that makes it difficult to use as a regulatory mechanism for the structuring of the labour market. But there is no doubt that, if millions of people leave their countries for an uncertain destiny, thousands of miles away from their homes, it is because they cannot reproduce themselves, not at least under adequate living conditions. This is especially evident when we consider that half of the migrants are women, many married with children they must leave behind. From a historical viewpoint this practice is highly unusual. Women are usually those who stay, not due to lack of initiative or traditional restraints, but because they are those who have been made to feel most responsible for the reproduction of their families. They are the ones who have to make sure that the children have food, often themselves going without it, and who make sure that the elderly or the sick are cared for. Thus, when hundreds of thousands leave their homes to face years of humiliation and isolation, living with the anguish of not being able to give to the people they love the same care they give to strangers across the world, we know that something quite dramatic is happening in the organisation of world reproduction.

We must reject, however, the conclusion that the indifference of the international capitalist class to the loss of life which globalisation is producing is a proof that capital no longer needs living labour. In reality, the destruction of human life on a large scale has been a structural component of capitalism from its inception, as the necessary counterpart of the accumulation of labour power, which is inevitably a violent process. The recurrent 'reproduction crises' that we have witnessed in Africa over the last decades are rooted in this dialectic of labour accumulation and destruction. Also the expansion of non-contractual labour and of other phenomena that may seem like abominations in a 'modern world' – such as mass incarceration, the traffic in blood, organs and other human parts – should be understood in this context.

Capitalism fosters a permanent reproduction crisis. If this has not been more apparent in our lifetimes, at least in many parts of the Global North, it is because the human catastrophes it has caused have been most often externalised, confined to the colonies, and rationalised as an effect of cultural backwardness or attachment to misguided traditions and 'tribalism'. For most of the 1980s and 90s, moreover, the effects of the global restructuring in the North were hardly felt except in communities of color, or could appear in some cases (e.g. the flexibilisation and precarisation of work) as liberating alternatives to the regimentation of the 9-to-5 routine, if not anticipations of a workerless society.

But seen from the viewpoint of the totality of worker–capital relations, these developments demonstrate capital's continuing power to de-concentrate workers and undermine workers' organisational efforts in the waged workplace. Combined, these trends have abrogated social contracts, deregulated labour relations, re-introduced non-contractual forms of labour not only destroying the pockets of communism that a century of workers' struggle had won but threatening the production of new 'commons'.

In the North as well, real incomes and employment have fallen, access to land and urban spaces has been reduced, and impoverishment and even hunger have become widespread. Thirty-seven million are going hungry in the United States, according to a recent report, while 50 per cent of the population, by estimates conducted in 2011, is considered 'low income'. Add that the introduction of labour-saving technologies far from reducing the length of the working day has greatly extended it, to the point that (in Japan) we have seen people dying from work, while 'leisure time' and retirement have become a luxury. Moonlighting is now a necessity for many workers in the United States while, stripped of their pensions, many 60- to 70-year olds are returning to the labour market. Most significantly, we are witnessing the development of a homeless, itinerant workforce, compelled to nomadism, always on the move, on trucks, trailers, buses, looking for work wherever an opportunity appears, a destiny once reserved in the United States to seasonal agricultural workers chasing crops, like birds of passage, across the country.

Along with impoverishment, unemployment, overwork, homelessness, and debt has gone the increasing criminalisation of the working class, through a mass incarceration policy recalling the seventeenth-century Grand Confinement, and the formation of an *ex-lege* proletariat made of undocumented immigrant workers, students defaulting on their loans, producers or sellers of illicit goods, sex workers. It is a multitude of proletarians, existing and labouring in the shadow, reminding us that the production of populations without rights – slaves, indentured servants, peons, convicts, *sans papiers* – remains a structural necessity of capital accumulation.

Especially harsh has been the attack on youth, particularly working class black youth, the potential heir of the politics of Black Power, to whom nothing has been conceded, neither the possibility of secure employment nor access to education. But for many middle-class youth as well, the future is in question. Studying comes at a high cost, causing indebtedness and the likely default on student loans repayment. Competition for employment is stiff, and social relations are increasingly sterile as instability prevents community building. Not surprisingly, among the social consequences of the restructuring of reproduction, there has been an increase in youth suicide, as well as an increase in violence against women and children including infanticide. It is impossible, then, to share the optimism of those like Negri and Hardt, who in recent years have argued that the new forms of production that the global restructuring of the economy has created already provide for the possibility of more autonomous, more co-operative forms of work.

The assault on our reproduction has not gone unchallenged, however. Resistance has taken many forms, some remaining invisible until they are recognised as mass phenomena. The financialisation of everyday reproduction through the use of credit cards, loans, indebtedness, especially in the United States, should be also seen in this perspective, as a response to the decline in wages and a refusal of the austerity imposed by it, rather than simply a product of financial manipulation. Across the world, a movement of movements has also grown that, since the 1990s, has challenged every aspect of globalisation – through mass demonstrations, land occupations, the construction of solidarity economies and other forms of commons building. Most important, the recent spread of prolonged mass uprisings and 'Occupy' movements that over the last year has swept much of the world, from Tunisia, to Egypt, through most of the Middle East, to Spain, and the United States, have opened a space where the vision of a major social transformation again becomes possible. After years of apparent closure, where nothing seemed capable of stopping the destructive powers of a declining capitalist order, the 'Arab Spring' and the sprawling of tents across the American landscape, joining the many already set in place by the growing population of homeless, show the bottom is once again rising, and a new generation is walking the squares determined to reclaim their future, and choosing forms of struggle that potentially can begin to build a bridge across some of the main social divides.

REPRODUCTIVE LABOUR, WOMEN'S WORK, AND GENDER RELATIONS IN THE GLOBAL ECONOMY

Against this background, we must now ask how reproductive work has fared in the global economy, and how the changes it has undergone have shaped the sexual division of labour and the relations between women and men. Here as well, the substantive difference between production and reproduction stands out. The first difference to be noticed is that while production has been restructured through a technological leap in key areas of the world economy, no technological leap has occurred in the sphere of domestic work, significantly reducing the labour socially necessary for the reproduction of the workforce, despite the massive increase in the number of women employed outside the home. In the North, the personal computer has entered the reproduction of a large part of the population, so that shopping, socialising, acquiring information, and even some forms of sex work can now be done online. Japanese companies are promoting the robotisation of companionship and mating. Among their inventions are 'nursebots' that give baths to the elderly and the interactive lover to be assembled by the customer, crafted according to his fantasies and desires (Folbre 2006: 349–60). But even in the most technologically developed countries, housework has not been significantly reduced. Instead, it has been marketised, redistributed mostly on the shoulders of immigrant women from the South and the former socialist countries. And women continue to perform the bulk of it. Unlike other forms of production, the production of human beings is to a great extent irreducible to mechanisation, requiring a high degree of human interaction and the satisfaction of complex needs in which physical and affective elements are inextricably combined. That reproductive work is a labour-intensive process is most evident in the care of children and the elderly that, even in its most physical components, involves providing a sense of security, consoling, anticipating fears and desires. None of these activities is purely 'material' or 'immaterial', nor can be broken down in ways that make it possible for it to be mechanised or replaced by the virtual flow of online communication.

This is why, rather than being technologised, housework and care work have been redistributed on the shoulders of different subjects through its commercialisation and globalisation. As the participation of women in waged work has immensely increased, especially in the North, large quotas of housework have been taken out of the home and reorganised on a market basis through the virtual boom of the service industry, which now constitutes the dominant economic sector from the viewpoint of wage employment. This means that more meals are now eaten out of the home, more clothes are washed in laundromats or by dry-cleaners, and more food is bought already prepared for consumption.

There has also been a reduction of reproductive activities as a result of women's refusal of the discipline involved in marriage and child-raising. In the United States, the number of births has fallen from 118 per 1,000 women in 1960s to 66.7 in 2006, resulting in an increase in the median age of first time mothers from 30 in 1980 to 36.4 in 2006. The birth rate hit a record low in 2011 when it "dropped to its lowest level in 90 years" with a rate of 63.2 children per 1,000 women of childbearing age (Czekalinski 2013). The drop in the demographic growth has been especially high in Western and Eastern Europe, where in some countries (e.g. Italy, Spain and Greece), women's 'strike' against procreation continues, resulting in a zero growth demographic regime that is raising much concern among policy makers, and is the main factor behind the growing call for an expansion of immigration (Russell Shorto 2008; Jo Butler 2013). There has also been a decline in the number of marriages and married couples, in the US from 56 per cent of all households in 1990 to 51 per cent in 2006, and a simultaneous increase in the number of people living alone – in the US by 7.5 million, from 23 to 30.5 million—amounting to a 30 per cent increase. By 2011 only half of American adults were married (Cohn et al. 2011).

Most important, in the aftermath of structural adjustment and economic reconversion, a restructuring of reproductive work has taken place internationally, whereby much of the reproduction of the metropolitan workforce is now performed by immigrant women coming from the Global South, especially providing care to children and the elderly and for the sexual reproduction of male workers. This has been an extremely important development from many viewpoints. Nevertheless its political implications are not yet sufficiently understood among feminists from the viewpoint of the power relations it has produced among women, and the limits of the commercialisation of reproduction it has exposed. While governments celebrate the 'globalisation of care', which enables them to reduce investment in reproduction, it is clear that this 'solution' has a tremendous social cost, not only for the individual immigrant women but for the communities from which they originate.

Neither the reorganisation of reproductive work on a market basis, nor the 'globalisation of care', much less the technologisation of reproductive work, have 'liberated women' or eliminated the exploitation inherent to reproductive work in its present form. If we take a global perspective we see that not only do women still do most of the unpaid domestic work in every country, but due to cuts in social services and the decentralisation of industrial production, the amount of domestic work, paid and unpaid, that women perform may have actually increased, even when they have had a extra-domestic job.

Three factors have lengthened women's workday and returned work to the home.

First, women have been the shock absorbers of economic globalisation, having had to compensate with their work for the deteriorating economic conditions produced by the liberalisation of the world economy and the states' increasing disinvestment in the reproduction of the workforce. This has been especially true in the countries subjected to structural adjustment programs where the state has completely cut spending for healthcare, education, infrastructure and basic necessities. As a consequence of these cuts, in most of Africa and South America, women must now spend more time fetching water, obtaining and preparing food, and dealing with illnesses that are far more frequent at a time when the privatisation of healthcare has made visits to clinics unaffordable for most, while malnutrition and environmental destruction have increased people's vulnerability to disease.

In the United States, too, due to budget cuts, much of the work that hospitals and other public agencies have traditionally done has been privatised and transferred to the home, tapping women's unpaid labour. Presently, for instance, patients are dismissed almost immediately after surgery and the home must absorb a variety of post-operative and other therapeutic medical tasks (e.g. for the chronically ill) that in the past would have been done by doctors and professional nurses (Glazer 1993). Public assistance to the elderly (with housekeeping, personal care) has also been cut, house visits have been much shortened, and the services provided reduced.

The second factor that has re-centered reproductive labour in the home has been the expansion of 'homework', partly due to the de-concentration of industrial production, partly to the spread of informal work. As David Staples writes in *No Place Like Home* (2006), far from being an anachronistic form of work, home-based labour has been demonstrated to be a long-term capitalist strategy, which today occupies millions of women and children worldwide, in towns, villages and suburbs. Staples correctly points out that work is inexorably drawn to the home by the pull of unpaid domestic labour, in the sense that by organising work on a home basis, employers can make it invisible, can undermine workers' effort to unionise, and drive wages down to a minimum. Many women choose this work in the attempt to reconcile earning an income with caring for their families; but the result is enslavement to a work that earns wages 'far below the median wage it would pay if performed in a formal setting, and reproduces a sexual division of labour that fixes women more deeply to housework' (Staples 2006: 1–5).

Lastly, the growth of female employment and restructuring of reproduction have not eliminated gender labour hierarchies. Despite growing male unemployment, women still earn a fraction of male wages. We have also witnessed an increase in male violence against women, triggered in part by fear of economic competition, in part by the frustration men experience in not being able to fulfill their role as family providers, and most important, triggered by the fact that men now have less control over women's bodies and work, as more women have some money of their own and spend more time outside the home. In a context of falling wages and widespread unemployment that makes it difficult for them to have a family, many men also use women's bodies as a means of exchange and access to the world market, through the organisation of pornography or prostitution.

This rise of violence against women is hard to quantify and its significance is better appreciated when considered in qualitative terms, from the viewpoint of the new forms it has taken. In several countries, under the impact of structural adjustment, the family has all but disintegrated. Often this occurs out of mutual consent – as one or both partners migrate(s) or both separate in search of some form of income. But many times, it is a more traumatic event, when husbands desert their wives and children, for instance, in the face of pauperisation. In parts of Africa and India, there have also been attacks on older women, who have been expelled from their homes and even murdered after being charged with witchcraft or possession by the devil. This phenomenon likely reflects a larger crisis in family support for members who are seen as no longer productive in the face of rapidly diminishing resources. Significantly, it has also been associated with the ongoing dismantling of communal land systems (Hinfelaar 2007). But it is also a manifestation of the devaluation that reproductive work and the subjects of this work have undergone in the face of the expansion of monetary relations (Federici 2008).

Other examples of violence traceable to the globalisation process have been the rise of dowry murder in India, the increase in trafficking and other forms of coerced sex work, and the sheer increase in the number of women murdered or disappeared. Hundreds of young women, mostly *maquila* workers, have been murdered in Ciudad Juarez and other Mexican towns in the borderlands with the United States, apparently victims of rape or criminal networks producing pornography and 'snuff'. A ghastly increase in the number of women murder victims has also been registered in Mexico and Guatemala. But it is above all institutional violence that has escalated. This is the violence of absolute pauperisation, of inhuman work conditions, of migration in clandestine conditions. That migration can also be viewed as a struggle for increased autonomy and self-determination through flight, as a search for more favourable power relations, cannot obliterate this fact.

CONCLUSION

Several conclusions are to be drawn from this analysis. First, fighting for waged work or fighting to 'join the working class in the workplace', as some Marxist feminist liked to put it, cannot be a path to liberation. Wage employment may be a necessity but it cannot be a coherent political strategy. As long as reproductive work is devalued, as long it is considered a private matter and women's responsibility, women will always confront capital and the state with less power than men, and in conditions of extreme social and economic vulnerability. It is also important to recognise that there are serious limits to the extent to which reproductive work can be reduced or reorganised on a market basis. How far, for example, can we reduce or commercialise the care for children, the elderly, the sick, without imposing a great cost on those in need of care? The degree to which the marketisation of food production has contributed to the deterioration of our health (leading, for example, to the rise of obesity even among children) is instructive. As for the commercialisation of reproductive work through its redistribution on the shoulders of other women, as presently organised this 'solution' only extends the housework crisis, now displaced to the families of the paid care providers, and creates new inequalities among women.

What is needed is the re-opening of a collective struggle over reproduction, reclaiming control over the material conditions of our reproduction and creating new forms of co-operation around this work outside of the logic of capital and the market. This is not a utopia, but a process already under way in many parts of the world and likely to expand in the face of a collapse of the world financial system. Governments are now attempting to use the crisis to impose stiff austerity regimes on us for years to come. But through land takeovers, urban farming, community-supported agriculture, through squats, the creation of various forms of barter, mutual aid, alternative forms of healthcare – to name some of the terrains on which this reorganisation of reproduction is more developed – a new economy is beginning to emerge that may turn reproductive work from a stifling, discriminating activity into the most liberating and creative ground of experimentation in human relations.

As I stated, this is not a utopia. The consequences of the globalisation of the world economy would certainly have been far more nefarious except for the efforts that millions of women have made to ensure that their families would be supported, regardless of their value on the capitalist labour market. Through their subsistence activities, as well as various forms of direct action (from squatting on public land to urban farming) women have helped their communities to avoid total dispossession, to extend budgets and add food to the kitchen pots. Amid wars, economic crises and devaluations, as the world around them was falling apart, they have planted corn on abandoned town plots, cooked food to sell on the side of the streets, created communal kitchens – *ola communes*, as in Chile and Peru – thus standing in the way of a total commodification of life and beginning a process of re-appropriation and re-collectivisation of reproduction that is indispensable if we are to regain control over our lives. The festive squares and Occupy movements of 2011 are in a way a continuation of this process, as the 'multitudes' have understood that no movement is sustainable that does not place at its center the reproduction of those participating in it, thus also transforming the protest demonstrations into moments of collective reproduction and co-operation.

This is the lesson Marxists need to learn if Marxism is to speak to the struggles of the twenty-first century. If, as Marx taught us, communism is not an idea projected towards a constantly receding future, but 'We call communism the real movement which abolishes the present state of things' (Marx, *German Ideology*, 1847), then, the transformation of our everyday life must be the first irreplaceable step towards it. This, however, will require discarding some of Marx's key assumptions concerning the preconditions for the construction of communism, such as need for large-scale industry and for the integration of science and technology into every aspect of production. These objectives today are largely realised and we can see that rather than ushering a more just society they are threatening our life on this planet. This should not be surprising. As Audre Lorde powerfully put it, 'the master's tool cannot dismantle the master's house'. Indeed science, technology, and industry will have to undergo radical transformation before they can become instruments of human liberation, for in their present capitalist forms they cannot be redirected to positive goals more than nuclear weapons can be used to promote peace. Marx's theory will also need to venture into new domains that, so far, only Marxist Feminists, mostly women, have explored, such as relations with children and sexual relations, topics almost impossible to find in any contemporary Marxist texts. Yet, if a more egalitarian society is to be constructed we need to investigate how to put an end to the systematic degradation of children, how to rethink and transcend sexual differentiation, how to transform our sexuality so that sexual encounters are freed from the possessiveness and jealousies that tear so many proletarian relations apart. This is but a small sample of the many crucial issues that Marxist theory so far has ignored, for the most part being declined in the masculine, but it will have to confront if it is to be a guide for social transformation in our time.

NOTES

1. This critique was first articulated by activists in the Campaign for Wages For Housework, especially Mariarosa Dalla Costa, Selma James, Leopoldina Fortunati, and Silvia Federici, among others. On this subject see Federici (2004) and Federici (2012).
2. Meillassoux (1975). Meillassoux has argued that women's subsistence farming has been a bonus for governments, companies, and development agencies in that it has enabled them to more effectively exploit African labour, through a constant transfer of wealth and labour from the rural to the the urban areas (Meillassoux, 110–11).

REFERENCES

Amin, Samir (1970). *Accumulation on a World Scale: A Critique of the Theory of Underdevelopment*. New York: Monthly Review Press.

Barbagallo, Camille and Silvia Federici eds. (2012). '*Care Work' and the Commons*, Published as *The Commoner*, Issue N.15, (Winter 2012): 95–157, thecommoner.co.uk.

Burkett, Paul (2006). *Marxism and Ecological Economics: Toward a Red and Green Political Economy*. Boston: Brill.

Butler, Jo (2013). 'Birth Rate Drops to the Lowest Ever', *Daily Mail*, 28 July 2013.

Caffentzis, George (2013). *In Letters of Blood and Fire. Work, Machines, and the Crisis of Capitalism*. Oakland: PM Press.

Czekalinski, Stephanie (2013). 'U.S. Birth Rate Hits Record Low', *National Journal*, 30 May 2013, NationalJournal.com.

Cohn, D'Vera et al. (2011). 'Barely Half of U.S. Adults are Married. A Record Low', *Pew Research Social & Demographic Trends*, December 14, 2011.

Cox, Nicole and Silvia Federici (1975). *Counterplanning from the Kitchen*. Bristol: Falling Wall Press. Reprinted in Silvia Federici, *Revolution at Point Zero* (2012): 28–40.

Dalla Costa, Mariarosa (1974). 'Riproduzione e Emigrazione' In Alessandro Serafini ed., *L'Operaio Multinazionle in Europa*. Milano: Feltrinelli, 1974. [Translated into English by Silvia Federici and Harry Cleaver, and published as 'Reproduction and Emigration' in Camille Barbagallo and Silvia Federici eds. (2012) : 95–157].

Dalla Costa Mariarosa (1971). "Women and the Subversion of the Community." Published in Dalla Costa-James (1975).

Dalla Costa, Mariarosa and Selma James (1975). *The Power of Women and the Subversion of the Community*. Bristol: Falling Wall Press.

Dalla Costa, Mariarosa and Leopoldina Fortunati (1976). *Brutto Ciao. Direzione di marcia delle donne negli ultimi trent'anni*. Roma: Edizioni delle donne.

Davis, Mike (2006). *Planet of Slums: Urban Involution and the Informal Working* Class. London: Verso.

Engels, Friederich (1980). *The Condition of the Working Class in England*. Moscow: Progress Publishers. (First Published in 1845).

Federici, Silvia (2012). *Revolution at Point Zero. Housework, Reproduction and Feminist Struggle*. Oakland: PM Press.

Federici, Silvia (2011). 'On Affective Labour-, in Michael. A. Peters and Ergin Bulut (eds), *Cognitive Capitalism, Education and Digital Labour*. New York: Peter Lang, pp. 23–6.

Federici, Silvia (2008). "Witch-Hunting and Feminist Solidarity in Africa Today," *Journal of International Women's Studies* (October 2008).

Federici, Silvia (2004). *Caliban and the Witch. Women, the Body, and Primitive Accumulation*. Brooklyn: Autonomedia.

Folbre, Nancy (2006). 'Nursebots to the rescue? Immigration, automation and care.' *Globalizations* vol. 3, no 3 (2006) : 349–60.

Fortunati, Leopoldina (1995). *The Arcane of Reproduction. Housework, Prostitution, Labour and Capital*. Brooklyn: Autonomedia.

Glazer, Nona (1993). *Women's Paid and Unpaid Labour: Work Transfer in Health Care and Retail* (Philadelphia: Temple University Press, 1993).

Gunder Frank, Andre (1966). *The Development of Underdevelopment*. New York: Monthly Review Press.

Gunder Frank, Andre (1967). *Capitalism and Underdevelopment in Latin America: Historical Studies of Chile and Brazil*. New York: Monthly Review Press.

Hardt, Michael and Antonio Negri (2000). *Empire*. Cambridge (MA): Harvard University Press.

Hardt, Michael and Antonio Negri (2004). *Multitudes: War and Democracy in the Age of Empire*. Cambridge (MA): Harvard University Press.

Hinfelaar, Hugo F. (2007). "Witch-Hunting in Zambia and International Illegal trade," in *Witchcraft Beliefs and Accusations in Contemporary Africa*, ed. Gerrie Ter Haar. Trenton, NJ: Africa World Press.

James, Selma. (1975). *Sex, Race and Class*. Bristol: Falling Wall Press.

Mander Jeremy and Edward Goldsmith (1996). *The Case Against the Global Economy*. San Francisco: Sierra Club Books.

Marx, Karl (1977) *Grundrisse, Karl Marx: Selected Writings*, Oxford: Oxford University Press.

Marx, Karl (1990) *Capital*, vol. 1. London: Penguin Classics.

Marx, Karl (1847)*The German Ideology*.

McMurtry, John (1999). *The Cancer Stage of Capitalism*. London: Pluto Press.

Meillassoux, Claude. (1975). *Maidens, Meal and Money: Capitalism and the Domestic Community*. Cambridge: Cambridge University Press.

Mies, Maria (1986). *Patriarchy and Accumulation on a World Scale*. London: Zed Books.

Milwaukee County Welfare Rights Organization (1972). *Welfare Mothers Speak Out*. New York: Norton Co.

Moulier Boutang, Yann. (1998). *De l'esclavage au salariat. Èconomie historique du salariat bride* (Paris: Presse Universitaire de France, 1998).

Moyo, Sam and Paris Yeros, eds. (2005). *Reclaiming the Land: The Resurgence of Rural Movement in Africa, Asia and Latin America*. London: Zed Books.

Dimitris Papadopoulos et al. (2008). *Escape Routes. Control and Subversion in the Twenty-first Century*. London: Pluto Press.

Seccombe, Wally (1993). *Weathering the Storm. Working Class families Form the Industrial Revolution to the Fertility Decline*. London: Verso.

Salleh, Ariel ed. (2009). *Eco-Sufficiency and Global Justice: Women Write Political Ecology*. London: Pluto Press.

Shorto, Russell (2008). 'No Babies? Declining Population in Europe', *New York Times*, 29 June 2008.

David E. Staples, *No Place Like Home: Organizing Home-Based Labour in the Era of Structural Adjustment* (New York: Routledge, 2006), 1–5.

Yong Kim, Jim et al. (2000). *Dying for Growth. Global Inequality and the Health of the Poor*. Monroe (Maine): Common Courage.

part 2

CLASSICAL ISSUES: EXPLAINING WORKERS' RESISTANCE AND ORGANISATION

5

THE ROLE OF TRADE UNIONS IN BUILDING RESISTANCE: THEORETICAL, HISTORICAL AND COMPARATIVE PERSPECTIVES

Ralph Darlington

INTRODUCTION

For some hostile commentators trade unions (or 'labour' unions as they are termed in the US) have become a 'dinosaur' whose justifiable role in the past of protecting vulnerable and exploited low-paid workers has increasingly become irrelevant within the transformed world of employment relations and Human Resource Management (HRM) of the twenty-first century. But for many millions of workers the durability of trade unionism, and its continuing quintessential function of attempting to organise to defend their collective interests within the workplace and society more broadly, has undoubtedly been reinforced by recent developments across the world. Thus not only did independent trade unions in early 2011 play a crucially important contributory role to popular revolutions and uprisings to overthrow repressive regimes in the Arab world, but in many countries in Western Europe and elsewhere over the last two to three years there has been the resurgence of collective trade union mobilisation and resistance to the austerity measures governments have attempted to impose amid the global financial crisis. Nowhere has this been more evident than in Greece where there have been repeated one-day general strikes involving millions of workers protesting at the impact of austerity on their pay, conditions, jobs and pensions, combined with repeated mass demonstrations in Athens. Likewise the attempt to shift the burden of the biggest economic and financial crisis of post-war capitalism onto workers' shoulders has provoked mass public sector or general strikes in France, Spain, Italy, Belgium and Britain, while in the United States there was a three-week long occupation of Wisconsin's state government building in opposition to a Republican-based law curbing collective bargaining rights, with protests spreading from Indiana to Oklahoma. Such developments have opened up the possibilities for an upswing in trade union fortunes generally across the world.

However, the picture is varied, the revival of trade union organising and mobilising capacities has been partial, and there remain formidable economic, political and social constraints to unions' abilities to defend their members from the ravages of corporate globalisation and neo-liberalism. Moreover, over the last 30 years in many advanced industrialised countries around the world, but notably in the US and Europe, trade unions have been in decline, if not 'crisis'. Declining membership, density, bargaining coverage, strike levels, and political influence have all underlined their apparent inability to 'renew' themselves, with unions often tending to rely on institutional supports rather than developing proactive strategies for confronting their predicament. Indeed, while unions have suffered the blows of neo-liberalism they have generally proved unable to construct an effective industrial and political challenge or counter-response to turn back the tide.

Some have even willingly co-operated with or provided qualified support to neo-liberalism, and have merely sought to safeguard workers' interests from its worst effects but to the detriment of other workers elsewhere. Others have also accepted neo-liberalism in practice, albeit attempting to pursue sympathetic strategic state and supra-state action to adjust market pressures (for example, in relation to privatisation), alongside the advocacy of a restoration of modified social democracy with Keynesian economics. Only a small minority of unions have appraised neo-liberalism as antipathetic to strong trade unionism and advocated anti-capitalist and radical socialist solutions on a national and global basis as an alternative, combined with militant collective union mobilisation to stave off its effects (Gall et al. 2011). Thus the extent to which the 'age of austerity' unleashed by the global financial crisis of 2009, and the revival of trade union struggle it has recently provoked in many countries, provides not merely a challenge but also an opportunity for unions to qualitatively re-build their powers of resistance and advance their organisation is an open question, but one which is likely to be resolved with dramatic long-term consequences for years to come.

Such challenges and opportunities also make it imperative for broader reflection and revaluation as to the limits and potential of trade unions as anti-capitalist forms of organisation. In this respect, although Marx and Engels never developed a systematic and generalisable theoretical analysis of trade unions, they were nonetheless close observers and frequent commentators on the development and struggles of British trade unionism over 50 years in its formative period of the nineteenth century, and in the process made some incisive insights. Undoubtedly their main contribution was to draw attention to the highly contradictory nature of trade unionism, which both *expressed* and *contained* working class resistance to capitalism, such that the unions were at one and the same time agencies of working class *conflict* and *accommodation* with the power of capital.

On the one hand, they mobilise the collective strength that workers have in the workplace, and through the battles fought over wages, jobs, conditions and hours, workers via their trade unions can gain the organisation, confidence and class consciousness to challenge and ultimately overthrow the capitalist system; as 'schools of war' trade unions can make workers aware of their ability to completely transform society (Engels 1969: 251). On the other hand, trade unions tend to operate within the framework of capitalism; they seek not to overthrow it, but merely to improve workers' position within the context of the existing system; their aim is not to end exploitation but to re-negotiate the terms on which workers are exploited. As Marx (1970: 225) put it, 'They are fighting with effects, but not with the causes of those effects.'

Yet significantly the dual nature of trade unionism is not always equally balanced. The relative weight of conflict and accommodation within capitalism is deeply affected by the situation in which the unions operate, namely the dramatic changes in the level of class struggle and in the consciousness and fighting strength of the working class at different periods, and it was this that affected Marx and Engels' apparent contradictory assessments of the nature of trade unionism (Hyman 1971; 2001: 18; Cliff and Gluckstein 1986: 26–34; Kelly 1988: 11). Building on the work of classical Marxism, this chapter examines this contradictory nature of trade unionism, on the one hand its role in building resistance to capitalism, and on the other hand in limiting such resistance within the context of the existing system. In the process it explores the different types of trade union model of resistance that have developed historically in different countries around the world, as well as some of the contemporary challenges they face in a context of neo-liberal globalisation and austerity. While the chapter prioritises an analytical overview, it also provides some concrete examples of processes and developments where appropriate.

BASIC DEFENCE ORGANISATIONS OF THE WORKERS

Trade unions are historical products of workers' everyday experience of capitalism, an organisational expression of the irreconcilability of labour and capital. They embody workers' resistance (however tentative) to capitalist domination over the employment relationship, challenging employers' 'right' to hire labour at the cheapest price and to deploy, manage and control labour irrespective of workers' own wishes and aspirations (Hyman 1975a: 160). In the process, trade unions provide the means by which workers can attempt to gain some minimal degree of counter-control over the terms of their employment and the conditions under which they work. It is for this reason that unionisation has invariably emerged historically only in the face of hostile opposition by employers.

To fully understand the direct link between trade unionism and capitalism we need to recall some of the main distinguishing features of the employment relationship. First, in a market economy, labour is in one sense a commodity to be bought and sold like any other. In effect, in return for their wages, employees surrender their *capacity to work*, which in Marxist terminology is known as 'labour power'. The sale of labour power – the fixing of the workers' income and hence the employer's labour costs – necessarily involves an objective basis for conflict. While it is in the employers' interest to maximise profits by securing labour at the lowest possible economic cost, and to retain workers in employment only so long as they generate a profit, it is in employees' interest to sell their labour at the highest possible price and thereby maximise wages. Moreover, the distinction between labour power and the actual product of labour is important to the Marxist charge of 'exploitation' – the notion that it is the difference between the value of goods produced and the value of labour power (wages) which is the source of 'surplus value' (roughly, profit). Thus, trade unionism – in fighting to defend and improve workers' wages – represents a reaction against such economic exploitation, against the extraction of surplus value from workers' labour.

Second, unlike other types of commodity, labour is quite unique. The employment relationship may lay down the wages that the worker receives, but it does not define precisely what will be provided in return. The worker does not agree to expend an exact amount of labour; for the precise tasks to be performed and the nature of acceptable performance can never be fully specified in advance, and anyway the employers want to be able to make flexible use of their labour force as circumstances dictate. Crucially it is the function of management, through an authoritarian structure of discipline and control over work organisation and the exercise of 'performance management', to transform – or more specifically *exploit* – this capacity into productive activity, to effectively 'utilise' employees for 'their own ends' of generating profit (Hyman 1980: 304; 1989: 227; Sisson 2009; 44). As a consequence, there is also a conflict of interest in the performance of work and over the control of the labour process, just as there is over the sale of labour power.

There is an inevitable imperative for employers faced with competitive pressures (or 'value for money' in the public sector) to attempt to alter the 'wage-effort' bargain by constantly seeking to cuts costs, intensify work tasks, introduce more 'flexible' working practices and new labour-saving technologies, and reduce the numbers of workers employed (Hyman 1989: 228). Yet the nature of the employment relationship is contradictory; in as much as employees represent both a cost and an investment compromises inevitably have to be made, such that employers are obliged to attempt to motivate employees not just to follow managers' instructions in an act of subordination but also to exercise their own judgment and initiative (Sisson 2010: 209). So work effort, like wages, is negotiable – the limits of management authority and employee obedience are always open to a negotiation of order, with more or less constant pressures on and opportunities for the parties to act to adjust the exchange in their favour. It is precisely within this 'frontier of control' (Goodrich 1975) over which workers and employers battle for supremacy – over wages, work speed and intensity, between pay and work effort, and over compliance with and resistance to managerial control over the labour process – that trade unions can play a fundamentally important role as a basic form of workers' defence organisation.

But trade unionism is not only a collective expression of the fundamental conflict of interest that exists between workers and employers over the terms of conditions of employment; it is also a reflection of the asymmetry or inequality of power between labour and capital. Isolated individual workers have little defence or bargaining power vis-à-vis their employers because the economic strength of the two parties is vastly different. Hence the need for trade unions – a source and medium of power – to reduce competition among workers in the labour market and confront the concentrated economic power of employers with their own organised combination of labour power and solidarity (Hyman 1980: 321). Through such collective organisation, unions have the power to persuade employers to negotiate with them, to make real the threat of a withdrawal of labour through strike activity, and to ensure there is some *collective* (rather than *unilateral managerial*) regulation over the terms and conditions of employment. The logic of trade unionism is to mobilise power to redress the bargaining imbalance between capital and labour and render it more equal.

Thus it was that Marx and Engels were among the first socialists in the nineteenth century to see trade unions as basic defence organisations or 'ramparts for the workers' (Marx 1973: 150). Unions are based on the idea of *class* organisation; they help workers to see that 'we are not all in it together', that workers have common interests which are quite distinct and opposed to those of employers. They act to block the smooth passage of capitalist requirements within the workplace (Cohen 2006: 209) and provide the means by which workers can begin to act to combat exploitation. Their primary function is to secure the things that every worker needs – a job, good wage, safe conditions and decent hours. Their all-inclusive unity, organised around the most basic issues that all workers have in common, is the secret of union power. 'Unity is strength' as the old slogan goes.

Historically the primary day-to-day means by which trade unions have sought to limit the power of employers and attempt to defend and, where possible, improve the terms and conditions of employment of their members, has been collective bargaining. Collective bargaining involves union representatives in a process of negotiation, bargaining and rule-making with managers, in which each side seeks to apply pressure, including forms of industrial action such as strike activity, to resolve differences between them. It results in a joint regulation of the employment relationship, codified in collective agreements that regulate wages and a wide range of other issues relating to union members' jobs and working life. Although in the UK by the late 1970s collective bargaining had become the predominant method used to determine many aspects of the employment relationship, the percentage of the workforce covered by such agreements (more extensive than trade union membership levels *per se*) has been in steady decline ever since, embracing about a third of workers today, with a similar tendency in many other countries amid the neo-liberal drive for flexibility. Other means of attempting to regulate or influence aspects of the employment relationship that involve trade union activity include individual representation and joint consultation. In the process 'the constant underlying social purpose of trade unionism is participation in job regulation. But participation is not an end in itself, it is the means of enabling workers to gain more control over their working lives' (Flanders 1975: 42).

The complexity of the ways in which trade unions have attempted to regulate the employment relationship has been captured by using the metaphor of a double-edged sword (Flanders 1970: 14). One edge of the sword represents the pursuit of *vested interest* in as much as their immediate concern is with protecting and improving the pay and conditions of their particular members. But in addition they are a *sword of justice* because, in defending workers against the arbitrary use of managerial power, they promote democratic involvement (both through internal structures of workplace union representation, as well as participation in collective bargaining machinery) and a strong sense of idealism and social purpose, for example, campaigning for the rights of the most vulnerable in society irrespective of whether they are union members or not. Recent examples of this social dimension include union support for anti-racist campaigns and the defence of migrant workers entering the labour market.

There are four broad classifications that can help to explain the diversity of methods used by unions to achieve their ends (Dundon and Rollinson 2011: 136–7). First, as we have seen, there is *economic regulation*, which broadly consists of unions attempting to secure the highest possible real wages and monetary conditions (including overtime, bonus payments, etc.) for their members. The evidence suggests that union recognition in a workplace tends to bring with it a higher wage premium for unionised employees compared with non-union workplaces, albeit this can depend on other factors such as the size of the employing organisation, nature of the product market, extent of workers' bargaining power, and the state of the economy and level of unemployment.

Second, there is *job regulation*, which allows union representatives to become 'joint' authors of the rules and regulations that govern employment in the workplace, thereby limiting managerial freedom of power and decision-making authority. These include rules that specify working hours, health and safety and equal opportunities obligations, as well as procedures for handling collective disputes, individual grievances, disciplinary action, disclosure of information and facilities for workplace union representatives.

Third, there is the *exercise of power*. Clearly the combination of employees within a trade union, and even union recognition by employers, does not necessarily guarantee that they will have the ability to resist the actions of managers. This depends on the power resources they are able to mobilise, with a union's credibility and persuasiveness ultimately underpinned by its potential capacity to take retaliatory action in pursuing its aims. Factors that influence unions' powers include, among other things, the nature and level of the labour market and product market, workers' scarcity value and ability to disrupt production or service provision, the level of membership density, and the cohesion and degree of solidarity among the workforce.

Fourth, the pursuit beyond the workplace of wider social, economic and political change within society has also been a function of many unions, for example, by attempting to persuade governments to devise public policies and enact statutory regulation (over matters such as wage protection and equality of opportunity) that benefit all citizens within society. In many European countries unions have direct links with social-democratic or socialist parties that aspire to be elected to parliament to enact social change. Sometimes the link between unions and such parties takes a formal, institutional shape, as in the case in Britain, through union funding and union representation at every level of the party, sometimes an informal one, as in Germany.

Thus trade unions are workers' basic frontline defence organisations against capitalist exploitation in the workplace. They are part of how workers come to see themselves as a class, united in a common interest against the employers, and they provide the collective means through which workers can offset to some extent the arbitrary powers of the employer. But arguably it is through the organisation of strike action – involving the withdrawal of labour by workers – that the real power and strength of trade unionism becomes most evident.

TRADE UNIONS AND STRIKE ACTIVITY

In the vast majority of cases the collective bargaining process is successful in resolving differences between trade unions and managers arising from conflict over the wage-effort bargain. However, there are times when it is temporarily suspended because agreement cannot be reached. On these occasions, amid a breakdown of co-operation and goodwill between the two parties, and in an attempt to express workers' grievances and reinforce the trade union's bargaining position, a strike can take place. It involves the application of naked force against management in an attempt to get them to agree to concede an employment decision against their wishes which cannot be resolved by negotiation. While the strike is not the only form of industrial action that can be used by trade unions to exert pressure on managers (for example, there is the overtime ban and work-to-rule) it is (apart from full-scale workplace occupations) the most visible and ultimately powerful means by which they can prevent managers from riding roughshod over workers' interests. Despite the fact that over the past two decades there has been a significant reduction in the incidence of strike action in many OECD countries, with historically low levels of industrial struggle in both the UK and US, strikes remain an important and enduring feature of trade union resistance. Moreover, the new wave of Europe-wide mass strikes recently, including the 2011 one-day public sector stoppage of 2.5 million workers in the UK, suggests a reassertion of the strength of union power and capacity for resistance via the strike weapon.

Arguably in many respects one of the most important factors pushing the balance of power in favour of workers is their self-activity, organisation and collective struggle in the workplace, with the level and character of strike activity an important measure of trade union confidence and power. It is true that the lack of strike action by strategically placed groups of workers might reflect their strength, not their weakness – in that employers may feel obliged to concede union demands to avoid conflict. Also the relatively higher propensity of strike activity in any particular industrial sector, organisation or enterprise might also reflect recalcitrant employers' policies as well as union strength (although often employers' policies are themselves formulated partly on the basis of workers' strength). In addition, strikes are only the most obvious means of exerting power and might on occasion be less effective than industrial action short of a strike or more political forms of leverage (Martin 1992). But the fact remains that strikes often only take place when workers feel strong enough to challenge employers and – after taking into consideration whether they are offensive or defensive, victorious or defeated – they are, particularly in the context of 'labour quiescence' generally in advanced industrial societies over many years (Shalev 1992), a particularly salient (if partial) barometer of the nature and extent of shop floor trade union strength and power (Darlington 1994: 35).

Of course, whether strikes take place or not is not dependent on the existence of trade union organisation; conversely even in countries where there is a relatively low membership, such as France, unions are capable of mobilising considerable numbers of workers and exerting significant pressure when they are seen as crucial intermediaries for public policies. To explain why strikes occur we have to consider the ('objective') underlying structural nature of the contradictory social relations between workers and management within capitalist society that can give rise to industrial conflict, the specific and genuine grievances and justifiable demands that can motivate workers to protest at managerial action (see, for example, Gouldner 1955; Royal Commission 1968; Bean and Stoney 1986; Darlington 2006), and the variety of potential power resources and 'opportunity structures' (Tilly 1978; McAdam 1996) which can limit or empower collective actors, including the economic and political situation, state of product and labour markets, industrial and organisational context, extent of management provocation and nature of bargaining power.

Nonetheless, it is not enough for workers just to hold a grievance for strike action to occur, and while structural factors create a more or less favourable environment for the collectivisation of the workforce, they do not *in themselves* necessarily generate strike activity. Rather, as mobilisation theory (Tilly 1978; Kelly 1998) has shown, the workers concerned must hold a collective sense of injustice, recognise that their interests are different from those of their employers, and attribute the source of their grievance to the actions of their employers. But crucially a mechanism needs to exist, in the form of activist leadership which channels that discontent into collective action. It is this function that trade unionism can often fulfill. Thus, even if trade union activists do not in any sense *cause* the underlying material conditions that lead to antagonism and strike activity, they do often play a crucial role in stimulating awareness of grievances and the potential for collective action for redress, and in proposing and initiating such action (Darlington 2002a; 2006; 2009a; 2009b; 2012). In this sense union organisation and leadership can be seen to be as important as any structural or institutional complexity in shaping the nature of collective strike activity.

In terms of building trade union resistance a number of important potential positive characteristics of strikes have long been acknowledged. They can be a sign that workers have broken with a habit of submission and passivity, are beginning to question the authority of management and are willing to dare to defend their interests (Knowles 1952; Turner et al. 1967; Eldridge 1968; Beynon 1973; Darlington 1994). They can begin to cut though the competition that runs through the capitalist system that often divides workers on the basis of skill, gender and ethnicity, enabling workers to forge a common solidaristic identity against a common enemy, 'us and them' (Rogaly 1977; Fantasia 1988). They can give workers a sense of their own collective strength, demonstrating in practice the dependence of employers and the wider society on workers' labour; indeed it is the sheer impact of strikes – in terms of their capacity to disrupt/stop production of goods or services and thereby hit employers' profits – which explains the hostile counter-response they invariably engender (Lane and Roberts 1971; Beynon 1973; Thornett 1987; Gall 2003). They use workers' collective social power to force the employers to back down and to give ground, effectively obtaining immediate measurable material concessions over wages, jobs and conditions that would not otherwise have been achieved (Lane and Roberts 1971; Franzosi 1995; Darlington 2009b; 2012; Darlington and Lyddon 2001).

In this respect there is sometimes the assumption that the process of corporate globalisation has undermined workers' ability to stand up to multi-nationals. But while some multi-nationals can potentially close plants in one country and move operations to another to undermine trade union action, this is often not viable. Moreover, the technological and organisational changes of the last 25 years – such as the adoption by the world's car firms of Japanese 'just-in-time' (JIT) system of keeping very low stocks of parts – can operate to workers' advantage, for example with strikes at individual General Motors plants in the US quickly shutting down company operations in other countries (Moody 1997: 30–31). Meanwhile despite the fact that in the public sector strikes are primarily political, with even large-scale action not directly disrupting the workings of the economy or cutting profits, they can still put enormous pressure on the government ideologically and politically and in a mass campaign supported by wider layers of society force governments to make U-turns, as occurred in France in 1995 over plans to raise the pension age.

Another crucial potential feature of strikes is their link to building and strengthening trade union organisation (Friedman 2008). Certainly there is much historical evidence to suggest that periods of dramatic rises in union membership and density have coincided exactly with upsurges of militant industrial struggle and/or strike 'waves', for example, in Britain in the late 1880s, 1910–14 and 1968–74, as well as in the USA in the 1930s, France in 1936–7 and Poland in 1980–81. In Britain trade union organisation was completely transformed by the 1910–14 'Labour Unrest', during which strike activity ran at more than four times the level of the previous decade, with trade union membership rocketing by 50 per cent from 2.1 million to 4.1 million (Holton 1976: 73; Cronin 1979: 93; Hinton 1983: 84). Likewise between 1934 and 1937 American workers unleashed a strike wave in which the 'sit-down strike' became an essential weapon in the fight to build union organisation; union membership increased by 5 million with the formation of the Congress of Industrial Organisations (CIO) drawing in people who had never been seen as 'typical' union members – women and immigrant workers (Bernstein 1970; Preis 1972). In both countries

> unions became the beneficiaries of a virtuous circle of effectiveness and membership. As the scale of strike activity increased, so did the win rate, and as the win rate increased, bargaining coverage rose, more workers perceived unions to be effective and joined them, which in turn enabled them to be called ... and so on.
>
> (Kelly 1998: 101)

REVOLUTIONARY POTENTIAL OF TRADE UNIONISM

One of the crucial reasons why Engels described the unions as 'schools of war' was because when they organise strikes they can have a profound radicalising

effect on working class consciousness, by revealing the class nature of capitalist society and state power and the connection between the industrial struggle
of one group of workers against their employer and the working class movement against the capitalist class as a whole (Lane and Roberts 1971; Beynon
1973; Eldridge 1968; Hyman 1972; Barker 1987; Kelly 1988), and ultimately
the need for a socialist revolution that can usher in a new society based on
workers' control. Of course, by no means do *all* strikes radicalise workers,
and even when they do it may be only a small minority of workplace union
activists affected (Gall 2003: 260–65). The extent and breadth of radicalisa-
tion is often dependent on the size, duration and strength of the strike; on
whether it is offensive or defensive, victorious or defeated; on the broader
level of working class resistance within society; on how effective trade union
officials (and social-democratic party leaders) are in blocking or restraining
action; and the effectiveness of radical socialist intervention and leadership
(see below). Nonetheless during some historical periods (in the UK in 1915–22
and to a lesser degree 1968–74) there is evidence of trade union militancy
over wages and conditions producing political class consciousness among
quite wide layers of workers (Kelly 1988) and in certain exceptional circumstances (Russia 1917, Germany 1919–23, Spain 1936, Portugal 1974–5) there
have been periodic upsurges of revolutionary consciousness among millions
of workers (Barker 1987).

Significantly Lenin's *What is to Be Done?* (1902) has often been quoted
out of context (Anderson 1967; Clarke and Clements 1977) to suggest that
industrial struggle can only develop 'trade union consciousness' and does not
lead to *revolutionary* class consciousness, thereby underlining the 'inevitable
limitations' of trade unionism. Yet as with the pattern of Marx and Engels'
observations the apparent contradictions between Lenin's writings on trade
unionism were a reflection of the different contexts in which unions operated.
Amid the 1905 Russian revolution, when mass strikes swept St Petersburg and
combative trade unions came into existence, Lenin swung the emphasis very
much in the *opposite* direction, emphasising the extent to which economic
struggles could spontaneously become generalised and tend towards the class
struggle with revolutionary political implications (Cliff 1975; Harding 1981;
Lih 2006). Likewise Rosa Luxemburg (1986), the Polish–German revolutionary Marxist, also drew out the importance of the 'mass strike' in the development of trade unions and the revolutionary movement, with the artificial
separation between *economic* struggles (particularly over living and working
conditions that touch on issues of control) and *political* goals (for the transformation of society) breaking down, with a reciprocal interaction between

the two beyond the constricting limits of existing trade union (and reformist party) organisation.

As we noted earlier on, strikes are not the only form of anti-capitalist resistance. Other struggles, campaigns and mass social movements (whether organised local, nationally or internationally) can give people a collective sense of political identity and confidence, forge an important sense of 'us and them', and win gains. Indeed, the 'labour upsurge' in America during the 1960s and 1970s was profoundly influenced by (and helped to influence) the great social movements that swept the era, above all the civil rights, Black Power, feminist, student and anti-Vietnam war movements. Significantly the contemporary international 'Occupy' movement against corporate greed and social inequality has been shaped in part by the legacy of a relatively weak trade union movement; amid a decline over many years in the incidence and apparent potency of collective trade union action based in the *workplace*, the *street* has for many newly radicalised young people been viewed as the more appropriate public venue of protest. But the centrality of the workplace, of the point of production, is one of the most fundamental features of Marxism, both as a theory of society and as a strategy for socialist transformation. It is here that the wealth of society is generated, that exploitation – the daily extraction of surplus value – takes place, and here that the power of the capitalist class is based. Therefore, arguably any challenge to capitalism that is not rooted in the workplace or that adopts as its primary focus some aspect of the superstructure, be it parliament, local government, or the street, is ultimately restricted to dealing with the outward manifestation of ruling class power not its inner source and is therefore likely to be severely constrained in its effect unless linked to the social weight and industrial power of the working class. As Luxemburg (1971a: 397) put it: 'Where the chains of capitalism are forged, there they must be broken.'

A graphic illustration of this was provided with the Egyptian revolution in early 2011. While the millions of people who demonstrated across the country and occupied Tahrir Square in Cairo seriously undermined the power of the regime, a crucial role was also played by successive waves of workers' strikes organised by new independent unions over the preceding four years, which helped force the military to intervene to remove Mubarak. Since then, successive waves of workers' struggles have raised demands ranging from basic democratic slogans through to economic issues, which in turn have generated greater momentum for new political mobilisations. It is this dynamic, through which workers have sought not just to displace a dictator, but to shift the boundaries of democratic control in the workplace, that has created the potential for a shift from a *political* revolution to a *social* one, challenging the basis of capitalism (Naguib 2011). As one Egyptian activist remarked: 'The union is a shield and our sword is the strike' (Shafiq 2011).

In other words, in certain circumstances and historical periods mass strikes have the potential to not only paralyse the economy but also to stop large parts of the state itself from functioning, bringing together political and economic struggles into a revolutionary challenge to the capitalist system. They are what the international revolutionary syndicalist (or revolutionary union) movement[1] that emerged in the early twentieth century, amid an extraordinary upsurge in strike activity in many countries across the world, called 'revolutionary gymnastics'. For the syndicalists, strikes were training for the future social revolution which instructed workers in the realities of class struggle, exposed them to the viciousness of the employers, encouraged solidarity, reinforced class consciousness, and provided valuable lessons for the greater revolutionary battles to come. Moreover they helped increase workers' confidence to change society *themselves* rather than relying on trade union officials or parliamentary representatives to do it for them (Darlington 2008: 38–9).

Significantly the syndicalists had a dual conception of the trade unions as both an *organ of struggle* in the present and an *instrument of revolution* and embryo of the new hoped-for classless society of the future. On the one hand, they believed the *raison d'être* of trade unionism was the organisation of workers against employers, standing at the very point where the class struggle arises and challenges the class enemy. That meant seeking every opportunity to defend and improve workers' wages, hours and conditions of work in their everyday struggle against specific employers. On the other hand, they believed the unions could be transformed into militant organisations dedicated to fighting for the entire working class with the overall objective of overthrowing capitalism and establishing a new society. The road to the emancipation of the working class lay through an intensification of the industrial struggle to its logical culmination in a revolutionary *general strike* that would overthrow the capitalist system and replace it by workers' control of industry and society exercised by the trade unions. As the Confédération Générale du Travail's (CGT) 1906 *Charte d'Amiens* stated: 'The trade union, which is today a fighting organisation, will in the future be an organisation for production and distribution and the basis for social reorganisation.'

Although 'classical' revolutionary syndicalism no longer exists as a major organised force within the international union movement, various 'quasi-syndicalist' tendencies have re-emerged in more recent years in some of the most powerful and radical workers' movements in the world, including South Africa and Brazil during the mid-1980s. One of the most notable examples was the Solidarity movement in Poland in 1980–81, with its explicit commitment to class warfare as the central means by which to change society, combined with a conception of the union as the main vehicle of revolutionary struggle to overthrow the Communist Party-dominated state bureaucracy (McShane 1981; Barker 1986; Darlington 2002b).

LIMITATIONS OF TRADE UNIONISM

As previously signalled, the profoundly contradictory nature of trade unionism within capitalism means that the potential *strengths* outlined above are merely one side of the competing logics at work: any fully rounded analysis also needs to consider the very real *limitations* to trade union resistance to capitalism.

First, there is sectionalism. Thus while trade unions *unite* workers in a common labour process, they also *divide* them since the boundaries of any individual union encompass only a fragment of the working class. As organisations built on particular trades or industries, they mirror the divisions imposed on workers by the capitalist system, with the very name *trade* unionism implying sectionalism. Just as workers in various industries earn different wages and operate under different conditions of employment, trade unions only embrace certain categories of workers as members and exclude others, with a primary concern with the particular occupation or sectoral interests of those they represent rather than the working class as a whole. Hence the divisions between blue-collar and white-collar workers, private and public sector workers, teachers in one union and railway workers in another, and even between different unions in the same industry. Each of these different (often competing) unions tends to adjust to capitalism in a piecemeal, ad hoc way rather than as a *movement* (Lane 1974: 267), pursuing their own sectional claims against specific employers without reference to others (reflected in the fragmented structure of collective bargaining) rather than co-ordinating workers' organisation into a broader anti-capitalist front. The occasional public sector-wide/national strike that embraces a number of different unions does not fundamentally change this underlying sectionalist feature. In addition, unions have often failed to confront, or seek or build structures and policies to overcome, the ethnic and gender inequalities within the employment relationship.

Second, as Marx and Engels argued, even though trade unions provide the means and instrument through which workers' resistance to capitalism can be organised, they seek merely to improve the terms of workers' subordination to managerial control within the existing framework of society, opposing the *symptoms* rather than the underlying *causes* of workers' exploitation. 'As institutions, trade unions do not *challenge* the existence of a society based on a division of classes, they merely *express* it . . . They can bargain within the society, but not transform it' (Anderson 1967: 264–5). Hence the curious phenomenon of 'antagonistic co-operation': the constant inter-penetration of conflictual and co-operative aspects of trade unionism (Hyman 1974: 258). Their 'dual character' means that at one and the same time they resist capitalist exploitation and function as a source of social order which helps stabilise capitalist society (Zoll 1976).

Third, there is the problem of trade union bureaucracy (Luxemburg 1986; Michels 1915; Webb and Webb 1920). By confining the class struggle to the search for reforms within the framework of a capitalist society there is a presumption that the interests of capital and labour can be accommodated, with the consequence that workers' struggles, however militant, must ultimately result in a compromise. It is this situation that generates a permanent apparatus of full-time union officials who specialise in negotiating the terms of such compromises – a 'union bureaucracy' that occupies a unique social position with interests, perspectives and resources different from, and sometimes in antagonism to, the bulk of the rank-and-file members they represent (Darlington and Upchurch 2012). Crucially full-time union officials are subject to enormous pressure to preserve the tolerance of employers and governments by establishing a stable and co-operative bargaining relationship, and therefore to subordinate the autonomous and informal activity of workers to limit managerial prerogative by channelling grievances into innocuous forms, defining bargaining issues within a narrow focus so as to render the task of achieving compromise more tractable (Hyman 1975b: xxv; 1984: 141). As a result, union officials often tend to view strike activity which pushes 'too far' and unduly antagonises employers and the state as an unwelcome disruption to stable bargaining relations. This can lead them to act as 'manager[s] of discontent' (Mills 1948: 9), ending strikes on 'compromise' terms detrimental to rank-and-file aspirations (Hartley et al. 1983: 150; Melvern 1986: 187; Bramble 1995; Gall 2003: 175–9).

Full-time union officials are not simply 'fire extinguishers of the revolution' (Anderson 1967: 277). Depending on the pressures on them from employers and government on the one hand, and their own members on the other, officials (even right-wing officials) *do* sometimes threaten or organise strike action. The central problem is that while the rank-and-file of the union have a direct interest in fighting against the exploitation of employers and government, and indeed have everything to be gained by fighting for the success of militant strikes, full-time officials have a vested interest in the continued existence of a system upon which their livelihood and position depends, and so end up trying to reconcile the interests of labour and capital, which usually leads them to temper workers' resistance. While ideological and political differences between 'left' and 'right-wing' officials can be important in influencing their behaviour, they are *secondary* to the much more fundamental, common material social role, position and interests which bind *all* officials together as a distinct social group (Cliff and Gluckstein 1986: Darlington and Upchurch 2012). As the British 1926 General Strike confirmed, the in-built structural pressures mean that at the end of the day left-wing officials are just as capable of holding back workers' struggles as their right-wing counterparts.

Fourth, there can be significant potential limitations to strike activity as a means of trade union resistance to capitalism. Even significant concessions over wages, conditions and jobs are inevitably vulnerable to the vicissitudes of the market and economy, and the repeated nature of employers' counter-attacks and their impact on the balance of power and workers' confidence to resist. Thus Luxemburg (1971b: 105) compared trade unionism to the 'labour of Sisyphus', who in Greek legend was condemned to push a huge boulder up a hill only to watch adversaries roll it back down again. Moreover strike action in a non-revolutionary period does not usually challenge or alter property relations in society. Even a mass strike that emerges through spontaneous rank-and-file struggle from below (such as in France and Spain in 1936 and France in 1995) as opposed to a bureaucratic mass strike called on and off by officials from above (such as the British 1926 General Strike), while it can seriously undermine the functioning of capitalism, does not automatically abolish it and create a new economic, social and political order.

Fifth, trade unions imitate their adversary, reflecting back capitalism's sharp demarcation between 'economics' and 'politics'. Put crudely this leads to an attitude which argues that trade unions should narrowly constrain themselves to the pursuit of the economic struggle in the workplace over wages and conditions, while for political change in society workers must look to social-democratic parties to act through the parliamentary process on their behalf. It encourages the belief that the class struggle between capital and labour is a de-politicised, economic and social issue and that workers' interests are best served through negotiation and reform rather than through the revolutionary transformation of society. The idea that the unions might attempt to *utilise industrial militancy for political ends* to challenge the government is completely rejected. For example, in Britain loyalty to the Labour Party, especially when Labour is in office, has encouraged government ministers to place pressure on unions not to undermine 'their' government with industrial disputes, and even when out of office the Labour Party has been able to pressurise them into dampening down strike action on the basis that this would harm electoral prospects (Miliband 1972; Coates 1975; 1989; Taylor 1989; 1993).

It follows from the different limitations outlined above that, because of their very function of negotiation and accommodation with capitalism, the anti-capitalist and revolutionary potential of trade unionism is severely constrained. As Hyman (1989: 250–51) explained, they operate in an environment of hostile forces which condition and distort their character and dynamics: bureaucracy, collabouration, sectionalism and economism are all reflections of powerful and often overwhelming tendencies, albeit they are not uncontradictory and irresistible forces. The different polar opposites in the nature of trade unionism – between *conflict* and *accommodation* – are not a fixed proposition in terms of an 'either/or' logic, but constantly in motion reflecting and at the same time changing the social condition of which it is part. The result is a continuum of possible and overlapping responses, each dominant to a greater or lesser degree within individual unions and changing over time. Thus, the contrast between the militancy of unions generally in the UK and US in the 1970s (combined with important continuing elements of conservatism) compared with the early 1980s onwards when accommodative tendencies predominated (combined with important elements of militancy). As Antonio Gramsci (1977: 265), the Italian revolutionary Marxist, wrote: 'The trade union is not a predetermined phenomenon. It becomes a determinate institution; it takes on a definite historical form to the extent that the strength and will of the workers who are its members impress a policy and propose an aim that defines it.'

The key point being repeated here is that it is the changing balance of class forces between capital and labour that has a profound impact on the nature of trade unionism and its role and ability to mount resistance to capitalism, in terms of which side is more confident, stronger and successfully pushing the frontier of control to their advantage within the workplace and society more broadly.

IDENTITY AND ORIENTATION

We can now briefly turn our attention to some of the more concrete manifestations of the different models of unionism that have developed both historically and comparatively, as well as some contemporary issues of union strategy. To begin with, as a means of conceptualising broad national historical variations in trade union identity and ideology, Hyman (2001) uses the notion of the 'geometry' of trade unionism to argue that trade unions in Europe (and perhaps more widely) have had three distinct strategic and tactical orientations around the axis of 'market', 'class' and 'society'.

Market: this is a form of 'business unionism' in which unions rely upon collective bargaining to achieve their goals which are largely related to 'bread and butter' concerns of immediate pay and conditions, with an arm's-length relationship between the sphere of party politics and that of trade union action. It is a form of what Samuel Gompers, who founded the American Federation of Labour (AFL), termed 'pure-and-simple unionism', exemplified by the attempt made by many American unions in the 1950s to seek collaborative relationships with employers, and still practised today by some unions both in the US and elsewhere.

Society: this is a form of social-democratic unionism, typically to be found in countries such as Germany, the Netherlands and Britain, in which unions are vehicles for social integration that have as their priority raising workers' status and promoting gradual improvements in social welfare and social cohesion. While collective bargaining is of importance, such unions also have strong links with social-democratic political parties and parliamentary reform is viewed as a key instrument for achieving favourable conditions of work and life.

Class: this is a form of class struggle and anti-capitalist unionism characterised by the embrace of strikes and socio-political protest. Unions are viewed as being in an irreconcilable struggle between capital and labour; they act as an agency which ultimately can be effective only as a means of collective mobilisation of the working class, with the ultimate objective of a revolutionary transformation of society. While historically syndicalist, socialist and communist unions (Darlington 2008), for example, the CGT in France and Industrial Workers of the World (IWW) in America in the early twentieth century, would fall under this category, so today would SUD-Rail in France and the RMT in Britain (Connolly 2010; Connolly and Darlington 2012; Darlington 2009a; 2009b).

While every trade union faces in all three of these directions and cannot afford to ignore any of the orientations, particular histories and social frameworks lead to different tensions emerging in varying institutional contexts, with contrasting union movements having a tendency to prioritise different identities. Nonetheless the three models represent merely 'ideal types' of unions which are rarely, if ever, seen in practice, leading Hyman (2001: 4) to assert that most unions have 'tended to incline towards an often contradictory admixture of two of the three ideal types'. Thus market-based 'bread and butter' unionism cannot altogether neglect the broader social and political context of market relations; civil society-based social-partnership unionism cannot water itself down indefinitely in collaborative integration; and class unionism cannot avoid having to deliver some short-term economic results for their members and find some accommodation with the existing social order.

It should be noted that while there are a number of factors influencing the nature and extent of democracy within trade unions, including the degree of membership homogeneity, extent of skill, status and educational qualifications, strength of occupational identity, and size and distribution of membership, union government is also affected by the prevailing conception of union purpose, whereby the broader and more ambitious the union's objectives, the more likely the members will become active participants. For example in the UK the RMT's adversarial unionism has been both cause and effect to such democratic tendencies. The attempt to regularly mobilise members to take strike action, the vigorous encouragement of membership activism, the union organising drive, and the broader left-wing politically-informed objectives that shape union policy have encouraged democratic processes, and in turn such democratic processes have helped to shape the union's approach, its organising success and the energising of the activists (Darlington 2009a; 2009b; 2012).

Upchurch et al. (2009) have identified the way in which, with neo-liberal marketisation becoming the dominant *modus operandi* of Western European governments, there has developed a 'crisis of social democracy' as social-democratic parties have increasingly accommodated themselves to neo-liberal imperatives. This has been paralleled by a potential 'crisis of the social-democratic model of trade unionism' which predominated in many countries. In response, there has emerged a minority 'radicalised political unionism' tendency – for example, the SUD (*Solidaires, Unitaires et Démocratiques*) movement in France, the independent unions focused on workers' centres in Greece, and among sections of the IG Metall and Ver.di unions in Germany – characterised by a rejection of neo-liberalism and a break to the left from social democracy. It is associated with the repetitive mobilisation of members through strike action, left oppositionist leadership, the use of less bureaucratically-controlled forms of trade union action, and an attempt to engage members beyond the workplace in new social movements and networks against globalisation and privatisation. Crucially, even though it is often overlooked in studies on trade union renewal and revitalisation strategies, the fortunes of such 'radicalised political unionism' as a viable alternative identity and its subsequent consolidation is likely to be intricately connected with the development of an alternative *left-wing* political leadership and *class-based* notions of trade unionism as the pathway to both advancing workers' interests and to revitalising union organisation (Connolly and Darlington 2012).

Meanwhile, in terms of building the potential for union resistance there is clearly the need to organise and recruit many more *new* union members, particularly among the enlarged periphery of casual, short-term, insecure, and poorly-paid workforce. But while it is often claimed the growing importance of women and ethnic minority workers, service work, part-time and other 'atypical' forms of employment has led to the fragmentation of worker interests, placing pressures on the construction of traditional solidaristic union identities and interests, Hyman (2001: 165) has acknowledged 'differentiation, division and disunity have been omnipresent features of trade union development'. Moreover, there remain possibilities for unions to 're-imagine' their interests, to move away from the building of *mechanistic solidarities* where collective interests are determined and expressed relatively narrowly by core groups, and to develop more *organic solidarities* which integrate and promote a far broader and diverse set of interests and identities of a changing workforce and membership, and which unite different groups of workers both within and between workplaces. But to do this, unions need to change the emphasis from *workplace*-solidarities to embrace *class*-based solidarities – with class becoming a 'rallying cry' for understanding, expressing and promoting the commonality of workers' distinct interests in opposition to capitalism (Simms 2008). In this fashion unions could assert their identity as a 'sword of justice', campaigning over broad social and political concerns and contesting oppression, inequality and discrimination in *all* its forms.

With such considerations in mind, 'social movement unionism' (SMU) has often been presented as a model on which trade unions might re-invent their identities to survive and thrive in a hostile global environment (Waterman 1998; Robinson 2000; Clawson 2003). Emphasising the need for trade unions, which many people view as essentially representatives of 'old labour', to begin to work in alliance with other agents in civil society, SMU has stood out as an alternative pathway for unions that seeks to revitalise the autonomous, inclusive and critical dimensions of their practice in contrast to the subordinate, exclusive and uncritical practices of 'business unionism' and 'social partnership'. Thus Waterman (1998: 203) has argued that because 'a complex high-risk globalised information capitalism' has undermined the capacity to develop an effective labour movement around a class identity, unions should link with non-labour organisations (the 'new alternative social movements') to form a global social movement that can rise to the challenge of the 'immediate necessity of civilising a capitalist world order (p. 2).

Yet as some otherwise sympathetic critics have pointed out, while unions undoubtedly need to build links with broader social movements, there is an implicit tendency within SMU's strategic approach to relegate the trade union struggle in the workplace to the status of merely one among many others (Mathers 2007; Upchurch and Mathers 2011), in the process effectively endorsing the view that there is no longer anything special about workers' collective exploitation and resistance at work which creates labour's unique potential to transform the world. Likewise, rather than counterposing a supposedly declining, conservative organised working class to the genuine radicalism on the streets or among 'precarious' workers as some commentators have done (Standing 2011; Mason 2012), the real task is to bring together the radical energy, creativity and initiative of the young protestors on the streets with the day-to-day struggles and collective power of organised workers in their trade unions.

SOME CONCLUSIONS AND FURTHER REFLECTIONS

Despite the decline in membership that many unions have experienced in different countries around the world during the past 30 years, the rationale for the collective representation of workers as a means of building resistance to capitalism – namely their distinct set of interests and asymmetry of power vi-a-vis the employers – remains. This suggests that, notwithstanding the pressures of globalisation and neo-liberalism, the fundamental basis for trade union recovery remains present. The new wave of mass strikes and demonstrations that have occurred across Europe recently has both underlined unions' enormous power and continuing relevance as well as the possibilities that exist for a revival of their fortunes.

Ironically for years many commentators have argued that the only feasible way for unions to maintain, let alone develop, their influence within the workplace, amid the transformed world of work and HRM, is by behaving moderately and entering into partnership relationships with employers, effectively eschewing adversarial relations in favour of more consensual relations designed to produce 'mutual gains' for both parties (Roche and Geary 2006). Yet arguably such 'strategies of retreat' (Moody 2012: 24), which have characterised the decisions and practices of many union leaders in different countries, have merely seriously weakened trade unionism and left it vulnerable to employers' attacks because they have eroded the willingness and capacity of members to resist and to challenge employer demands. In the current 'age of austerity' the potential relationship between trade union militancy, effectiveness in protecting workers' interests, membership growth and union revitalisation could become more evident.

Nonetheless, for all the reasons we have explored, trade unionism is essentially oriented on merely coming to terms with the power of capital rather than attempting to overthrow that power. Thus, the universal tension that has been identified between the contradictory elements of 'movement' and 'organisation' (Herberg 1943; Hyman 2001; Cohen 2006). On the one hand, trade unionism *as an organisation* enshrined in formal, official and often bureaucratic 'representative' structures that prioritise collective bargaining and institutional survival (the protection of material and financial assets). On the other hand, trade unionism *as a movement*, an organisational form that prioritises workplace resistance, direct democracy, membership mobilisation and radical economic and political aspirations. In other words, while there are some features of revolutionary potential to trade unionism, their accompanying in-built limitations mean that *on their own* they cannot be the vehicle of capitalism's abolition.

Clearly strong rank-and-file organisations within the unions are absolutely crucial to the task of building effective resistance inside the working class movement. For example, during an upturn in the level of workers' militancy in Britain in the early late 1960s and early 1970s, strong independent workplace union organisations, often in the form of the shop stewards' system of lay representation of rank-and-file members, acted as an important counteracting tendency against the bureaucratisation and accommodation of official union leaderships (Darlington and Lyddon 2001). While they have not been immune from similar pressures towards accommodation and bureaucracy affecting full-time union officials, and with their confidence to organise independently of officials from below considerably undermined in the wake of the massive strike defeats that occurred in the 1980s and 1990s, shop stewards and other lay workplace union reps have generally remained *qualitatively different* from officials in their potential responsiveness to rank-and-file pressure (Darlington 2010; Darlington and Upchurch 2012). If the recent Europe-wide revival of industrial struggle and trade union confidence is sustained, it raises the possibility for the revitalisation of such rank-and-file organisation.

An important historical model was provided by the way in which during the First World War networks of local shop stewards were able to operate both *within* and *outside* official union structures, walking on two legs, official and unofficial, to transform shop stewards' fragmented forms of *organisation* in different workplaces into a national rank-and-file *movement* which linked together hundreds of thousands of workers across the engineering industry, and thereby provided an alternative leadership to the full-time union officials who could act independently of them. As the Clyde Workers' Committee declared in 1915: 'We will support the officials just so long as they rightly represent the workers, but will act independently immediately they misrepresent them' (Hinton 1973). Almost a century later, this remains a useful guide to how the relationship between rank-and-file workers and full-time union officials can work, with union activists focusing less on attempting to capture the union machine (by electing left-wing officials into office) than on fostering independent collective action by workers themselves.

Nonetheless, from a Marxist perspective, no trade union organisation, however militant, is enough to defeat capitalism. Workers' struggles can deal with the power of the capitalist class only if they *break out* of the confines of trade unionism. Only by ignoring the division of economics and politics and by making their target the capitalist state, can the working class hope to win a lasting victory. But despite the fact that in periods of mass struggle the division between economic and political issues can break down, there is an 'organisational condition' for this to become durable and far-reaching. Hence, the role of radical left political parties and broad left groupings (such as Syriza in Greece, Front de Gauche in France and Die Linke in Germany). There will be a need for new layers of political militants, motivated by ideologies of social justice, who are able to take up not only workers' immediate struggles over pay, conditions, jobs and pensions, but also broader political questions about the crisis of political legitimacy; who can link trade union industrial struggles to a concerted anti-capitalist movement that has as its central strategic aim the need to overthrow the existing system. In the process, such left-wing *political* trade unionism can begin to provide a political and organisational alternative to social-democratic politicians and official union leaders.

Furthermore, historical evidence suggests that within certain extraordinary *revolutionary situations* there is the potential for rank-and-file movements to develop into new types of bodies of workers' power which can supplement or even supplant the unions to challenge the economic and political power of the ruling class – in a similar fashion to the workers' councils (or 'soviets') that became a central feature of the Russian revolutions of 1905 and 1917, the revolutions in Germany, Hungary and Italy in 1919–20, and during the Spanish Civil War of 1936, as well as in other countries in more recent times such as Poland 1980–81.

In conclusion, while trade union bureaucracies and social-democratic parties are essential shock absorbers for modern capitalism and its states, because of their capacity to smooth out and contain opposition, at various times different balances are struck between conflict and accommodation in workers' action and consciousness, and given that the seedbed of class conflict is re-sown and re-fertilised by the everyday experience of exploitation, the containment of workers' resistance to capitalism is anything but a simple and automatic process, even in quiet times (Barker 1987: 222). At the same time as the Occupy movement of resistance to global corporate power and social inequality has reignited a debate about the very nature and legitimacy of capitalism as a form of society, trade union struggle is also returning to the centre stage, with the rising curve of resistance to government austerity measures in many European countries putting the organised working class back on the agenda as a fundamental agent of change in society.

NOTE

1. Of course 'syndicalism' is necessarily only a very broad term for a number of related but rather different revolutionary union movements that flourished across the world in a variety of national forms which utilised contrasting terms, including: 'revolutionary syndicalism' (France and Britain), 'industrial unionism' (America) and 'anarcho-syndicalism' (Spain and Italy). Nonetheless, arguably the colloquial description of such different movements as 'syndicalist' is both useful and justified because it draws attention to basic fundamental ideological and practical *similarities* between them, notwithstanding the specific strategic approaches and organisational forms adopted by individual movements (Darlington 2008: 4–7).

REFERENCES

Anderson, P. (1967) 'The limits and possibilities of trade union action', in R. Blackburn and A. Cockburn (eds) *The Incompatibles*, Harmondsworth: Penguin, pp. 263–80.
Barker, C. (1986) *Festival of the Oppressed: Solidarity, Reform and Revolution in Poland 1980–81*, London: Bookmarks.
——. (1987) 'Perspectives', in C. Barker (ed.) *Revolutionary Rehearsals*, London: Bookmarks, pp. 217–45.
Bean, R., and P. Stoney (1986) 'Strikes on Merseyside: A regional analysis', *Industrial Relations Journal*, vol. 17, no. 1, 9–23.
Bernstein, I. (1970) *Turbulent Years: A History of the American Worker 1933–1941*, Boston: Houghton Mifflin.
Beynon, H. (1973) *Working for Ford*, Harmondsworth: Penguin.
Bramble, T. (1995) 'Deterring democracy? Australia's new generation of union officials', *Journal of Industrial Relations*, vol. 37, 401–26.
Brenner, A., R. Brenner and C. Winslow (eds) (2010) *Rebel Rank and File: Labour Militancy and Revolt From Below During the Long 1970s*, London: Verso.
Clarke, T. and L. Clements (eds) (1977) 'The raison d'être of trade unionism', in *Trade Unions Under Capitalism*, Glasgow: Fontana/Collins, pp. 7–23.
Clawson, D. (2003) *The Next Upsurge: Labour and the New Social Movements*, Ithaca; ILR Press.
Cliff, T. (1975) *Lenin, Vol. 1: Building the Party*, London: Pluto Press.
Cliff, T. and D. Gluckstein (1986) *Marxism and the Trade Union Struggle. The General Strike of 1926*, London: Bookmarks.
Coates, D. (1975) *The Labour Party and the Struggle for Socialism*, Cambridge: Cambridge University Press.
Cohen, S. (2006) *Ramparts of Resistance: Why Workers Lost Their Power and How to Get it Back*, London: Pluto Press.

Connolly, H. (2010) *Renewal in the French Trade Union Movement: A Grassroots Perspective,* Oxford: Peter Lang.

Connolly, H. and R. Darlington (2012) 'Radical political unionism in France and Britain: A comparative study of SUD-Rail and the RMT', *European Journal of Industrial Relations,* vol. 18, no. 3: 13–23.

Cronin, J.E. (1979) *Industrial Conflict in Modern Britain,* London: Croom Helm.

Darlington, R. (1994) *The Dynamics of Workplace Unionism.* London: Mansell.

——. (2002a) 'Shop stewards' leadership, left-wing activism and collective workplace union organization', *Capital and Class,* vol. 76, 95–126.

——. (2002b) 'Revolutionary syndicalism: Classical and contemporary forms', Paper presented to 4th European Social Science History Conference, Netherlands Congress Centre, The Hague, Holland, 27 February–2 March.

——. (2006) 'Agitator "theory" of strikes re-evaluated', *Labour History,* vol. 47, no. 4: 485–509.

——. (2008) *Syndicalism and the Transition to Communism: An International Comparative Analysis,* Aldershot: Ashgate.

——. (2009a) 'Leadership and union militancy: The case of the RMT', *Capital and Class,* vol. 33, no. 3, 3–32.

——. (2009b) 'Organising, militancy and revitalisation: The case of the RMT', in G. Gall (ed.) *Union Revitalisation in Advanced Economies: Assessing the Contribution of 'Union Organising',* Basingstoke: Palgrave Macmillan, pp. 83–106.

——. (2010) 'The state of workplace union reps organisation in Britain today', *Capital and Class,* vol. 34, no. 1, 126–35.

——. (2012) 'The interplay of structure and agency dynamics in strike activity', *Employee Relations,* forthcoming.

——. and D. Lyddon (2001) *Glorious Summer: Class Struggle in Britain, 1972,* London: Bookmarks.

——. and M. Upchurch (2012) 'A reappraisal of the rank-and-file versus bureaucracy debate', *Capital and Class,* vol. 36, no. 1, 77–95.

Dundon, T. and D. Rollinson (2011) *Understanding Employment Relations,* London: McGraw-Hill Higher Education.

Eldridge, J.E.T. (1968) *Industrial Disputes: Essays in the Sociology of Industrial Relations.* London: Routledge.

Engels, F. (1969) *The Condition of the Working Class in England,* St Albans: Panther.

Fantasia, R. (1988) *Cultures of Solidarity: Consciousness, Action and Contemporary American Workers.* Berkley: University of California Press.

Flanders, A. (1970) 'Trade unions in the Sixties', in A. Flanders (ed.) *Management and Union: The Theory and Reform of Industrial Relations,* London: Faber, pp. ??–??.

——. (1975) *Management and Unions: The Theory and Reform of Industrial Relations,* London: Faber and Faber.

Franzosi, R. (1995) *The Puzzle of Strikes: Class and Class Strategies in Postwar Italy.* Cambridge: Cambridge University Press.

Friedman, G. (2008) *Reigniting the Labour Movement,* London: Routledge.

Gall, G. (2003) *The Meaning of Militancy? Postal Workers and Industrial Relations.* Aldershot: Ashgate.

Gall, G., A. Wilkinson and R. Hurd (eds) (2011) *The International Handbook of Labour Unions: Response to Neo-Liberalism,* Cheltenham: Edward Elgar.

Goodrich, C.L. (1975) *The Frontier of Control,* London: Pluto Press.

Gouldner, A.W. (1955) *Wildcat Strike: A Study in Worker-Management Relations.* New York: Harper Torchbooks.

Gramsci, A. (1977) 'Unions and Councils', in *Selections from Political Writings 1910–1920,* London: Lawrence and Wishart, pp. 265–8.

Harding, N. (1981) *Lenin's Political Thought: Vol. 2: Theory and Practice in the Socialist Revolution,* New York: St Martin's Press.

Hartley, J.J. Kelly and N. Nicholson (1983) *Steel Strike: A Case Study in Industrial Relations*, London: Batsford.

Herberg, W. (1943) 'Bureaucracy and democracy in labour unions', *Antioch Review*, vol. 3, 405–17.

Hinton, J. (1973) *The First Shop Stewards' Movement*, London: Allen and Unwin.

——. (1983) *Labour and Socialism: A History of the British Labour Movement 1867–1974*, Brighton: Wheatsheaf Books.

Holton, B. (1976) *British Syndicalism 1900–1914*, London: Pluto Press, 1976.

Hyman, R. (1971) *Marxism and the Sociology of Trade Unionism*, London: Pluto Press.

——. (1972) *Strikes*, London: Fontana.

——. (1974) 'Workers' control and revolutionary theory', *Socialist Register*, vol. 11, 241–78.

——. (1975a) *Industrial Relations: A Marxist Introduction*, Basingstoke: Macmillan.

——. (1975b) 'Foreword to the 1975 edition', in C.L. Goodrich [first published 1920] *The Frontier of Control: A Study in British Workshop Politics*, London: Pluto Press, pp. vii–xli.

——. (1980) 'Trade unions, control and resistance', in G. Esland and G. Salaman (eds) *The Politics of Work and Occupations*, Milton Keynes: Open University Press, pp. 303–34.

——.(1984) Strikes, 4th edn, London: Macmillan.

——. (1989) 'Class struggle and the trade union movement', in *The Political Economy of Industrial Relations*, London: Macmillan, pp. 224–53.

——. (2001) *Understanding European Trade Unionism: Between Market, Class and Society*, London: Sage.

Kelly, J. (1988) *Trade Unions and Socialist Politics*, London: Verso, 1988.

——. (1998) *Rethinking Industrial Relations. Rethinking Industrial Relations: Mobilisation, Collectivism and Long Waves*, London: Routledge.

Knowles, K.G.J.C. (1952) *Strikes: A Study in Industrial Conflict*, Oxford: Blackwell.

Lane, T. (1974) *The Union Makes Us Strong*, London: Arrow Books.

Lane, T. and K. Roberts (1971) *Strike at Pilkingtons*, London: Fontana.

Lenin, V.I. (1970: first published 1906) 'What is to be done?', *Selected Works*: Vol. 1, Moscow: Progress, pp. 122–270.

Lih, L.T. (2006) *Lenin Rediscovered: 'What is to be Done?' in Context*, Brill: Historical Materialism.

Luxemburg, R, (1971a) 'Our programme and the political situation', *Selected Political Writings*, New York: Monthly Review Press, pp. 377–408.

——. (1971b) 'Social reform or revolution', *Selected Political Writings*, New York: Monthly Review Press, pp. 52–134.

——. 1986) *The Mass Strike, the Political Party and the Trade Unions*, London: Bookmarks.

McAdam, D. (1996) 'Conceptual origins, current problems, future directions', in D. McAdam, J.D. McCarthy, M.Y. Zald (eds), *Comparative Perspectives on Social Movements. Political Opportunities, Mobilizing Structures, and Cultural Framings*, Cambridge: Cambridge University Press, pp. 23–40.

McShane, D. (1981) *Solidarity: Poland's Independent Union*, Nottingham: Spokesman.

Martin, R. (1992) *Bargaining Power*, London: Clarendon Press.

Marx, K. (1970) 'Wages, price and profit', in K. Marx and F. Engels, *Selected Works*, Moscow: Progress. pp. 185–226.

——. (1973) *The Poverty of Philosophy*, Moscow: Progress Publishers.

Mason. P. (2012) *Why It's Kicking off Everywhere: The New Global Revolutions*, London: Verso.

Mathers, A. (2007) *Struggling for a Social Europe: Neoliberal Globalisation and the Birth of a European Social Movement*, Aldershot: Ashgate.

Melvern, L. (1986) *The End of the Street*, London: Methuen.

Michels, R. (1915) *Political Parties: A Sociological Study of the Oligarchical Tendencies of Modern Democracy*, (republished) New York: Collier Books, 1962.

Miliband, R. (1972) *Parliamentary Socialism: The Politics of Labour*, London: Merlin Press.

Mills, C.W. (1948) *The New Men of Power: America's Labour Leaders*, New York: Harcourt Brace.

Moody, K. (1997) *Workers in a Lean World: Unions in the International Economy*, London: Verso.

——. (2012) 'Contextualising organised labour in expansion and crisis: The case of the US', *Historical Materialism*, vol. 20, no. 1, 3–30.

Naguib, S. (2011) *The Egyptian Revolution: A Political Analysis and Eyewitness Account*, London: Bookmarks.

Preis, A. (1972) *Labour's Giant Step: Twenty Years of the CIO*, New York: Pathfinder Press.

Robinson, I. (2000) 'Neoliberal restructuring and US unions: Towards social movement unions', *Critical Sociology*, vol. 26, no. 1/2, 109–38.

Roche, W.K. and J.F. Geary (2006) *Partnership at Work: The Quest for Radical Organisational Change*, London: Routledge.

Rogaly, J. (1977) *Grunwick*, Harmondsworth: Penguin.

Royal Commission on Trade Unions and Employers' Associations (1968) *Report.* Cmnd 3624. London: HMSO.

Shafiq, M. (2011) 'The union is shield and our sword is the strike', *Socialist Review*, vol. 364, 22–4.

Shalev, M. (1992) 'The resurgence of labour quiescence', in M. Regini (ed.) *The Future of Labour Movements.* London: Sage, pp. 102–32.

Simms, M. (2012) 'Imagined solidarities: Where is class in union organising?', *Capital and Class*, vol. 36, no. 1, 97–115.

Sisson, K. (2009) 'Industrial relations and the employment relationship', in R. Darlington (ed.) *What's the Point of Industrial Relations? In Defence of Critical Social Science,* Salford: BUIRA.

——. (2010) *Employment Relations Matters.* Available at: http://www2.warwick.ac.uk/fac/soc/wbs/research/irru/erm/.

Standing, G. (2011) *The Precariat: The New Dangerous Class*, London: Bloomsbury Academic.

Taylor. A.J. (1989) *Trade Unions and Politics: A Comparative Introduction,* Basingstoke: Macmillan.

Taylor, R. (1993) *The Trade Union Question in British Politics: Government and Unions Since 1945,* Oxford; Blackwell.

Thornett, A. (1987) *From Militancy to Marxism*, London: Left View Books.

Tilly, C. (1978) *From Mobilization to Revolution*, New York: McGraw-Hill.

Turner, H.A., G. Clack, and G. Roberts (1967) *Labour Relations in the Motor Industry*, London: Allen and Unwin.

Upchurch, M., G. Taylor and A. Mathers (2009) *The Crisis of Social Democratic Trade Unionism in Western Europe: The Search for Alternative*, Aldershot: Ashgate.

Upchurch, M. and A. Mathers (2011) 'Neoliberal globalisation and trade unionism: Toward radical political unionism?', *Critical Sociology*, vol. 38, no. 2, 265–80.

Waterman, P. (1998) *Globalisation, Social Movements and the New Internationalisms*, London: Mansell.

Webster, E. (1988) 'The rise of social movement unionism: The two faces of black trade union movements in South Africa', in P. Frankel, N. Pijnes and M. Swilling (eds) *State, Resistance and Change in South Africa*, London: Croom Helm, pp. 174–96.

Webb, S. and B. Webb (1920) *History of Trade Unionism 1666–1920,* London: Longmans, Green and Co.

Zoll, R. (1976) *Der Doppelcharakter der Gewerkschafen*, Frankfurt: Suhrkamp.

6

WORKERS ORGANISING WORKERS: GRASS-ROOTS STRUGGLE AS THE PAST AND FUTURE OF TRADE UNION RENEWAL

Sheila Cohen

INTRODUCTION

In the wake of the long-term decline, or at least stasis, in trade union membership and effectiveness in the 'advanced countries', researchers, commentators and trade union leaders have produced a series of remedies: financial incentives; employer-union 'partnerships'; the Organising Model; and, most recently in the UK, 'leverage' (Cohen 2006; Wright 2011b). Yet despite extensive support from trade union leaderships for at least some of these approaches, much research is forced to acknowledge a failure, at least to date, to do more than at best stem the rate of membership loss. This contribution on workers' grass-roots organising and its potential for union growth examines historical trends of 'spontaneous' resistance and workplace activism in order to uncover the class dynamics of union renewal past and future.

'NO UNIONS AT ALL'?

As an example of such movement-based rather than 'top-down' struggle, workers in the newly industrialising countries (NICs) are fighting back against their super-exploitation and ill-treatment; and such resistance is so far rooted primarily *in the workplace*. Official trade union leaders, particularly in China, oppose this militant grass-roots action as much as do employers and the state. Yet repression has not stemmed these desperate struggles. The *China Labour Bulletin* recorded an 'upsurge' in strike action by transport workers in April 2012, along with a 17 per cent rise in strikes in manufacturing. This followed continued strikes and protests throughout February that year, with the Hanzhong Iron and Steel Group hit by two separate strikes on the 14 and 23 April over low pay and poor working conditions (Cheung 2012a; 2012b).

Yet what is really going on within such resistance is often barely understood in the West. A recent report by a US trade union activist describes a meeting at which, in response to reports of 'the unprecedented strike and protest wave occurring throughout [China] . . . led by workers [with] 90,000 of such "mass incidents" taking place last year alone', those at the meeting were 'much . . . surprised' to learn that 'these strikes are being led by workers with no unions at all' (Ruiz 2012).

This 'surprise' is in itself significant in an audience of experienced and sophisticated trade unionists. But there are further contradictions. The conclusion drawn by these trade unionists and by labour lawyers at the meeting is that 'If . . . China adopts some type of U.S.-style labour law, it will be done for the very reason that the U.S. government and employers acquiesced to [US] labour law in the first place – because it will lead to "industrial peace" and quell the strike wave' (Ruiz 2012). In other words, these resurgent, workplace-based, essentially democratic forms of direct action will be subordinated to an 'institutional' approach acceptable to government and employers.

A Contradictory Role

This response is significant for two reasons: first, and most importantly, a lack of awareness that strikes can be, and historically often have been, carried out by workers with 'no unions'; and, second, the indication that the ruling class and trade union bureaucracy sees legislation and its historical corollary, trade union institutionalism, as a way out of such insurgent, unregulated class conflict.

Yet historically it has always been exactly such conflict that has led to the establishment of trade union organisation and recognition in apparently the most oppressive and hopeless circumstances. One attendee at the meeting described above compared the Chinese strikes to 'those in the

US which were led by the Wobblies in the 1920s'; and it was not only the 'Wobblies' (the syndicalist Industrial Workers of the World, or IWW) who led non-institutionalised strike waves of this kind in the US. Such upsurges can be dated back to the 'Great Upheaval' of the 1870s and earlier, and indeed forward to the rank and file strikes of the 1930s, which were disowned by the existing American Federation of Labour (AFL) bureaucracy on the grounds of incipi-ent militancy as well as craft snobbery (see below), and led to the foundation of a – briefly – more activist-oriented trade union federation, the Congress of Industrial Organizations (CIO).

Optimism or Pessimism?

To return to the present day, in an environment of ongoing global capital-ist crisis and – in some cases – militant resistance, trade unions continue to play a contradictory role. In fact trade unions themselves are a contradictory and ambiguous agency for the advance of workers' interests (Cohen 2006); that ubiquitous label 'the unions' can be said to conceal and obscure a dual reality in which two opposed processes are merged within one organisational form. As Hyman (1971) and Anderson (1967) have noted, this two-sided character has routinely given rise to conflicting 'optimistic' and 'pessimistic' views of the political and social potential of trade unionism. In addition, the common critique of trade union activity as 'economistic' stems from a reluc-tance by many socialists to accept that workplace-based resistance over pay or working conditions can ever take political, let alone revolutionary, form. Yet this 'left' dismissal of the political significance of workplace struggles is contradicted by historical accounts of workers' councils and other poten-tially revolutionary grass-roots formations (Cohen 2011; Ness and Azzellini 2011).

In line with this ambiguity in the nature of trade unionism is the two-sided perspective of optimism and pessimism noted not only by Hyman and Anderson but also by Kelly (1988) in his overview of the potential connections between trade unionism and socialism. In fact the 'optimistic' perspective, raising revolutionary opportunities as it does, has routinely been evaded by trade union leaderships, who have more than once quailed at the 'abyss' opened up to them by historical episodes of resistance such as, in Britain, the 1926 General Strike. Thus, while it is unquestionable that workers remain at least potentially the 'gravediggers' of capitalism, their organisational – and political – leaders continue to deny or even to recognise that role. The perspec-tive offered here suggests a return to the history and analysis of working-class, workplace-based resistance in order to restore a dynamic and class-based analysis.

In carrying out its critical analysis, this paper will focus on the underlying logic and purpose of trade union organisation, particularly at its base in the workplace, and will question assumptions in the literature that 'trade unions' are hegemonic and one-dimensional entities. By contrast, the analysis starts from the perspective referred to above that trade unionism carries a dual character as 'institution' and as 'movement' (Cohen 2006), and that union-as-institution need not be a necessary condition for the formation of workplace-based structures which resemble, and ultimately become, trade unions. In other words, as a number of commentators have observed in various formulations, there is often 'a union before the union got there' in dynamic, collectively-based processes of worker organisation (Fink 2003: 54).[1]

'The Only Silver Bullet'

The approach offered here investigates these processes through a historically-based exploration of worker-organising which emphasises three major dynamics: that union growth is historically linked with strike waves and other incidences of major class resistance; that such waves are workplace- and grass-roots-based; and that as such they tend to challenge unions-as-institutions while simultaneously, in effect, establishing the foundations of such structures. This indicates a 'paradox' noted by Friedman (2008) in terms of a 'Faustian bargain . . . Unions expand through the unrest that they then pacify; they pacify the unrest that feeds their growth' (p. 72). But this emphasises only one side of a complex dialectic in which the sources of unpredictable and class-structured conflict continue within the workplace – a process that demands recognition and development by analysts committed to the cause of effective worker organisation.

The argument put here is neither hostile or indifferent to officially-based processes of trade union recruitment and recognition; but it recognises and emphasises the key dynamic of worker self-organisation as overwhelmingly rooted in unofficial, 'spontaneous' forms of worker resistance which predate more institutionalised structures. Such grass-roots organising processes are also associated with the most active, healthy and effective forms of ongoing workplace trade unionism – those that unambiguously make a difference to workers' everyday experience.

This point emphasises the question of 'agency', and indeed recent years have seen an increased focus on this side of the movement/institution dialectic (Kelly 1998; Darlington 2002; Atzeni 2010; Cohen 2013). Yet at the same time there are objective factors underlying the relatively 'spontaneous' and subjectively-felt dynamic of workplace resistance: the *structural* reality of exploitation and its associated factors of labour intensification, worker victimisation etc; and, second, the existence of a layer of committed activists able to provide the necessary leadership for such 'explosions' of conflict.

Strike Waves and Organisation

Worker self-organising efforts throughout history have been motivated less by abstract idealism than by concrete, workplace-based resistance to exploitation. Such dynamics have meant that more than any other factor, surges of trade union organisation and growth are based on strike waves, often involving workers not already in trade unions, along with their related surges of militant, grass-roots, independent trade union organisation. To put this in its clearest statistical context, Kelly's (1998) overview of industrial relations and worker mobilisation states succinctly:

> Even the most cursory inspection of British trade union membership and density statistics shows that the periods of dramatic union growth seem to have coincided exactly with the major and minor strike waves... [E]xamining the relationship between strike activity and union membership... shows that strike frequency and union membership changes went hand in hand (up or down together) in 70 per cent of the years from 1889 to 1993 in Great Britain.
>
> (Kelly 1998: 89, 94)

Such upsurges themselves demonstrate a number of key common factors. First, they are almost always unpredictable and, in a contested conception (Leopold 2007), 'spontaneous'. Second, they often, if not always, involve sections of workers previously categorised as 'unorganisable' (dockers, twentieth-century car workers, etc.). Third, that such organisations are routinely formed by workers who, as with a recent movement of migrant carpenters in California, 'didn't know what a union was yet' (Clawson 2003: 104). And, fourth, central to the argument developed here, it is such upsurges and strike waves, more than any other dynamic, that organise workers on a significant scale. It is curious that the alchemists of today's organising strategies seem not to have investigated what was happening during membership surges such as those that took place in the UK during the strike wave of the late 1960s and 70s, when, as one trade union official put it, 'we could not cope with the influx of members wanting to join' (Murray 2003: 44).

It is strike action – the withdrawal of the labour that produces goods, services and most of all profits – that provides the greatest threat to capital (Kelly

1998; Buttigieg et al. 2007), operating in a way that might be compared, melo-dramatically, with the reaction of Dracula to the cross – or, as one airline activist put it more subtly, making management concessions was 'like taking sweets from a baby' (Cohen 2009). While strike figures at the time of writing have fallen to historically low figures, along with trade union density and union effectiveness, they do of course persist, and their rationale continues to reflect Marx's aphorism that workers are potentially 'the gravediggers of capitalism' in posing the ultimate threat to that system, the withdrawal of labour. As one worker put it during a recent UK dispute with the American giant Heinz, 'the only silver bullet the working man has is to strike' (Carter and Clifton 2010).

It is hardly surprising that the most class-conscious, neo-liberal capitalist politicians – Reagan, Thatcher – took steps to rapidly undermine the effectiveness of this major class weapon and one of its most central conditions, working-class solidarity. Nevertheless, even the draconian UK anti-union legislation has not prevented successful examples of industrial struggle in which workers simply 'walked through' those laws, as in the construction engineering disputes of 2009, with little or no retribution from the state (Morris 2009).

It is this independent, exploitation-based dynamic of resistance that informs the most successful of current struggles, and has also most effectively built union organisation in the past. History informs us of renewed surges in unionisation throughout capitalism among workers in sectors previously thought non-organisable – and that such surges were based on strike action even in some of the most apparently passive, 'weak' and inexperienced sectors. We therefore turn here to a historical survey of such episodes, in both Britain and the US, and their lessons for would-be organisers today.

'IT JUST WENT LIKE TINDER'

While Britain was, of course, the cradle of trade unionism, this form of organisation did not extend to its less privileged workers until the late nineteenth century. The 1850s to 1880s were a time when struggle and organisation were at a dispiritingly low ebb. Even an apparently successful wave of organisation among low-skilled workers like agricultural labourers, gas-stokers and railway workers in the early 1870s 'did not last . . . Trade began to worsen in 1874, and in the following years severe depression hit one industry after another . . . The Trade Union movement, *on the morrow of its great expansion*, shrank up again' (Cole 1937, emphasis added).

Yet even in these unpromising circumstances, the beginnings of organisation among non-unionised workers 'could come from the most unpredictable and apparently unpromising source. Call centre personnel? Supermarket till staff? Well, not in 1888! It was 12 to 15 year old kids in the match industry!' (Charlton 1999: 27).

In this way, the wave of unionisation of the unskilled and semi-skilled in late 1880s Britain was almost literally 'sparked' by some of the most oppressed workers in society – 13- to 15-year-old girls working in appalling conditions for poverty pay in the match-making factory of Quaker 'philanthropists' Bryant and May. Contrary to myth, this strike was neither managed nor instigated by contemporary socialists (Raw 2011) but, like strikes throughout the history of capitalism, broke out unexpectedly and 'spontaneously' on the sacking of one of these extraordinarily ill-treated workers. As one teenage militant put it, 'It just went like tinder; one girl began, and the rest said "yes", so out we all went' (Charlton 1999: 131).

This historic strike was rooted in anger and resentment reaching back for a number of years (Charlton 1999: 20–1; Raw 2011); and such hidden resentment is almost certainly a characteristic of today's super-exploited and apparently 'passive' workplaces. The shared issues include the everyday impact of exploitation, the element of *unpredictability* – upsurges are rarely expected – and the existence or otherwise of workplace activists who, even today, are committed to building effective workplace organisation in the long term.

'ORGANISATION . . . FAILED, AND . . . THE WORKERS' MOVEMENT GREW'

Thus, from the depressing decline in organisation described by Cole, serious worker resistance surged again in the late 1880s. The great Dock Strike of 1889, which launched the organisation of supposedly 'unorganisable' workers in the great general unions, the National Union of General and Municipal Workers (today's GMB) and the Transport and General Workers' Union (now reconstituted as Unite after a merger with the engineering union in 2010) was a direct follower of the victorious struggle of the 'matchgirls' in 1888. As Raw (2011) and others have demonstrated, the Bryant and May workers were tightly connected through families and friendships within the poverty-stricken East End communities with dockers and other workers who went on during this period to generate historic waves of working-class organisation.

Although socialists like Eleanor Marx were involved in and supportive of these developments, the waves of struggle which launched New Unionism were born not out of political principle but of concrete, exploitation-related workplace issues. The 1889 Great Dock Strike began over the operation of a form of piecework known as the 'plus' system which dockers suspected – rightly – of being manipulated so that they were denied a bonus payment for extra tonnage moved. One final example of this chicanery, when piece-work rates were refused to workers loading a ship called *The Lady Armstrong*, 'was the effective issue on which action started to roll' (Charlton 1999: 38). Yet as so often, the strike was not only over the iniquities of this payment system but a whole set of underlying grievances relating to dockers' casualisation, underemployment and dire poverty.

The story of the Great Dock Strike is one of propaganda and moral pressure rather than one of direct struggle – although the withdrawal of all labour from the Port of London by 50,000 dockers was of course no small event. In the end the strike was won more by the intervention of Australian dockers and their fellow trade unionists, who sent the then enormous sum of £30,000 to sustain the strike, than by the strength of the dockers alone. Yet the impact of the strike and the links to Will Thorne's unwavering efforts to organise gas workers, which finally bore fruit after the dockers' victory in winning their 'tanner' (a rise of six old pence an hour) resulted in an explosion of membership growth; despite the disdain of the British Trades Union Congress for these unskilled masses, affiliated TUC membership had grown by 200,000 or 25 per cent in one year (Charlton 1999: 109).

This initial surge was not sustained. As one history recounts, 'Trade union membership grew only very slowly in the 1890s and 1900s, and [there was] a marked reduction in worker successes during strikes ... From the 1890s there was a clear trend amongst the ... unions to accept institutionalised collective bargaining with employers ... and to oppose militant direct action' (Kenefick and McIvor 1996). In 1909–10, weakness and 'apathy' among oppressed sectors could be mourned in Robert Tressall's celebrated novel of working-class life and politics (Tressall 1914, 2004). But, by the time that classic was published, the explosion of militancy between 1910 and 1914 – the 'Great Unrest – had begun; during the conflict union membership increased by over 500,000. The issues which prompted workers into action in the Great Unrest period were very similar to those confronting workers today – acute labour intensification, wage freezes or reductions, and in general an employer agenda of almost sadistic aggression. Thus, in a syndrome sometimes despised by the intellectual left, workers were forced into struggle by the actions of employers, rather than forming any kind of conscious 'political' agenda of resistance as a precondition.

'DESPITE . . . UNIONS RATHER THAN BECAUSE OF THEM'

The same dynamic can be seen when looking at the extraordinary upsurge of worker struggle and trade union organisation which erupted in the US of the 1930s at the height of the Great Depression. Historical orthodoxy suggests that this wave of organising was instigated by then-president Roosevelt's 1935 National Labour Relations Act (NLRA), with its legal safeguards for workers attempting union organisation. Yet the analysis of Piven and Cloward (1979) reveals that, while the NLRA did indeed lead to a flood of worker applications for union membership, the highly conservative AFL (American Federation of Labor) refused to allow this mass of semi- and unskilled workers into their ranks. The rationale appears to have been fear of these workers' militancy as much as rejection of their less-skilled status; as Tobin, head of the Teamsters' union, put it: 'We do not want the men today if they are going on strike tomorrow' (Piven and Cloward: 117). Yet as a result of this cold-shouldering approach:

> Factory workers . . . extract[ed] their most substantial concessions . . . *before they were organized into unions.* Their power was not rooted in [trade union] organisation, but in their capacity to disrupt the economy. For the most part strikes, demonstrations and sit-downs spread during the mid-1930s despite existing unions rather than because of them.
>
> (Piven and Cloward: 96, emphasis in original)

As Piven and Cloward summarise the situation, 'At this stage, organization [into unions] failed, and perhaps for that reason, the workers' movement grew' (p. 119). It would be difficult to find a more telling endorsement of the logic and dynamic of grass-roots worker organisation – of union-as-movement in contradistinction to union-as-institution.

A less dramatic, but nevertheless telling, example of this dynamic can be found in an account of early unionisation in Pressed Steel, a UK factory supplying the car industry (Edwards 1979). This began with an 'apparently docile workforce which seemed resigned to "free enterprise"' until 'to the astonishment of Pressed Steel management, who thought everything was going admirably, the spontaneous explosion of 1934 happened . . . On July 17, 180 workers in the press shop walked out'. The story continues to reflect familiar features of such 'spontaneous' explosions: 'At first they had no clearly defined demands . . . there was no recognised leadership of any kind. No union existed to call in . . . The strike was . . . a spontaneous expression of revolt.'

Yet despite the absence of experienced activists, the necessary forms of organisation swiftly suggested themselves in a characteristic 'union before the union got there' dynamic: 'After some confused discussion among the unorganised workers someone proposed that a provisional strike committee be elected. *Thus the traditional form of strike organisation was created before any formal union organisation existed*' (emphasis added). As the author rightly comments, 'This was a remarkable illustration that, in essence, the union is no more than the determination of the workers to act in union for the betterment of their conditions of labour' (Edwards: 5). Possibly the most anti-trade union company on the world stage, Ford Motors, was unionised in both America and Britain in the early to mid-1940s via exactly the conflict-ridden process exemplified at Pressed Steel (Cohen 2013).

Many of these accounts of apparently impossible organising feats in the face of employer hostility and worker resignation evoke the dynamic of 'mobilisation theory', an influential perspective proposed by Kelly (1998) in his comprehensive 'rethinking' of industrial relations and trade union dynamics. Yet while the concept of 'mobilisation' clearly applies to the grass-roots organising actions described above, there are problems with the trajectory outlined by Kelly, in which decisions and experience-based shifts in consciousness appear as part of an almost 'stageist' process based on an explicit and somewhat moralistic apprehension of 'injustice' (Atzeni 2009; 2010). While workers can often been seen to adopt a strong justice-based morality, the dynamic of mobilisation 'does not proceed', in the words of Rosa Luxemburg, 'in a beautiful straight line but in a lightning-like zigzag' (Luxemburg 1925: 73).

'UNIONS NOT ALWAYS THE BEST ORGANISERS'

It is this 'lightning-like' dynamic, this 'suddenness' and unpredictability of worker organisation – based always in workplace conditions and contradictions, rather than beamed-from-above organising strategies – which has, over and over, enabled unionisation in sectors once thought unorganisable. Labour historian G.D.H. Cole, writing in the 1930s, commented gloomily on prospects for unionisation in the then 'new industries' such as 'motor-car manufacture and other mass-production trades . . . Many of the big motor firms refuse to recognise any sort of combination' (Cole 1939: 108). Along similar lines, 'In certain important sections, notably the big motor-manufacturing firms, organisation is almost non-existent except among fully-skilled workers'. Again, Croucher's (1980) detailed study of union organisation in the period up to and including World War Two in Britain shows how the 'new industries' of the South East, created in the wake of near collapse in traditional industries like shipbuilding and mining in Scotland and the North, were regarded as pessimistically in terms of unionisation as, say, call centres today.

Yet, as we now take for granted, industries like aerospace and car production had become bastions of trade unionism by the end of World War Two and, particularly in the case of the car industry, were to be instrumental in the 'upsurge' of workplace-based revolt from the mid-to-late 1960s which resulted, by the end of the period, in Britain's highest historic levels of trade union density.

Thus, simply through comparing periods of strong trade union growth with levels of militant strike activity and mass worker involvement, a clear correlation emerges between the dynamics of grass-roots worker struggle, strike waves and significant increases in union membership. This kind of explosive, unplanned process is indisputably more associated with union growth than the careful, leadership-instigated strategies of today's union leaders in the West. To summarise, a brief glance at trade union history instantly informs us that the most successful periods of trade union organisation are those when workers themselves, rather than the unions, do the organising.

'FAIRNESS IN THE TWENTY-FIRST CENTURY?'

Yet the dynamic of *workplace-based* conflict in trade union renewal remains often unacknowledged by either trade union leaders or, in many cases, by researchers and writers in the field of industrial relations. In fact, a shift in strategy in a very different direction is signalled by recent statements on 'community unionism' by Unite, Britain's largest general union, in the radical magazine *Red Pepper*. Here, its new General Secretary, Len McCluskey, reports that the union had recently agreed

> a new 'community membership'... for 'non-working people': not just unemployed, but non-working people. It's to demonstrate that we want to reach out, we want to engage not just in our workplaces but with our communities... Unite should be identified with everything that's going on in the community... [because] whenever we have an industrial struggle I want the community to be there for us.

While McCluskey concedes that 'we're a trade union. And a trade union is about organising workers at work', a central aspect of this new strategy is said to be the creation of 'area activist committees' which are 'supposed to draw people together within a geographical confine [sic] to develop common issues about what's going on in their locality' (Power et al. 2011: 16–18).

Unfortunately, such idealism is not supported by practical reality. As one writer on contemporary British industrial relations comments, 'there are practical limits to the capacity of civil society organisations to influence employer practice because, unlike unions, they do not have a direct presence in the workplace . . . these groups are primarily campaign organisations . . . rather than provid[ing] continuous bargaining and workplace representation' (Wright 2011: 9).

Interestingly, McCluskey concludes his paean to 'the community' by commenting: 'Rather than talking about the repeal of the anti-trade union laws, which is the kind of slogan that we've been coming out with for thirty years, we need to freshen up our language. I'm interested in talking about fairness in the 21st century.' The postmodernist rhetoric is all the more ironic in that McCluskey himself comes from a tradition of militant workplace organisation in the Liverpool docks, becoming a steward at the age of 19 in 1969, the height of the shop steward-based 'upsurge' in Britain (Wilson 1972).

There seems little question that the rhetorical flourishes of leaders like McCluskey cannot substitute for the raw power of that upsurge. As one ex-print worker commented on the recent anniversary of the historic 1986 Wapping dispute (and its defeat), 'Whatever you think of the print unions, whether they did have too much power – and lots of people thought they did – you look at the situation now, and you can only say: there's no worker protection at all. None' (Henley 2011). Once workers lose, or appear to lose, what gave rise to the 1970s aphorism 'Trade Unions have too much power' – clearly linked to precisely the incidence and efficacy of strikes in that tumultuous decade – they lose, also, any real means to defend themselves against the inherent aggression of capital.

'THE TOOLS OF SOLIDARITY'

By a melancholy contrast, the current period from at least the mid-1990s, if not earlier, has exhibited an almost 'flat-lining' incidence of significant industrial struggle, in Britain and United States at least. Strike statistics demonstrate historic lows, while such strikes as do take place are tied down with the ball and chain of trade union legislation which Tony Blair, on entering office in 1997, proudly defined as 'the most restrictive in the Western world' (Taylor 1997).

As opposed to McCluskey's airy dismissal of the issue of these laws, which have crippled the ability of workers to fight back for over 30 years, a number of analyses emphasise the centrality of the strike to the process of union renewal. One recent US publication (Burns 2011) makes the emphatic point, backed up by considerable empirical evidence, that 'organisation' per se, in the sense of trade union recognition and membership density, is insufficient to truly build the movement in such a way that it can effectively fight back against what are, once again, almost intolerable pressures on the working class.

Burns notes the distinction between passive and limited forms of 'organisation', between the term's use by some union leaderships simply to indicate recruitment into trade unions and its more combative meaning in terms of the workplace-based processes described above. As he writes, current US union strategy in the sphere of 'organizing the unorganized' is rooted in the concept of ' "union density" ... Unfortunately, [this] model ... addresses only one ... [factor], the numbers of employees unionized in an industry, while failing to address the need for labour to possess the necessary tools to force an employer to reach an agreement'. Burns suggests reversing the strategy, as indeed has historically been the case in periods of strong union growth and workplace power: 'If labour wielded the economic tools of solidarity and stopping production – ie an effective strike – it would then be able to organize workers and achieve density' (Burns 2011: 96).

It is significant that Burns qualifies 'strike' with 'effective'. The pattern in Britain, certainly in the twenty-first century if not before, has been to substitute one- and two-day strikes for more lasting periods of industrial action. This, along with the kind of 'propagandistic' strikes which have tended to be sponsored by union leaderships in contrast to the more organic and dynamic pattern of previous years, has rendered TUC and union leadership announcements of strikes against 'the cuts' more of a ritual than the genuine threat to capital posed during the late 1960s to late 1970s upsurge.

Burns' argument also suggests a still more fundamental point – that where union 'density' is obtained by virtue of co-operation and partnership with employers – as is the case with the American Service Employees' Industrial Union (SEIU) – this factor itself undermines the real purpose of trade unionism – to protect and advance workers' interests. As Moody (2010) shows, the SEIU's coup in organising apparently non-unionisable immigrant janitors in 1990 remained just that – a feat of 'organising' rather than of even basic improvements in the workers' terms and conditions. Ten years later, low-paid janitors were still just that: 'The second five-year agreement with the contractors ... scheduled an increase ... from $6.80 [an hour] in April 1995 to $7.20 in February 2000. This was an increase of little more than 1% a year ... in real terms a *drop* of 6% over five years' (Moody 2007, emphasis in original). Accounts by Moody and others emphasise, not coincidentally, the bureaucratic oppression of the LA janitors after they were recruited into a massive, state-wide California 'local' (Cohen 2006: 109).

TAKING UNION LEADERS BY SURPRISE

A contemporary struggle in the UK building industry underlines the connection between institutionalised organising and the lack of democracy afforded union members involved in such 'over-their-heads' forms of union membership. In the words of construction industry activists caught up in current struggles against employers' threatened withdrawal from a relatively favourable industry agreement:

> This struggle ... has taken the union leaders by surprise. They have been content to bury their heads in the sand for years. They sat back while the industry was deregulated and splinted by subcontractors and agencies ... The union leaders were content as long as the employers played ball with them and paid over the union dues through a check-off system. Instead of building up a strong rank and file site organisation, they relied on the good will of the employers ... Predictably, the bosses have reneged on their agreement. They have led the union leaders a merry dance with their cushy relationships and cups of coffee ... without the involvement of the rank and file ... All this played into the bosses' hands.
>
> (Kelly and Blakely 2011)

Here we have union density, indeed organisation of a kind – but the lifeblood of effective trade unionism, workplace organisation, has been undermined. Yet the dispute currently raging within this industry, marked by mass demonstrations and walkouts, shows such accommodation to be a contradictory process in which the much-feared hydra head of rank and file trade unionism resurfaces below the bureaucratic crust. The construction industry employers' attempt to unilaterally break up a longstanding national pay structure has 'sparked', to use a predictable metaphor, a wave of militancy among construction electricians – one comparable to the engineering construction workers' walkouts of 2009.

Those walkouts were in direct, and as it turned out unpunished, defiance of the UK anti-union laws which have bound trade union action in increasingly tight restraints over more than 30 years. Such demonstrations of the efficacy of 'wildcat' action stands in sharp contrast to the timid response of a leading Unite organiser to the suggestion that strikes might play a key role in organising: 'We will use industrial action, but it has to be within legal boundaries. It's a last resort...We have had a number of ballots but these have been coupled with leverage, legal challenges, etc. We have to use our collective strength but...industrial action is not the only type of use of collective strength' (quoted in Cohen 2009).

This apparent disengagement from traditional industrial action by a leading union organiser, along with recent failures in the same union to support sustained action even by strong groups like airline workers, raises the contrasting question of which aspects of the increasing burden of immiseration and workplace oppression could have the force to spur workers into significant struggle despite official union opposition – struggle that can go beyond the workplace and trade union bureaucracy to illustrate the historic function of labour as a 'gravedigger' of capital.

'TWENTY-FOUR HOURS AWAY FROM MELTDOWN'

A still recent but now largely forgotten episode illustrates the force of that hidden giant, working-class power. In the UK in September 2000 a motley crew of road haulage workers, farmers and taxi drivers, but most of all unionised oil tanker drivers, staged military-style protests against ever-higher fuel tax rates. Within a few days supermarkets were running out of food, ambulance services had imposed speed limits, and funeral directors were reporting that they had enough petrol to pick up bodies, but not to bury them. The apocalyptic potential of this 'seven days that shook Britain' is illustrated in one near-contemporary account: 'Blair was...warned what would happen if the blockades continued to the end of the working week: the shops would be empty and essential services crippled...There would be no food. The health service was going to collapse. We were twenty-four hours away from meltdown' (Rawnsley 2001: 409–10).

Yet, within the 10 days seemingly allocated for such events, the 'revolution' ended. Union leaders were central to cobbling the final compromise, in which drivers at the Grangemouth refinery were persuaded to take out the tankers on the basis of guaranteeing their 'safety'. The withdrawal of unionised drivers broke the back of the movement, and Labour Prime Minister Blair was duly grateful: 'I have had many harsh things to say about the unions over the years, but I have to say that on this crisis they reacted magnificently...For the first time in memory, I was praising John Edmonds of the GMB and Bill Morris of the TGWU, and was actually really grateful to the TUC' (Blair 2011: 297).

So, not for the first time in history, trade union leaders stepped in to save capital, not to destroy it. This willingness of the working class movement's leadership to act as rescuer of the system which exploits and oppresses its members should not come as a surprise – trade unionism per se has always been reformist rather than revolutionary – but it illustrates once again the weight of union-as-institution in suppressing rather than advancing the basic class interests of workers.

'BEING PART OF THE UNION'

This statement may appear ungracious in the face of recent concerted action taken by a range of British trade unions against government 'reforms' which reduce public sector workers' pensions. A one-day strike across Britain on 30 November 2011 which brought out hundreds of thousands of workers across the country evoked journalistic comparisons with the UK's 1978–9 'Winter of Discontent' in terms of the numbers taking part. Yet such arithmetical parallels miss the point. The Winter of Discontent was a wide-ranging and sustained strike wave which (like the 2000 fuel protests) evoked aspects of 'dual power' (Beckett 2009) and, unlike the 30 November strike, won significant gains across the working class.

Thus, while union representation in the UK and similar economies continues to be of overwhelming value to workers, its overall impact on the crucial areas of remuneration, working hours and labour intensification is at a historic low point in comparison to the last period of worker militancy and union renewal, the mid-1960s to late 1970s. One ex-shop steward at the historic Ford Dagenham plant evoked the culture and expectations of this period trenchantly:

> Coming to Fords, being part of the union was the thing to do . . . If you became a rep you were very political, and the politics on the shop floor was very simple – everybody accepted that you took strike action to get more money – everybody was ready for it. And in those days when people took industrial action it worked. Most people were clear what the fight was about – in those days if you picked up a newspaper there was always somebody winning something in an industrial action – all around you, you could see that someone had won money because they took industrial action.
>
> (Quoted in Cohen 2013)

This energetic and traditionally 'militant' culture stands in poignant contrast to today's scenario, in which strikes are overwhelmingly one-day affairs or so constrained by current legislation that workers' initially militant impulse is caught in a web of legal barriers based on forensically detailed examination of balloting procedures. As one steward in the train drivers' union ASLEF put it, 'Nowadays they try to look for any little alleged discrepancy in a strike ballot, like if there's one spoilt paper, or one person's not at the address they've sent the ballot ... they [go for an] injunction. They can play God, these judges' (Moynihan 2011).

Yet there are a number of factors that can be brought together to rescue the current analysis from pessimism as to future trade union action and efficacy. First, the *unpredictability* of waves of working-class struggle was recently reaffirmed in the upsurge of quasi-revolutionary activity in some of the most oppressed sectors of the Arab world. This upsurge was both prefaced and associated with strike waves and other aspects of trade union action; as one key activist put it, 'This day in the revolution could be named for the labour unions' (Abbas 2011).

Second, and in apparent contradiction to the 'spontaneity' of many of these upsurges (see above), stands the layer of indomitable workplace activists, persisting even in these troubled times, who are motivated primarily by the need to build the movement rather than by any wish to rise within it on an individual basis (although unfortunately no impermeable barrier yet exists which can halt this trajectory). Such activists are key to the movement in two ways: in sustaining what independent trade union organisation and struggle remains even in the troughs of trade union action, and in providing a potentially class-conscious leadership when, as history appears to show it will, struggle does resurface.

In fact, initial research on trade union organising in the US emphasised the importance of 'worker to worker' campaigns in which well-organised groups visited or otherwise engaged non-members in their immediate areas (Bronfenbrenner and Juravich 1998: 25). The approach was supported by further empirical research which confirmed the importance of rank and file tactics: 'Unions are most likely to win ... when they ... [utilise] a grass-roots, rank-and-file intensive strategy' (Bronfenbrenner 2003: 41). The importance of this 'strong-to-weak' dynamic is confirmed in later accounts of 'greenfield' organising where successful campaigns involved the support of networks of activists (Simms 2008; Findlay and McKinlay 2003). In general, research shows that already existing and committed activists are crucial to recruitment and organising (Kelly 1998; Heery et al. 1999).

Third, there is the role of workplace trade unionism of building awareness and consciousness even among the most inexperienced who put themselves forward for trade union activity. Sian Moore's (2011) study of 'new' workplace representatives such as Union Learning Reps (ULRs) demonstrates that even forms of workplace representation that can be justly criticised as 'an implausible path to union revitalisation' (McIlroy 2008) can generate a wider political consciousness. As one (previously inexperienced) ULR put it:

> I've probably become a socialist through my union work . . . politics have never been something that I was interested in, I've never thought about it . . . it's only when I joined the union and . . . was facing all those things [that] I thought This can't be right surely . . . I can't say I am a socialist now . . . I don't know, I need to learn more about it and I've read lots, and I think I am a socialist . . . but I'm not educated politically. As trade unionists our time is coming again . . . the working landscape is changing all the time, and people will come to us the unions again for protection and help!
>
> (Moore 2011: 162)

These interrelated elements – the unpredictability of working-class struggle, its power to organise the 'unorganisable' and heighten consciousness, the continued existence through upsurge and downturn of a key layer of committed workplace representatives – constitute the key force which can offer a solution to Friedman's 'paradox' cited above, one which essentially repeats the logic of Michels' Iron Law of Oligarchy. That force consists of the class power lent by withdrawal of labour, the solidarity generated by grass-roots struggle whatever the force of 'the law', and perhaps most of all the *direct democracy* characteristic of 'spontaneous' workers' struggles and their common structures throughout the history of capitalism (Cohen 2011). Conscious recognition of such structures and the key element of direct accountability they embody is key to a strategic perspective for the grass-roots of the movement (Parker and Gruelle 1999).

CONCLUSION

As the argument of this paper suggests, despite the refrain of the old IWW song

> *Solidarity for ever,*
> *For the union makes us strong*

'the union' can in many cases make us weak, where 'we' are its basic membership or rank and file. The gigantic SEIU in the United States, for example, has 'locals' (branches) larger than an American state, while its members are left to deal with their grievances via call centres; recognition deals are frequently concluded on a basis of 'partnership' with predatory employers like private hospital chains which leave workplace members open to abuse and intensified exploitation (Early 2011).

Yet the dangers of bureaucratisation and its associated 'weakening' of the trade union formation are not cited here in order to suggest opposition to trade unionism per se – quite the contrary. The very hostility of many employers to any hint of trade union organisation, illustrated perhaps most clearly in the 'union-busting' activities common in the United States (Moody 2012) demonstrates without question the intrinsic anti-capitalist logic of trade unionism.

In this context, strategic awareness of the need for sustained democratic accountability to union members in the workplace by the movement's representatives is crucial. The old adage of the 1915 Clyde Workers' Committee leaflet – 'We will support the officials just so long as they rightly represent the workers, but we will act independently immediately they misrepresent them' (quoted in Hinton 1973: 119) remains if anything more relevant today than at its inception. And it is exactly today's equivalent of the World War One shop stewards who remain the key to union renewal.

The three key factors highlighted in this study of the dynamic and potential of worker organisation and resistance – its roots in the *structural* realities of workplace-based exploitation, the dialectic between the often 'spontaneous' action sparked by such factors and the role of already existing workplace activists, the historical *unpredictability* of mass upsurges with their accompanying peaks of union growth – combine to compel a focus on the one stable factor in this scenario, that of already-existing activism. Even at the lowest points of working-class trade union involvement and struggle, a core of conscious activists committed to workplace union effectiveness and, frequently, direct democracy is always present within the movement (Charlwood, Greenwood and Wallis 2006; Fairbrother 2000; Cohen 2007). It is these activists, whatever their number, who will provide the invaluable resource of experience and cross-union commitment to any future resurgence of struggle.

NOTE

1. 'We didn't organize anybody', a LIUNA (Labourers' International Union of North America) representative in the Morgantown campaign of 1995 recalled. 'There was a union before the union got there' (Clawson 2003: 54).

REFERENCES

Abbas, K. (2011) Centre for Trade Union and Workers' Services, Egypt.

Anderson, Perry (1967) 'The limits and possibilities of trade union action' in R. Blackburn and A. Cockburn (eds) *The Incompatibles: Trade Union Militancy and the Consensus*, Penguin, London.

Atzeni, M. (2009) 'Searching for injustice and finding solidarity? A contribution to the mobilization theory debate', *Industrial Relations Journal*, vol. 40, no. 1, 5–16.

Atzeni, M. (2010) *Workplace Conflict: Mobilization and Solidarity in Argentina*, Palgrave Macmillan, Basingstoke.

Beckett, Andy (2009) *When The Lights Went Out*, Faber and Faber, London.

Blair, Tony (2011) *A Journey*, Random House, London.

Bronfenbrenner, K. and Juravich, T. (1998) 'It takes more than house calls: Organizing to win with a comprehensive union-building strategy' in Bronfenbrenner, K., Friedman, S., Hurd, R.W., Oswald, R.A. and Seeber, R.L. (eds) *Organizing to Win*, Cornell, ILR Press.

Bronfenbrenner, K. (2003) 'The American labour movement and the resurgence in union organizing' in Fairbrother and Yates (eds) *Trade Unions in Renewal: A Comparative Study*, London, Routledge

Buttigieg, D., Deery, S. J. and Iverson, R. D. (2007) 'Union mobilization: A consideration of the factors affecting the willingness of union members to take industrial action', *British Journal of industrial Relations*, vol. 46, no. 2.

Burns, J. (2011) *Reviving the Strike: How Working People can Regain Power and Transform America*, Ig Publications, New York.

Carter, H. and Clifton, H (2010) 'No need to hoard beans, says Heinz', *The Guardian*, 30 December, London, p. 6.

Charlton, J. (1999) *It Just Went Like Tinder: The mass movement of New Unionism in Britain 1889*, Redwords, London.

Charlwood, A., Greenwood, Ian and Wallis, Emma (2006) 'The dynamics of trade union activism in Great Britain 1991–2003', paper presented to the 24th Annual International Labour Process Conference, London.

Cheung, J. (2012a) 'Strikes and worker protests continue throughout February', China Labour Bulletin, March.

Cheung, J. (2012b) 'Pay disputes and factory relocations the focus of strike action in April, China Labour Bulletin, May.

Clawson, D. (2003) *The Next Upsurge: Labor and the New Social Movements*, ILR Press, New York.

Cohen, S. (2006) *Ramparts of Resistance: Why Workers Lost Their Power, and How to Get It Back*, Pluto Press, London.

Cohen, S. (2007) ' "Activating the activists" in union futures: How can we best build a vibrant, growing trade union movement?', TUC Union Ideas Network.

Cohen, S. (2009) 'Opening Pandora's box: The paradox of institutionalised organising, in G. Gall (ed.) *The Future of Union Organising: Building for Tomorrow*, Palgrave Macmillan, Basingstoke.

Cohen, S. (2011a) 'The red mole: Workers' councils as a means of revolutionary transformation', in Ness and Azzellini (eds) *Ours to Master and to Own: Workers' Control from the Commune to the Present Haymarket*, Chicago.

Cohen, S. (2011b) 'Left agency and class action: The paradox of workplace radicalism', *Capital and Class*, vol. 35, no. 3.

Cohen, S. (2013, forthcoming) *Notoriously Militant: The History of Ford Central Branch at Dagenham*, Merlin, London.

Cole, G.D.H. (1939) *British Trade Unionism To-Day*, Gollancz, London.

Croucher, R. (1980) *Engineers at War*, Merlin.

Darlington, R (2002) 'Shop stewards' leadership, left wing activism and collective workplace union organization', *Capital and Class*, vol. 76.

Darlington, R. (2010), 'The state of workplace union reps' organization in Britain today', *Capital and Class*, vol. 34, no. 1, 126–35.

de Turberville, S. (2007) 'Union Organizing: A Response to Carter', *Work, Employment and Society*, 21(3): 565–76.

Early, Steve (2011) *The Civil Wars in U.S. Labour: Birth of a New Workers' Movement or Death-Throes of the Old?*, Haymarket.

Edwards, D. (1979) 'How trade unionism came to Pressed Steel', Militant Publications, London.

Fairbrother, Peter (2000) 'British trade unions facing the future', *Capital and Class*, vol. 71.

Findlay, P. and McKinlay, A. (2003) 'Organising in electronics: Recruitment, recognition and representation – shadow shop stewards in Scotland's "Silicon Glen" ' in G. Gall (ed.) *Union Organising: Campaigning For Trade Union Recognition*, Routledge, London.

Fink, L. (2003) *The Maya of Morgantown: Work and Community in the Nuevo New South*, University of North Carolina Press.

Friedman, G. (2008) *Reigniting the Labour Movement: Restoring Means to Ends in a Democratic Labour Movement*, Routledge, London and New York.

Gall, G. (2011) 'The backward march of labour halted? Or, what is to be done with "union organising"? The cases of Britain and the United States', *Capital and Class*, vol. 36, no. 2.

Gall, G. and Dundon, T. (eds) (2014) *Global Anti-unionism: Nature, Dynamics, Trajectories and Outcomes*, Basingstoke: Palgrave Macmillan.

Heery et al. (1999), 'Organising unionism comes to the UK', *Employee Relations*, vol. 22, no. 1, 38–53.

Heery, E. and Simms, M. (2008), 'Constraints on union organising in the United Kingdom', *Industrial Relations Journal*, 39(1): 24–42.

Henley, J. (2011), 'It was a war and we lost it', *The Guardian*, London.

Hinton, James (1973) *The First Shop Stewards' Movement*, George Allen and Unwin

Hyman, Richard (1971) *Marxism and the Sociology of Trade Unionism*, Pluto Press.

Kelly, J. (1988) *Trade Unions and Socialism*, Verso, London.

Kelly, J. (1998) *Rethinking Industrial Relations: Mobilization, Collectivism and Long Waves*, Routledge, London.

Kelly, Steve and Blakely, Ross (2011) *Siteworker*, Autumn.

Kenefick, W. and McIvor, A. (1996) *Roots of Red Clydeside 1910–1914: Labour Unrest and Industrial Relations in West Scotland*, John Donald, Edinburgh.

Leopold, L. (2007) *The Man Who Hated Work and Loved Labour*, Chelsea Green, Vermont.

Luxemburg, R. (1925) *The Mass Strike 1925*.

McIlroy, J. (2008) 'Ten years of New Labour: Workplace learning, social partnership and union revitalization in Britain', *British Journal of Industrial Relations*, vol. 46, 283–313.

Moody, K. (2007) *US Labour in Trouble and Transition: The Failure of Reform from Above, the Promise of Revival from Below*, Verso, London and New York.

Moody, K. (2012) 'Beating the union: Union avoidance in the U.S., 1945 to the present', in Gall, G. and Dundon, T. (eds) (2014) *Global Anti-unionism: Nature, Dynamics, Trajectories and Outcomes*, Basingstoke: Palgrave Macmillan.

Moore, Sian (2011) *New Trade Union Activism: Class Consciousness or Social Identity?*, Palgrave Macmillan, Basingstoke.

Morris, O. (2009), 'The return of the wildcats?' *Solidarity*, Issue 25.

Moynihan, M. (2011) 'Management changed the rules – not us', *Solidarity*, Issue 28.

Murray, A. (2003) *A New Labour Nightmare: The Return of the Awkward Squad*, Verso, London.

Ness, I. and Azzellini, D. (eds) (2011) *Ours to Master and to Own: Workers' Control from the Commune to the Present*, Haymarket, Chicago.

Parker, M. and Gruelle, M. (1999) *Democracy is Power: Rebuilding Unions from the Bottom Up*, Labour Notes, Detroit.

Piven, F.F. and Cloward, R.A. (1979) *Poor People's Movements: How they Succeed, How they Fail*, Vintage, New York.

Power, Nina et al. 2011 'New life in the unions?' *Red Pepper*, vol. 179, 16–18.

Raw, Louise (2011) *Striking A Light: The Bryant and May Matchwomen and their Place in History*, Continuum, London.

Rawnsley, A. (2001) *Servants of the People: The Inside Story of New Labour*, Penguin Books, London.

Ruiz, A.C. (2012) 'The US labour movement and China'. Available at: http://www.counterpunch.org 27 April.

Simms, M and Holgate, J (2010), "Organising for what? Where is the debate on the politics of organising?" Work, Employment and Society 24:157, London.

Taylor, R. (1997), 'Election '97: Backtracking embitters old guard', *Financial Times*, London, 7 April.

Tressall, R. (2004) *The Ragged Trousered Philanthropists*, first published 1914, Penguin Books, London.

Wilson, D. (1972) *Dockers: The Impact of Industrial Change*, Fontana, London.

Wright, C. (2011) 'What role for trade unions in future workplace relations?', Advisory, Conciliation and Arbitration Service, UK.

Wright, C.F. (2011a) 'Organising beyond the employment relationship: unions, collective bargaining and supply chain coordination' TUC.

Wright, C.F. (2011b) 'Beyond the employment relationship: collective bargaining and supply chain coordination', TUC.

7

THE WORKERS' CONTROL ALTERNATIVE*

Maurizio Atzeni

INTRODUCTION

There is a shared view among business people that considers it is almost common sense to organise work in a hierarchical, management-led way. Notwithstanding fashionable managerial programmes about employee's participation and involvement, which in the best of the cases collapse as sandy castles under the storm of economic crises, within capitalism 'management has the right to manage'. That somebody needs to be empowered in the interest of business to take quick decisions and impose the execution of these on working people, is a principle hardly contested and indeed commonly accepted by workers themselves as the normal state of things. This acceptance is further reinforced by a system of work organised on the basis of a separation between planning and execution that concentrates knowledge (and consequently decision-making power) in the hands of a few. This conception about the accepted, effective and thus 'natural' way of organising work in our societies is so embedded in the way we live that to think about a different, more democratic, equalitarian, less hierarchical and authoritarian way of organising work is at best treated as a utopia.

Historical research on the labour movement and on workers' contentious actions provides a good antidote to this dominant view about organising work

---

*This is an abridged version of the introductory chapter of my edited book, *Alternative Work Organizations* (Basingstoke: Palgrave Macmillan, 2012).

and represents a fundamental tool in the process of critique to the existing system. Although with differences in terms of socio-political and geographical context and within a wide range of ideological perspectives, workers with their actions have often reverted taken for granted assumptions about property, management, work organisation, wages, and have overall contested, in daily practice, the almost natural character of capitalist work relations while contemporaneously creating alternative forms of work organisation. From Owen and the socialist utopians to the co-operative movement of the late nineteenth century, from the Russian soviets to the revolutionary factories' occupations in Italy in the 1920, from the spread of self-management in Cataluña during the Spanish Republic of 1936–9 to the institutionalisation of self-management in the post-war communist Yugoslavia, from the promotion of workers' control in industry in the 1970s to the contemporary cases of worker-run production and democratic decision-making at Tower Colliery and Suma in the UK, from the recent experiences of self-management in Argentina born out of an economic crisis to Venezuelan state-supported factories' expropriation and nationalisation under workers' control, all these geographically and historically diverse contexts nonetheless have represented cases and experiences of workers with alternative forms of work. Workers' control or self-management, workers' democratic decision-making power on production and administration, has often been the way through which workers have demanded or attempted to change the traditional way of organising work. In general terms, workers' control can be then considered as epitomising the search for an alternative. Indeed, with its emphasis on democracy in the decision-making process, on workers autonomy in the management of the labour process, on solidarity and equality among producers and on the idea of work as purposive and creative, workers' control stands directly opposite the authoritarian, alienating, job de-skilled, profit-driven reality of a capitalist work organisation.

What is the theoretical relevance of all these historical attempts to revert the 'natural' state of things of capitalist work relations?

In order to answer this question the chapter will first present a discussion about the capitalist nature of the labour process and of how this material and ideological structure works, affecting the possibility of workers' control. Production within capitalism is rationally organised, both technically and socially, to produce and increase profit. This logic of production changes the nature of the labour process, which from a process, just like any other, in which human labour transforms things, becomes a united whole of production and valorisation. Management control of the labour process, authoritarian and hierarchical decision-making, a tendency to task specialisation, job segmentation and de-skilling, increased individualism and divisions among workers, are just few of the consequences that the need for profitability can impose on the organisation of work.

In the second part of the chapter, a number of important theoretical aspects associated with workers' attempts to control production will be addressed. The pervasiveness of capitalist social relations makes exceptional any deviations from the capitalist model of work organisation. Historical experiences have nonetheless evidenced how the existence of structural conditions favours the emergence of an alternative and how this alternative is, by its own nature, transformative of the status quo and thus, potentially, revolutionary.

Despite this potential, workers experiments with new forms of organising work have inevitably always been inserted within the present capitalist socio-economic system and its dynamics of market competition. This has a twofold consequence. On the one hand, the mere existence of a radical alternative in the form of a direct control by workers of the whole production and decision-making process has always been opposed by the dominant classes. Workers' control in capitalism is indeed critical. With its emphasis on grass-roots democracy, collective property and self-management it directly challenges the capitalist labour process, giving space to the formation of new, by nature more radical, forms of workers organisation, the workers councils or committees. On the other hand, once the alternative remains within the remits of the system, as has been typical of any long-standing experience of workers' self-management and of the co-operative movement, the competition in the market imposes the adoption of capitalist managerial rules that limit the extent of democracy and participation within the organisation.

The theoretical debate about the fate of workers' attempts to build an alternative within the system has been dominated by the thesis that the incorporation in the market would lead to a degeneration of the potentially revolutionary character of workers' control of production. However, while it is true that capitalism strongly distorts or eliminates any serious attempts at changing the organisation of work, all experiences of alternative work have represented an advance in terms of workers' emancipation and empowerment. This is the starting point if we aim to make the search for an alternative and more democratic organisation of work central to the social science and policy agenda.

THE NATURE OF WORK WITHIN CAPITALISM

There seems to be a coincidence among overlapping disciplines in the social sciences about the nature of work within capitalism. Work is generally seen as a negative, alienating and unchangeable condition of life. In mainstream labour economics, for instance, in the last 300 years, work has been described as a pain or disutility and mainly seen as an activity workers would happily avoid for a life of leisure and consumption. As a consequence, rather than looking at the intrinsic characteristics of the work activity itself, labour economists have placed great emphasis on monetary rewards as an instrument to convince workers to work (Spencer 2009).

That workers need to be motivated to perform work is a view also shared by contemporary human resource management literature. While monetary incentives linked to the monitoring of employees' performance remain central to increase productivity, discourses about job satisfaction and enrichment, employees involvement and the mutual gain enterprise, have stressed the importance of gaining workers' motivation to work through psychological and ideological incentives (Guest 2002; Kochan and Osterman 1994). Adding to this, it has been argued that in today's more dynamic and knowledge-based work environment, autonomy, mastery and purpose are the most fundamental motivators of people at work (Pink 2011). From a different perspective, workplace ethnographic and qualitative studies have often given voice to workers' unconformity to work. The degradation of work produced by the repetitiveness of tasks, the intensification of rhythms and conditions of work, management authority and control and its use of race and ethnicity to divide workers, insufficient wage levels and threats to job security are all aspects of work that constantly surface from within the employment relation, structuring collective action and resistance (Linhart 1981; Beynon 1984; Fantasia 1989; Turner 1995; Cohen 2006; Sherman 2007; Mollona 2009; Atzeni 2010; Lopez 2010).

While work represents an important moment in the social life of people and it is in itself a potentially creative and fulfilling activity, there is no doubt that workers' compulsion to sell their labour power for a wage, the main social form through which work has been subsumed under capitalism, creates (for the majority of workers) a negative attitude toward work. Rather than an end in itself, waged work is performed and accepted just because it represents the only method available to reproduce the workers, giving them access, via exchange in the market, to the consumables required to satisfy the variable sets of material and social human needs:

> But beneath this apparent habituation, the hostility of workers to the degenerated forms of work which are forced upon them continues as a subterranean stream that makes its way to the surface when employment conditions permit . . . it renews itself in new generations, expresses itself in the unbounded cynicism and revulsion which

a large number of workers feel about their work, and come to the fore repeatedly as a social issue demanding solution.

(Braverman 1974: 151)

Marx argued that the double nature of the capitalist labour process, contemporaneously a process of production of a use value and a process of valorisation of this through living labour, and the treatment of labour as a commodity to be exchanged in the market, produces a number of consequences, specific to the capitalist labour process, that affect the material reality of work and structures the way people think and behave in relation to their work. On the one hand, by entering into exchange with the capitalist, workers are separated from the product of their labour and lose control of the labour process. This becomes, with the development of industry, increasingly segmented, repetitive and subjected to a hierarchical system of managerial/technical control, functional to efficiency and profitability, based on the division between intellectual/directive and manual work. On the other hand, these material changes increase the alienation of workers from their work up to the point that 'the instrument of labour confronts the worker during the labour process, in the shape of capital, dead labour, which dominates and soaks up living labour power' (Marx 1976: 548).

The work of Braverman, published in his seminal book, *Labour and Monopoly Capital*, and the so-called labour process debate that followed from this publication have been discussed in detail by Spencer in this book (Chapter 1). Empirical studies in the labour process tradition have provided important insights into changes and transformations occurring in the world of work, particularly with the new work processes associated with flexibilisation and lean production (Delbridge 1998; Elger and Smith 1994, 2005) and the new knowledge and service economy (Korczynski 2002; Taylor and Bain 2005; Warhurst, Grugulis and Keep 2004; Bolton 2005; Bolton and Houlihan 2009). Despite the importance of this body of work in explaining the complexity of social processes occurring in the workplace, the framework provided by Marx and, successively, Braverman to understand the specificity of the labour process should be defended (Cohen 1987; Spencer 2000; Tinker 2002). First, the tendencies outlined in this framework have proved to be, to a large extent, resistant to the passing of time. In this sense, de-skilling remains an inevitable tendency especially in the accelerated global production process (Taylor 2008). Second, it is still probably the best model we have to establish linkages between the abstract and the concrete, the theoretical and the empirical. Marx's view of the labour process as contemporaneously a production and valorisation process, connects the specificities of social relations at the workplace with the general dynamics of a system based on class relations in which the labour process is set in motion to create profit. This logic tends to shapes the entire organisation of work but is limited, among other factors, by workers' opposition and resistance to it. This is indeed omnipresent and rational since the exploitation of labour by capital is inherently contradictory and conflictive (Hyman 2006).

It might be argued that in any social system based on class division, labour would be always coerced and work would be always organised in a way functional to the interest of the dominant classes in appropriating the surplus produced by workers. In this sense there would be nothing specific to the capitalist system and producers would always perceive work as a pain and a cost. However, as Burawoy rightly shows in his comparison with the feudal system (Burawoy 1979: ch. 2), there are a number of specificities of the labour process under capitalism that make this system different and consequently structure subjective attitudes to work. The appearance of the payment of the wage as an equal compensation for the expenditure of labour power, while giving an impression of equal exchange in reality conceals the automatic appropriation by capitalist of both necessary and surplus labour. Different to feudalism, here there is no clear division between the time spent by workers to produce their means of existence (necessary labour) and the time dedicated to produce the surplus. Workers cannot reproduce themselves independently, not just because under capitalism the means of production belong to the employer, who is the decision-maker and organises the labour process, but also because, in a social system that presents itself as 'an immense accumulation of commodities' (Marx 1976: 1), workers are forced to sell in the market their commodity, labour power, if they want to obtain the means of their existence. The market it is thus the necessary mediator for both the worker and the capitalist whose relations become dominated by economic rather than political and institutional factors. 'The production of commodities is, simultaneously, the reproduction of the relations of production, whereas, under feudalism, production for the lord is connected to production for the serf through political and legal mechanisms' (Burawoy 1979: 25). Finally, important differences are to be found at the level of control, co-ordination and conflict. While during feudalism productive activities were fixed and legally regulated, allowing workers to keep to a large extent control of the labour process, in capitalism, due to the indeterminacy of labour power, management control is essential to securing profitability. At the same time, whereas changes to the production model and the organisation of work were in feudalism the outcome of struggles at the political/institutional level, the economic nature of the relation between capital and labour imposes a process of constant renegotiation of the effort/reward directly where production takes place. All these specificities, deriving from the nature of the capitalist labour process, act upon the subjective experience of work and shape individual and collective responses to it, creating the conditions for the existence of a continuous tension between the opposing interests of capital and labour (Hyman 1975).

Although the exchange between labour power and wages has become the historically dominant form through which commodities' production within capitalism has taken place, different forms of workers' subordination and thus different modes of production/labour processes do co-exist within the same system (van der Linden 2008 and Chapter 3 in this book). Producers might be more or less autonomous and independent from the sale of their labour, they might or might not be the owner of the labour power (as with the many forms of indentured or bonded labour), they might be economically or non-economically tied to their employer or they might or might not possess their own means of production. This historical reality has consequences in terms of the practical arrangements regulating the labour process and the efforts/reward, requiring, for instance, the use of more or less extended forms of direct control and supervision, giving space to different forms of conflict and labour management relations. However important these differences are, within a system globally organised on the basis of commodity production and quite independently of the form through which labour has been commodified, the labour process will continue to remain influenced by the capitalist environment in which it takes place. Even outside 'traditional' wage labour, work will be performed, organised and shaped to produce not just useful but also exchangeable things in the market. Thus, the need to realise profit through exchange in the market will tend to continue shaping the labour process even in those cases in which collective ownership of the means of production and self-management have substituted the more traditional forms of capital ownership and control of production. The recent case of the recovered factories in Argentina is just the last concrete example of the influence of market forces on workers' genuine attempts to organise work in an alternative, more democratic and participative way (Atzeni and Ghigliani 2007). I will however consider the extent of these influences and the possibilities for alternative work in the final part of this chapter.

Work under capitalism remains for the majority of people a negative experience. A situation of 'structural unfreedom', to use the expression of the political philosopher G.A. Cohen (Cohen 1983), is what characterises the daily conditions of workers under capitalism. Lacking access to the means of production, they are compelled to work and to 'offer' themselves in a labour market in order to guarantee their survival. They need to accept a type of work organisation that while functional to profitability tends to impoverish their daily work experience simplifying and repeating task, reducing their intellectual contribution to the production process, increasing the physical and mental exploitation of the worker. At the same time they spend their working day in an environment which is not just limiting their participation to decision-making but is often authoritarian. Furthermore, their job stability and salary levels, on which their living directly depends, are subordinated to decisions taken under the pressure imposed by an impersonal market, which is by its own nature, unstable and uncontrollable.

A world historical perspective on the labour movement provides evidence of workers' attempts to limit these negative consequences on work and rebalance class relations at the level of society (Silver 2003). However, workers' struggles have tended to remain within the limits imposed by the system. Fair wages and working conditions, rather than workers' control, have indeed been the historical demands trade unions have put forward as agents representing workers in the negotiation of the price of labour. Why then have workers tended to maintain their struggles within the wage system and consequently, why have examples of workers'control been numerically less important in the history of workers' struggles?

Many contingent factors can explain the emergence, the success or the failure of these experiments, as I will attempt to do in the next section of the chapter by presenting an historical overview of cases. But an answer to these questions necessarily means, to use the expression of Michael Lebowitz, an understanding of what 'keeps capitalism going' (Lebowitz 2004) and thus an understanding of the structural conditions that do not allow a worker envisaging an alternative, notwithstanding workers' negative perception about work. Following Marx, three conditions are outlined by Lebowitz: the exploitation of workers is not *obvious* as this is hidden by the very structure of the wage relation which presents itself on surface as an equal exchange; capitalism mystifies social relations, capital appears as the producer of all wealth and workers see themselves as dependent on capital; finally, workers do not only appear as dependent upon capital, they really are dependent on it for their own survival. Moreover since capitalism is based on individual capitals in competition, workers will be interested in the economic profitability of their own employers and in the light of this they will accept economic sacrifices.

Notwithstanding these obstacles, workers have contested, in the course of the last 100 years, from different ideological perspectives and in different geographical and socio-political contexts, the inevitability of capitalist forms of work organisation and provided examples of workers' control as an alternative. It is to the theoretical relevance of these that we now turn our attention.

THE TRANSFORMATIVE SIDE OF WORKERS' CONTROL

The history of the labour movement is rich in examples of workers' control (for recent reviews and analysis see Atzeni 2012 and Ness and Azzellini 2011). But the ways in which this control has been attempted and eventually put into practice have been varied and often contradictory, reflecting the different origins and contexts, political ideals and pragmatic decisions, but also the difficulties inherent to the sustainability of workers' control within capitalism.

Without pretending to be exhaustive, and partly following Bayat's categorisation (Bayat 1991), we could, however, identify six main variations in the concept and forms of control that have appeared and overlapped in different geographical contexts through the last 100 years or so of (mainly) industrial capitalism. The first variation corresponds to workers' control as a mean to revolutionary transformation. Linked to the theoretical positions of the different historical streams of libertarian and emancipatory communism (council communism, views of the workers' councils, anarcho-syndicalism, Italian *Autonomia Operaia*), workers' control is seen as the organisational pillar for the transition to and establishment of a new classless, democratic, communist society. The second variation, exemplified by the activity and debates promoted by the Institute of Workers' Control in the 1970s in the UK, while not directly envisaging a new, communist, workers' controlled society, intended control as a means to limit capital prerogative in the workplace, in what would be a trade union led strategy for encroaching control. The third variation, mirrored in the history of the co-operative movement, considers workers' control or self-management as the natural consequence of workers' collective ownership of co-operatives. The fourth variation, closely associated to national states' conciliatory industrial relations policies, sees control as a form of workers' participation and sharing in the management of companies. The fifth variation corresponds to the planned and/or implemented workers' control or participation in the management of companies within the planned economies of real socialism. Lastly, but probably most importantly for its transformative potential, workers' control can be seen as a radical, often spontaneous and unintended form of collective action through which workers defend achieved rights or demand new.

These variations should not be considered as clear cut. Very often in the same context different meanings have been associated to workers' control. Existing ideological or political differences orienting workers' action, the unstable social and economic climate in which workers' control was inserted, the extent of opposition from dominant classes, the need to compete in a capitalist market, but also the unexpected consequences unleashed by the very act of occupying and taking control of factories, have often resulted in contradictory developments. However, in an attempt to generalise from historical examples, we could say that the theoretical importance of workers' control lays in its potentially transformative nature. Workers control is and has been transformative in many ways. First, it has often been highly disruptive of the previously accepted systems. Private property, authoritarian workplace management, taken-for-granted patterns of production and distribution and the entire system of capitalist relations, as in coincidence with revolutionary or political turmoil, have been directly challenged by workers' control of production. This destabilising effect has always meant that workers' control has been opposed by the dominant classes and practical attempts to establish it have been short lived and almost invariably repressed. Second, workers' control has been characterised by a high degree of spontaneity, direct democracy, workers delegates' accountability, independence and autonomy from trade unions and political parties. In this sense the historical manifestation of workers control has been the proof of alternative, more direct ways of representing and organising workers' interests that precede and eventually go beyond trade unionism. Third, workers' self-management, workers' democratic decision-making power on production and administration, is transformative in envisaging a capital-free form of work organisation built on values and practices radically opposed to those of a traditional capitalist organisation. Most importantly, however, is that workers control, with its related transformative potential, is linked to structural conditions of the labour capital relation. Indeed, very often workers' occupation of factories and the following attempts to directly manage production, have been the unintended consequences of grass-roots collective action based on economic claims. The most recent and direct example of this can be seen in the cases of the Argentinean recovered factories. Here, the occupation of the companies' premises initially were a defensive, unplanned, response by workers to job losses and unemployment in the middle of a huge economic and political crisis, but they were transformed into self-managed production during the course of action. So what started originally as a grass-roots, defensive action transformed itself into a real class-based alternative to defend workers' interests, this process strengthening also workers' own consciousness.

While structural conditions external to the workplace have often created a fertile soil for the emergence of workers' control, as has been the case with acute and deep economic crises, with periods of revolutionary turmoil, with state support or socialist politics oriented to promote workers' control, it has, however, been the conflictual nature of the labour– capital relation that constantly made possible the reappearance of forms of workers' control and self-management. Driven by the requirement to satisfy basic economic needs, grass-roots-based organisations, already existing or spontaneously formed in the course of action, have been crucial in co-ordinating workers' practical experiences with a new system of work oriented toward direct democracy, equality and diffused decision-making power (Cohen 2011). Thus, the real alternative to the traditional capitalist organisation is anchored in the structure of capitalist relations. This, rather than blueprints of alternative work systems, should be the fundamental departure point in evaluating the future perspectives of workers control.

WORKERS' CONTROL AND SELF-MANAGEMENT AS AN ALTERNATIVE WITHIN CAPITALISM

What we have defined as the transformative side of workers' control is most clearly visible in those cases in which workers' attempts to control production are inserted within a dynamic of workplace or socially diffused collective action. But apart from these latter cases in which fertile soil exists for workers' action to create disruptive effects, control of production and self-management has been the historical claim of the working class, finding the most direct expression in the co-operative movement. Producers' co-operatives, in particular, eliminating managerial control of the labour process and giving to each producer/owner equal representation and rights in the decision-making process, represented for Marx a real advancement for workers and the 'practical demonstration that capital was not necessary as a mediator in social production' (Lebowitz 2003: 89) and thus pointed to an alternative to the existence of the wage/labour system. This emancipatory potential of the co-operative movement, however, has always been the object of debate, especially among Marxists. The core of criticism pointed to the limits market competition imposes on co-operatives since these 'naturally reproduce in all cases, in their present organisation, all the defects of the prevailing system, and must reproduce them' (Marx 1981: 571). Following from this, Rosa Luxemburg underlined the dual face of co-operatives which were, as small islands of socialism in a sea of capitalism, unable to keep unaltered the democratic principles of their organisations within the market economy. From a revolutionary perspective co-operatives were then not able to offer a stable, alternative solution. This negative view has long dominated among Marxist writers. Mandel's outright rejection of any revolutionary strategy based on factory occupation and self-management has probably represented the most extreme example of this view (Mandel 1970; 1974).

By contrast, more recent contributions, while recognising the limits that even the most democratic experiences of self-managed co-operatives encounter in a capitalist market, have emphasised the importance, in a perspective of social change, of devising strategies for strengthening the role of producers' cooperatives. Thus, while Egan (1990), for instance, has stressed the importance of the existence of a radical self-organising environment as a way to counteract the degenerating effects of market forces, Baldacchino (1990) has pointed to the need to build an institutional framework to actively promote and defend the democratic practice of self-managed workplaces. In a more reformist vein, other authors, while also acknowledging the limitations imposed by competition, have focused, however, on the positive effects that the expansion of the co-operative sector can have on the market economy, both in terms of generalising the diffusion of co-operative values (for instance, Mellor, Hannah and Stirling 1988; Melnyk 1985) and inspiring alternative forms of work organisation (for instance, Schneiberg, King and Smith 2008; Cheney, 2002).

Leaving aside for the moment the debate about the roles of co-operatives as agents of social change and the strategies that should be adopted in relation to this, what all critical works have certainly underlined is that competition effectively distorts the democratic practices and values adopted by workers in self-managed or co-operative workplaces. What all these experiences show is that there are practical, tangible situations in which market forces influence workers' control and democratic decisions about production, thus creating a divergence between workers' independent will and existing structural conditions. To emphasise the existence of this distortive dynamic, and how, through this, market logic is reasserted, is particularly important in the analysis of cases of self-management as it warns against explanations of changes based exclusively on workers' subjective attitudes. In this sense, independent workers' control and democratic decision-making in self-managed workplaces is weakened not just because workers are, for instance, culturally prone to delegate functions or obey orders. There are material, objective, tangible pressures related to the everyday business of the self-managed company that drive decisions toward centralisation and delegation. Similarly, even in those cases in which workers have developed a collective consciousness of the distortive effects of the market on their organisation, they will still need to face material obstacles and overcome barriers to assert their own will and control on the organisation. To put this in Marxist terms, while workers, in the sphere of production, can freely and democratically take decisions about the life of their organisation, when buying raw materials and resources, selling the outcome of their production, or securing their families' reproduction, that is, when they engage in the sphere of circulation, they will remain exposed to system-based factors on which they have no or scarce control (prices, crisis, offer and demand).

As developed in greater detail elsewhere with reference to the recent cases of factory occupations and self-management in Argentina (Atzeni and Ghigliani 2007), the pressure of competition can be detected in different forms and at different levels of analysis. It certainly manifests itself in the form of time constraints on the democratic decision-making processes adopted by workers. Delivery deadlines fixed by clients, a quick answer to catch a business opportunity, extended working shifts imposed by the lack of capital, all represent concrete obstacles to the democratic participation of workers in the everyday management of the organisation. This democratic deficit leads then to a tendency to delegate and, overall, to a centralisation of decisions. The same time constraints affect the possibility of changes in the labour process. Job rotation, a practice to which many workers would aspire, requires time and resources to retrain workers but this conflicts with the need to produce on time and at the required quality level. As a consequence of this, the separation between manual/productive and intellectual/directive work is reinforced. On a different level, labour market competition for skilled workers threatens the equal salary policy which was adopted by workers at the beginning of their experiences with self-management to strengthen solidarity and co-operative values.

Notwithstanding these limitations, the example of the Argentinian self-managed workplaces do show important alternative practices. Favoured by the elimination of managerial/supervisory posts and by the central role of workers in the decision-making process, the system of control has been changed and the labour process has been de-centralised. Rather than the top-down style of capitalist companies, workers organise production by communicating through formal and informal channels and this takes place throughout the process of production. Co-operation rather than imposition seems to be the leading motive used to solve problems in a less authoritarian environment dominated by shared responsibility and in which workers feel empowered and effectively participate, even if with important limitations, in the decision-making process.

From the wide range of historical experiences with workers' control we can see how there is always an interplay between market forces, workers' collective efforts to establish a more empowering workplace and the socio-political context surrounding the different experiences. Subjective, cultural or context-based factors have often played a substantial role in shaping positively the outcome of workers' experiences with self-management and control of production. However important the combination of one or more of these factors might be in explaining the dynamics and outcomes of self-management, in an attempt to generalise, we have, once more, to emphasise how the existence of structural factors influences different experiences. The exposure to market competition and the effects this provokes on the organisation of work and collective decision-making are unavoidable conditions to which any self-managed experience needs, to a lesser or greater extent, to confront with on a daily basis. This should then be considered as the departure point in any future analysis.

WORKERS' CONTROL IN PERSPECTIVE

The path toward the establishment and consolidation of a new democratic, enriching and participatory model of work organisation is disseminated with ideological and material obstacles. For workers depending on a wage to live, who grew up in an education system organised to provide skills for a labour market and whose experience of work has always been within a capitalist labour process, it is difficult to imagine a system of work going beyond this and directly empowering them. For the same reasons, despite the fact that workers' attitudes toward work have often been negative, rarely have trade unions considered workers' control as a way to address these issues, preferring to concentrate on the negotiation of the price of labour. Equally rare, apart from a few cases, has been the role of state institutions in advancing a real participation of workers in the management of companies. Paradoxically, the idea of a more motivating and inclusive work environment, which has been promoted in many industries as a way to capture the knowledge and creativity of workers, has been central to the interests of capital rather than labour.

However, as we have seen, in the history of the labour movement these ideologically built obstacles have often been superseded, in coincidence with a moment of local political turmoil, economic and business uncertainty, by the spontaneous, transformative impetus of workers' struggles. The seizure of factories and the subsequent attempts to produce under self-management have represented the practical alternative proposed by workers to overcome the capitalist organisation of work. Short-lived and repressed for their anti-systemic nature, these experiences are the proof not just of the possibility of building a more democratic, empowering and thus alternative system of work, but also of how this alternative is rooted in the contradictions of the capitalist system.

While ideological obstacles can be temporarily removed in the course of action, in disclosing to workers the possibility of re-inventing themselves and their work and then innovating in the sphere of production, material conditions are somehow more solid obstacles in the path toward the consolidation of an alternative system of work. The survival of worker-managed workplaces will be in fact, as companies generating an income in the market, increasingly dependent on the goals of efficiency, productivity and profitability that will, in turn, put pressure on the democratic, participatory, more equalitarian values adopted by workers.

The history of the co-operative movement is rich in examples of how workers' genuine attempts to direct and take decisions on production have been transformed and shaped by the necessity to operate in a market. The level of this transformation has been varied and certain co-operatives values and practices, particularly the ones concerned with the organisation of work, have been affected more than others. The size of the companies, the sector of activity, geographical location, exposure to the global market, institutional support and workers' ideological awareness and commitment to emancipatory values have been important factors in determining the outcome of these transformations. But certainly the initial emancipatory power common to the majority of experiences of self-managed workers' co-operatives has tended to disappear and to be subsumed under the market logic.

This is a fundamental departure point in assessing the future of alternative workers' controlled and directed production within the capitalist system. While it does not necessarily imply that all companies democratically managed will degenerate into a traditional, authoritarian and centralised capitalist organisation, it clearly focuses on material obstacles to the establishment of alternative organisational forms.

Beyond these limits, writing about the experiences of workers' control and self-management tells us, however, of the great potential for transforming the workplace and society that these may have and of the fears that these transformations have often provoked among the ruling classes. Far from any utopian view, workers have been able to provide real examples of more democratic, enriching and participatory organisations of work, but these have been the outcomes of real class confrontations rather than of smooth negotiations. To the extent that capitalism is an undemocratic but also a contradictory system, alternative proposals for the future organisation of work in production and the role of work in our societies will recurrently emerge but will also need to be recurrently defended.

REFERENCES

Atzeni, M. (2010), *Workplace Conflict: Mobilization and Solidarity in Argentina*, Basingstoke, Palgrave Macmillan.

Atzeni, M. (ed.) (2012) *Alternative Work Organisations*, Basingstoke: Palgrave Macmillan.

Atzeni, M. and Ghigliani, P. (2007), 'Labour process and decision making in factories under workers' self-managment: empirical evidence from Argentina', *Work, Employment and Society*, vol. 21, no. 4, 653–72.

Baldacchino, G. (1990), 'A war of position: ideas on strategies for workers cooperative development', *Economic and Industrial Democracy*, vol. 11, no. 4, 463–82.

Bayat, A. (1991), *Work, Politics and Power. An International Perspective on Workers' Control and Self-management*, London, Zed Books.

Beynon, H. (1984), *Working for Ford*, Harmondsworth, London, Penguin Books.

Bolton, S. (2005) *Emotion Management in the Workplace. Management, Work and Organisations*, Basingstoke, Palgrave Macmillan.

Bolton, S. and Houlihan, M. (2009), 'Are we having fun yet? A consideration of workplace fun and engagement', *Employee Relations*, vol. 31, no. 6, 556–68.

Braverman, H. (1974), *Labour and Monopoly Capital*, New York, Monthly Review Press.

Burawoy, M. (1979), *Manufacturing Consent*, Chicago, University of Chicago Press.

Cheney, G. (2002), *Employee Participation Meets Market Pressure at Mondragon*, Ithaca, New York, Cornell University Press.

Cohen, G.A. (1983), 'The structure of proletarian unfreedom', reprinted in 1988 in a revised form in *History, Labour and Freedom*, Oxford, Clarendon Press.

Cohen, S. (1987), 'A labour process to nowhere', *New Left Review*, vol. 1, no. 165. Available at: http://www.newleftreview.org/?view=229 (accessed 23 July 2013).

Cohen, S. (2006), *Ramparts of Resistance: Why Workers Lost Their Power and How to Get it Back*, London, Pluto Press.

Cohen, S. (2011), 'The red mole: Workers' councils as a means to revolutionary transformation', in Ness, I. and Azzellini, D. (eds), *Ours to Master and to Own. Workers Control from the Commune to the Present*, Chicago, Haymarket Books, pp. 48–65.

Delbridge, R. (1998), *Life on the Line in Contemporary Manufacturing*, Oxford, Oxford University Press.

Elger, T. and Smith, C. (1994), *Global Japanisation? The Transnational Transformation of the Labour Process*, London, Routledge.

Elger, T. and Smith, C. (2005), *Assembling Work: Remaking Factories' Regimes in Japanese Multinationals in Britain*, New York, Oxford University Press.

Egan, D. (1990), 'Toward a Marxist theory of labour-managed firms: Breaking the degeneration thesis', *Review of Radical Political Economics*, vol. 22, no. 4, 67–86.

Fantasia, R. (1989), *Culture of Solidarity. Consciousness, Action and Contemporary American Workers*, Berkeley, University of California Press.

Guest, D. (2002), 'Human Resource Management, corporate performance and employee wellbeing: Building the worker into HRM', *Journal of Industrial Relations*, vol. 44, no. 3, 335–58.

Hyman, R. (1975), *Industrial Relations, A Marxist Introduction*, London, Macmillan.

Hyman, R. (2006), 'Marxist thought and the analysis of work', in M. Korczynski, R. Hodson and P. Edwards (eds) *Social Theory at Work*, Oxford, Oxford University Press, pp. 26–55.

Linhart, R.(1981), *The Assembly Line*, Amherst, University of Massachusetts.

Lopez, H.S. (2010), 'Workers, managers, and customers: Triangles of power in work communities', *Work and Occupation*, vol. 37, no. 3, 251–71.

Lebowitz, M. (2003), *Beyond Capital, Marx's Political Economy of the Working Class*, 2nd edn, Basingstoke, Palgrave Macmillan.

Lebowitz, M. (2004), 'What keeps capitalism going?', *Monthly Review*, vol. 56, no. 2. Available at: http://monthlyreview.org/2004/06/01/what-keeps-capitalism-going accessed 23 July 2013).

Kochan, T.A. and Osterman, P. (1994), *The Mutual Gains Enterprise: Forging a Winning Partnership Among Labour, Management and Government*, Harvard Business School Press.

Korczynski, M. (2002) *Human Resource Management in Service Work*, Basingstoke, Palgrave Macmillan.

Mandel, E. (1970), 'Self-management: dangers and possibilities', *International*, vol. 2, no. 4, 3–9.

Mandel, E. (1974), *Control obrero, consejos obreros, autogestion*, Mexico, Ediciones Era.

Marx, K. (1976), *Capital*, volume 1, London, Penguin Books.

Marx, K. (1981), *Capital*, volume 3, London, Penguin Books.

Mellor, M., Hannah, J. and Stirling, J. (1988) *Worker Co-operatives in Theory and Practice*, Milton Keynes, Open University Press.

Melnyk, G. (1985), *The Search for Community, From Utopia to a Cooperative Society*, Montreal-Buffalo, Black Rose Books.

Mollona, M. (2009), *An Ethnography of Industrial Work and Politics*, New York, Oxford, Berghahn Books.

Ness, I. and Azzellini, D. (2011), *Ours to Master and to Own. Workers' Control from the Commune to the Present*, Chicago, Haymarket Books.

Pink, D.H. (2011), *The Surprising Truth of What Motivates Us*, New York, Riverhead Books.

Schneiberg, M., King, M. and Smith, T. (2008), 'Social movements and organizational form: Cooperative alternatives to corporations in the American insurance, dairy, and grain industries', *American Sociological Review*, vol. 73, no. 4, 635–67.

Sherman, R. (2007), *Class Acts: Service and Inequality in Luxury Hotels*, Berkeley, University of California Press.

Silver, B. (2003), *Forces of Labour, Workers' Movement and Globalisation since 1870*, Cambridge, Cambridge University Press.

Spencer, D. (2000), Braverman and the contribution of labour process analysis to the critique of capitalist production, twenty-five years on, *Work, Employment and Society*, 14: 2, 223–43.

Spencer, D. (2009), *The Political Economy of Work*, Abingdon, Routledge.

Taylor, M. (2008), *Global Economy Contested: Power and Conflict Across the International Division of Labour*, London and New York, Routledge.

Taylor, P. and Bain, P (2005), India calling to the far away towns the call center labour process and globalisation, *Work Employment & Society* 19: 2, 261–82.

Tinker, T. (2002), 'Spectres of Marx and Braverman in the twilight of postmodernist labour process research', *Work Employment & Society*, vol. 16, no. 2, 251–81.

Turner, C. (1995), *Japanese Workers in Protest: An Ethnography of Consciousness and Experience*, Berkeley, University of California Press.

Van der Linden, M. (2008), *Workers of the World. Essays Toward a Global Labour History*, Leiden, Brill.

Vieta, M (2012), 'From managed employees to self-managed workers: the transformations of labour at Argentina's worker-recuperated enterprises', in Atzeni, M. (ed.) (2012), Alternative Work Organisations, Basingstoke, Palgrave Macmillan, pp. 129–156.

Warhurst, C., Grugulis, I. and Keep, E. (2004), *The Skills that Matter*, Basingstoke, Palgrave Macmillan.

part 3

CONTEMPORARY ISSUES: WORKERS ORGANISING IN THE GLOBAL WORLD

8

INFORMAL LABOUR, FACTORY LABOUR OR THE END OF LABOUR? ANTHROPOLOGICAL REFLECTIONS ON LABOUR VALUE

Massimiliano Mollona

ANTHROPOLOGICAL REFLECTIONS ON LABOUR VALUE

What is labour? How do we use it and value it? And why do societies care so much about it? These are some of the questions that I will deal with in this paper. The notion of 'labour' is difficult to define because it applies to virtually all human activities – material and immaterial – through which societies reproduce themselves: the physical labour of steelworkers or of parents who raise their children; the immaterial labour of employees in call centres and IT firms; the production of symbols, stories and ideologies by priests, shamans and politicians and the 'affective' labour of nannies, nurses, maids and of all those who care for the others. Because labour is both symbolical and material – affective and pragmatic – we are often confused as to how to value it.

A great portion of human labour goes into the reproduction of people in the present life and in the afterlife (food, clothing, education, mourning); on the other hand, a great deal of it is spent in the reproduction of objects and wealth – which also includes war, oratory and lush rituals of gift exchange. Most societies keep these two spheres of labour separated into different moral orders (Bloch and Parry 1989). In Malaysia, the cash produced through the labour of male fishermen can be used for the household only after women purify it by cooking it on the household hearth (Carsten 1989); in Benares, India, the Brahmins priests performing death rituals accept money only after an elabourate ritual of refusal performed to avoid spiritual pollution (Parry 1989). The different orders of morality associated with these spheres of labour create inequalities between those who perform them. The handling of money, wages or gifts or the involvement in war, government and diplomacy is called 'work' and performed by people (usually men) with high status and rank in public and often ostentatiously. The activities that go into the reproduction of people are normally performed by women and children in the domestic or informal realm and are considered as less valuable and defined 'labour'. This distinction between valuable 'work' and non-valuable 'labour' is conductive to social inequality. On the one hand we attribute to *work* nearly a supernatural value, considering it as a magic and transformative force possessed by talented individuals or an inalienable property that gives to their 'owners' the right to citizenship or the dignity of personhood. On the other hand we talk about *labour* as a source of alienation, material dependence and social exclusion. This is evident in the way we often make connections between black, unregulated and illegal labour and foreigners or marginal people.

Anna Arendt defines this opposition between labour (intended as alienated activity) and work (intended as purposeful one) as 'the human condition' and argues that this split concerning the value of human production runs deep in all societies (Arendt 1988). It emerges already in Aristotle's *Polis* where the aristocrats, artisans, demiurges, politicians, and notables were considered skilled craftsmen (Sennett 2008) whose 'work' (oratory, writing or accounting) was central to the nation's economy (*oikonomeia*). On the other hand, the labour of slaves, manual workers and servants was classified as unskilled, un-human 'sufferance' (*ponein*) and good 'only' to keep the household economy going. Industrial capitalism took the dichotomy between work and labour even further. It classified all human activities taking place in the enclosed and enforced space of the factory as valuable 'work' and those taking place outside as valueless or informal 'labour'. The capitalists' drive to profit led to a systematic devaluation of work within the very wage relation. Taylorism was a scientific system of factory organisation aimed on the one hand, at formalising and standardising work and on the other, at devaluing those human activities that were not conductive to profit, such as collective labour, mutual credit or friendship. Chronometers, stopwatches and photography froze the workers' movement into 'units of effort'. Statistical correlations were made between the workers' efforts and their wages. Industrial wages become monetary equivalents of their value and were standardised both at the level of the factory and of the nation. The capitalists were interested in standardising the workers' wages and their organisation because in so doing they increased their profits. But workers supported standardisation and formalisation of labour too, because they believed that this would increase their living standards and prevent the exploitation of the 'informal labour' of children and women. The activities that went in the reproduction of people – such as caring for children, cooking, cleaning or making clothes, gardening, trading local goods – were relegated in the valueless realm of the domestic economy or the informal economy – a dangerous moral zone. Those out of work or performing informal and unskilled labour were considered as marginal citizens and even socially dangerous. 'Total institutions' such as prisons, clinics, poorhouses, labour camps, the police, the medical and legal professions and various state apparatuses in charge of the economy developed to regulate those unproductive classes. Indeed, one of the central concerns of Smith's economic theory was to put in place mechanisms of state valorisation of the labour of unproductive classes.

Still today there is a sense that work performed outside the workplace and informally – with friends or family, out of pleasure or improvisation – is less valuable and respectable than wage work. But for many outside the capitalist quarters, at least for many anthropologists, the term informal labour has a positive appeal because it highlights a 'grey area' – between work and unemployment – in which people live meaningfully, fully value their actions (although not economically) and create wealth for their communities escaping the control of capitalist states and markets. This positive view of informal labour could be self-defeating. Does not the idea that some human activities are not accountable imply that others can be calculated and given an economic value to? And was not Marx right in claiming that it was industrial capitalism that, by making labour accountable in monetary terms, institutionalised the dichotomy between formal and informal labour? For Marx the dialectics of 'work' and 'labour' is a product of class struggle. Powerful people decide which human activities are valuable and commodifiable and which are not, maximising the value of (productive) work, while devaluing (reproductive) labour. By claiming a greater share of the capitalist profits, workers subscribe to such system of labour commodification. But are workers' co-operatives and mutualist arrangements the same as informal labour or may be more like the end of labour?

Is the term worth keeping? I suggest that the notion is worth retaining, if anything because it reflects the belief of many people around the world that human activities should not be accounted for economically. But I will present ethnographic and historical evidence of how informality is normally associated with labour precarisation (casualisation). In what follows I will show the dynamics of 'labour' and 'work' intended respectively as devalued and valuable under capitalism and colonialism, and I map this dynamics spatially and temporally. In the first section, I look at the process of industrialisation and related informalisation in post-colonial of Africa. In the second and third sections, I discuss the neo-liberal shift of the 1980s – associated with the liberalisation of labour and capital markets, flexible production, supranational financial institutions of governance and the attack to the working-class – respectively in the North and the South. I argue that flexible production spreads informal and precarious labour both in the North and the South but that in the North the labour movement was not able to oppose it, partly because of the weakness of its working class. In the South the labour movement created a strong opposition, thanks to its links with peasant movements with an alternative social and economic vision. In the last section, I discuss the recent development of new conglomerates and of wage work in BRIC countries, which I read as a new form of capitalist organisation, this time taking place in the South, which follows the collapse of the financial model of the 1980s. I conclude by arguing that the dialectics of formal and informal labour reproduces the oscillatory dynamics of capitalism and try to imagine an alternative to it.

MODERNISATION AND LABOUR COMMODIFICATION IN AFRICA

As I have mentioned above, industrial capitalism can be described as the systematic exploitation of reproductive labour by those in control of the reproduction of wealth based on moral discourses that value work over labour. The capitalist distinction between work and labour historically moulded the economic relations between the North and the South, too. Labourers in the South are generally involved in informal, rural, domestic, community-based and 'low valued-added' labour, whereas the North is in charge of the valuable wage economy – including modern factories, high-tech jobs and luxury commodities.

For a long time racial superiority was *the* moral discourse legitimising the systematic exploitation of labour in the South by the North. But with colonial independence, and especially the decolonisation that followed WWII, western companies adopted a moral discourse rooted in economics, in order to continue to exploit the labour and commodity markets in the ex-colonies. The 'modernisation theory' of economist Rostow provided one such moral legitimisation of neo-colonialism. The theory formulates a relationship between economic growth and modernisation that follows a linear trajectory – from traditional societies, based on simple technologies and social institutions to ones adopting sophisticated technologies and institutions. This flowed model describes economic growth as a powerful force that impacts on traditional societies like a time-travelling machine, turning small and self-sufficient nomadic packs into high-tech multi-national corporations. Linking development and industrialisation, Rostow's theory legitimated forced industrialisation in the ex-colonies. Harriss and Harriss (1989) show clearly the links between 'modernisation' and proletarianisation in the South. The flow of foreign capital and technology – often in the form of 'aid' – forces peasants to intensify and specialise their farming. The least entrepreneurial peasants drop out from self-production and become impoverished, having to sell their labour either within their community or migrate to cities in search for wage work. Ultimately, for the authors, this 'modernisation' process pushes rural communities from self-sufficiency to market dependency and proletarianisation.

Keith Hart's famous article on the informal economy (1973) in Accra, an ex-colonial town in Southern Ghana, describes the effects of forced industrialisation on the livelihood of the Frafras, an ethnic group living in slums and drawn into informal activities by price inflation, low wages and surplus in the labour market. The official statistics of the time showed that 40 per cent of the active male and 95 per cent of the active female population were out of employment. But these statistics on formal employment had little heuristic value since both unemployed and wageworkers were actively involved in the informal sector. Hart shows that the so-called 'formal labour' (made up of private and public sector wages) was a very small portion of people's work which, in fact, mostly consisted in informal legal activities (farming, gambling, market gardening, building, tailoring, transport, petty trade) or illegal activities (usury, smuggling, bribery, theft). Besides, due to the low level of industrial wages, expenditures in food, clothing and lodging exceeded monthly wages so that even those in formal employment sought supplementary sources of income. Most Frafras had more than one job at the time and some of them even managed to become successful entrepreneurs like Atinga, a slum dweller who transformed his living room into a bar, setting up an informal retail business in crude gin.

In Ghana industry created very little and polarised wealth and alienated work. It was the informal sector that generated wealth and meaningful work, embedded in family and ethnic networks. Hart uses this evidence for a trenchant critique of the western notions of 'work' and 'unemployment'. Are the busy and productive informal workers of Accra really unemployed? Are wageworkers with multiple informal jobs really formal sector workers? And is unemployment really a problem? And if yes, whose problem is it? Is it the economists' problem? For Hart, the stigma that western society puts on people outside formal employment is misleading. The term 'unemployment' conjures images of people queuing at the dole office. But in Accra people out of employment are not without labour. In Accra, the economists' notions of work and unemployment are 'foreign' because labour has no abstract, moral or monetary value and it cannot be owned, lost, or given away. The article unveiled the ethnocentric nature of economics and more particularly of the kind of Keynesian capitalism – based on state-led industrialisation – that was being exported to the developing world. Hart reads the informal economy as an anti-colonial and anti-state 'space'. The spread of the informal economy, he claims, is a sign that people are taking their lives in their own hands and rejecting the economic morality of rich countries based on the glorification of 'work' and the commodification of human labour.

Like Hart, anthropologist MacGaffey (1987) looks at the informal economy of Zaire in the context of foreign-led industrialisation. In the 1980s, prices of export commodities were falling, imports increasing, industrial production slowing down and industrial wages precipitating. This disastrous state of the economy was partly linked to Mobutu's corrupted post-colonial government that was meeting the interests of foreign companies, in spite of its nationalisation policy. Low industrial wages in relation to prices forced urban dwellers, including wageworkers, into informal jobs. Among these jobs MacGaffey lists the legal production of goods and services concealed to avoid taxes, the production of illegal services and goods and the smuggling of diamonds, coffee and ivory with Sudan, Congo and Angola. Smuggling, according to the author, was the 'real economy' of Zaire.[1] The industrial economy supported by Mobutu and by global financial institutions created little wealth for the local people. On the contrary smuggling – 'the illegal crossing of national borders and the evasions of tariffs, customs dues and regulations' – operated through kinship and ethnic networks, empowering marginal subjects. Especially, those many rural women who, excluded from formal education and the labour market both under the Belgian and the Mobutu regimes, controlled these informal economic networks.

By crossing national borders and avoiding trade restrictions, tariff and price controls, smuggling was also an anti-colonial praxis, aimed at reasserting those fluid trade and political routes that existed before colonialism. MacGaffey makes it clear that the small farmers, hunters, rural workers and village chiefs operating in the informal economy were against corrupted states and corporations but not against capitalism and indeed some of them became successful entrepreneurs in the agro-business, transport and real estate sectors. Generalising, she argues that in all 'mercantilist regimes'[2] the informal economy creates small-scale, self-directed and creative forms of livelihood and hence, constitutes a radical alternative to ethnocentric models of development. Echoing the point of view of many liberal thinkers of the time,[3] she describes the informal economy as a revolutionary movement but without an anti-capitalist agenda. Both Hart and MacGaffey show instances of people who have carved a space of informal labour relations against the colonialist framework of the wage relation. This argument is compelling and yet problematic because, as both Hart and MacGaffey note, the official and the secondary economies are interrelated in many ways including in terms of labour exploitation. For instance, the asymmetrical relations existing between traders and farmers or among informal traders reflect the competitive pressures put upon them by foreign corporations. Given that capitalism and colonialism are two sides of the same process, is it possible to reject one and retain the other? And if capitalism always creates inequality, does it matter if it is local or foreign?

Janet Roitman (2005) gives a more nuanced reading of the relations between informal economy, capitalism and colonialism, in the context of Cameroon in the 1990s. Under pressure by the international community, the corrupted regime of Biya, linked to the anti-colonial party Cameroon National Union (CNU), instituted multi-party politics but also the state of emergency and militarisation. In 1991 against these measures, the association of the opposition parties organised the operation *Villa Mortes*, a campaign of civic activism based on fiscal disobedience (*incivisme fiscal*) – a mixture of fiscal evasion, general strikes and the informalisation of previously formal jobs and commerce. The aim of the movement – co-ordinated by university students, lawyers and journalists but involving the whole of the population – was to shake the state's finances through mass tax evasion. Indeed, the movement was very successful causing a 40 per cent drop in GDP. Fiscal activism had an important historical precedent in Cameroon, where the French rule used tax imposition as a way of controlling the local population. To the French colonial administrators the local amorphous substratum of nomads, bandits, seasonal workers, iterant traders, brokers, speculators and petty capitalists constituted a political threat. Imposed through corrupted tribal leaders, the tax system forced this 'floating population' (*popolation flottante*) to formally register with the administration and hence, to become legal subjects. Today, bandits, local leaders, iterant merchants, brokers, market boys and petty capitalists challenge this fiscal colonial apparatus through smuggling, illegal deals, informal trade and undeclared production. It could be argued that the movement of fiscal disobedience and informal labour disrupted the relation between work, tax and citizenship, which is at the very core of colonialism and capitalism. But for Roitman informalisation is a self-defeating strategy, if anything because it legitimises the regime's crackdown on illegality and support to foreign capitalists. She argues that this network of invisible political agents is one of many regulatory forces of capitalism in post-colonial Cameroon.

These three studies on informal economy in post-colonial Africa look at labour as a realm of value separated from that of work. But this picture radically changes if they are seen as inter-dependent. Claude Meillassoux (1981) looks at the dialectics of work and labour in the context of North/South relations. He starts with a simple question: 'Why are industrial wages low in developing countries?' De-politicising the answer, economists would relate low wages to excess of labour supply, overpopulation or North/South trade imbalance. For Meillassoux, global corporations have low wages in Africa because its strong domestic economy sustains the reproduction of labour. Capitalism is essentially a mechanism of 'labour brokerage' (see also Ong 2006) based on the exploitation of the differential in labour costs between rich and poor countries – or social strata – though organic connections between wage work and domestic labour. Labour migration (or movement) is central for labour brokerage. First, foreign companies uproot rural farmers from their villages and turn them into factory workers. But by offering them industrial wages below their subsistence costs they force them 'back' into the domestic economy of their villages. These workers' movements between factories and villages inflate the value of work through invisible domestic labour. As a consequence, the workers of developing countries are half proletarians and half domestic workers. This is the case of the Guro people in Ivory Coast, West Africa who work in factories for half of the year and return to their villages for the other half. Foreign capitalists keep the Guro's wages low because they know that they can survive on their domestic economy. Unlike the urban under-proletarians of Accra, the Guro do not find informal work in the city and must return to their villages. If the Frafras are half industrial workers and half entrepreneurs in the informal economy, the Guro are half industrial workers and half household dependent. For the former the informal as a form of empowerment, for the latter it is a form of enslavement. For Meillassoux, informal labour is an integral part of the wage relations, rather than a separate realm of value production. Labour brokerage has important gender and generational implications. The labour of women and younger members of the community performed in the domestic sphere is the core of capitalist surplus value but this labour is unaccounted for and often controlled by the elder men of the family ('the wageworkers') who became capitalists in their own families.[4] In fact, labour brokerage can be described as a form of primitive accumulation based on the externalisation of coercion from the company to the workers' families.

The scale of labour migration is variable. Some labourers migrate from neighbourhood to neighbourhood; others migrate across continents. This is the case of the North African workers for a global car maker in Paris who, unlike their Parisian co-workers, have very low wages, short-term contracts, no union rights and are often on illegal visas.[5] Managers justify their lower remuneration with racist and xenophobic discourses that construct them as unskilled and unreliable (and which sometimes are subscribed to by the trade union, too). Unable to make up for their low wages through informal labour, these migrants are forced to return if only temporarily, to their hometowns. Informed by the work of Rosa Luxemburg, Meillassoux makes it clear that the informal economy is not a space of anti-colonial and anti-capitalist resistance, but a grey area in which capitalism and colonialism – wage labour and slavery – come together. Both capitalism and slavery impose a forced separation between home and workplace and between the realm of people and the realm of the economy. Both rely on a combination of force (kidnapping, deportation or forced adoption) and economic persuasion. Like slaves, the employees of the global manufacturer are forced to move between Paris and Africa in order to survive. By making home and work two separate spheres of value production but at the same time bridging them through the movements of labour, the informal economy lies at the core of capitalist brokerage.

TOYOTISM AND FLEXIBLE PRODUCTION: THE RETURN OF MARSHALL TO SHEFFIELD

Broadly speaking, Fordism is based on standardised labour process, 'economies of scale' and mass consumption. Capitalists cannot implement labour standardisation or mass consumption, especially in foreign markets, without the help of states.[6] When states are weak, industries suffer too. At the end of the 1970s capitalist profits in the North were shrinking and markets were oversaturated. The colonial independence of oil-producing countries exacerbated such crisis in the North. When they set up cartels to control the price and supply of crude oil the cost of energy boomed and the profits of western multi-nationals collapsed. Fordism, as a way of producing and a vision of society entered into deep crisis.

Looked at historically, for every capital re-organisation aimed at maximising labour brokerage, a labour reconfiguration follows, leading to an intricate layering of labour capital relations (see Silver, Chapter 2 in this book). Colonial independence was one such reconfiguration, which reduced the profits of western companies by the rents, bribes and investments imposed upon them by post-colonial elites. Anti-colonialism made Fordism obsolete. In order to generate profit capital now had to circulate without the heavy apparatus of the factory and in shorter cycles. The mechanical factory of Henry Ford, based on fixed machines and stable workforces operating in a physically circumscribed space and producing high volumes of standardised goods, gave way to the flexible factory. This operates simultaneously in different countries, different markets and with a reduced and constantly changing pool of workers in geographically dispersed productive chains of externalised labour. Initially implemented by the Japanese Toyota car maker (and hence, know as 'Toyotism') 'flexible' or 'lean' production inverts the principles of Fordism. If 'Fordism' relies on the de-skilling and fragmentation of the labour process, 'Toyotism' relies on its recomposition. In the former system each worker performs the same task on the same machine (they are de-skilled), in the latter they perform different tasks on different machines (they are multiskilled). The former operates through the assembly line based on linear and inter-dependent tasks and hierarchical positions, the latter through horizontal and self-organised teams. Fordism relies on big workforces with equal rights and obligations, Toyotism on a small numbers of core workers and an army of external subcontractors. Core workers have a job for life, high pensions and benefits and salaries upwardly adjusted according to their performances. Subcontractors have virtually no rights. The Fordist firm is based on a military ethos, Toyotism on the idea of the family.

New Information Technology (NIT) and capital deregulation led to this shift in production paradigm. With NIT, flows of information replaced flows of goods and people, erasing the boundaries between firms and markets and increasing the mobility of capital vis-à-vis labour. For instance, the just-in-time (JIT) system establishes a direct communication line between custumers and line workers, making these responsible of operative targets and market orders. In lean firms, bosses operate simultaneously in different locations and with changing pools of workers. In a typical flexible scenario, an American marketing manager working in Hong Kong would simultaneously supervise employees in Singapore and invest in the London stock exchange, while instructing his employees in Bangkok to cut the local workforce. The liberalisation and deregulation of the capital market in the 1980s led to the proliferation of new financial subjects other than banks offering a whole new range of financial services such as bank landings, loans, grants, commercial credits and new derivatives including swaps, futures and options. This proliferation of virtual money on a global scale broke the connection between buyers and sellers, creditors and debtors and between the provenance and destination of money, de-territorialising and de-personalising capital and de-stabilising poorer economies, as in the cases of the currency crises in Mexico and Asia in the 1990s. At the level of the firm, capital mobility made labour more precarious. Under the so-called 'stock market' model the financial Return on Investments (ROI) replaced profit as corporate benchmark. In order to maximise the ROI, firms slashed labour costs through various forms of numeral and functional flexibility (flexi-work, work-share, temporary-work, co-work, agency work). Linking top managers' salaries and bonuses to stock market performance rather than to corporate profits, many of them drove themselves into insolvency.

Pressurised to increase financial returns, companies dismantled the 'traditional' wage contract and substituted it with alternative forms of casual and even indentured labour. For instance, if the wage contract of industrial capitalism was a direct agreement between employer and employees, today labour contracts are brokered by temporary agencies, lifting employers from contractual responsibility and leaving temps with no labour right. Temporary agencies have become global corporations (armies of labour brokers!) such as the Switzerland-based Adecco, one of the world's biggest private corporations. Second, under industrial capitalism the labour contract was established through collective bargaining (an agreement between a category of workers and the employers) whereas today it takes place between employers and individual workers. Left without collective bargaining power, these are often asked to opt out from their most basic rights, such as pensions, sick leave and paid overtime, as a precondition of getting the job. Third, the classical industrial contract involved an agreement from the employees to work for a set amount of time and for a set wage – essentially it is a commodification of the employees' time. But today the time that the workers have to give up in order to get the job is unlimited. In such temporary contracts as the 'zero-hour' the employees are not sure how many hours, if any, they will work and how much they will be paid. Having to make themselves available at all times they, in effect, commercialise their entire existence. Finally, in the old capitalist framework workers, like machines, were considered as fixed (although human) capital, whereas today they are considered as variable costs to be minimised through a combination of *offshoring* and *inshoring*. With industrial wages shrinking, workers increased their personal debts in real estate and consumption. The financialisation of salaries that paralleled the financialisation of profits (Marazzi 2011) led the workers into a permanent state of indebtness (Lazzarato 2012). Many American companies, like MacDonald and Walmart, entirely rely on unskilled and temporary workers with no union rights and forced to join 'yellow unions'.[7] In this dystopian capitalist scenario – suspended between pre- and post-Taylorism – wageworkers are forced to make themselves available at all times, accept salaries that oscillate like commodity prices and travel like nomads through different workplaces.

While most studies on industrial downsizing in the North focus on unemployment or new forms of intellectual labour, very little has been written, and mainly by anthropologists, on how de-industrialisation led to new forms of precarious and often indented labour in traditional industries. Anthropologist Tom Gill (2000) shows an instance of neo-bondage in contemporary Yokohama, Japan. Gill's contribution came at a time when economists enthusiastically supported Japan's economic model. For instance, sociologist Ronald Dore famously described Japanese capitalism as 'shareholder-oriented', based on labour 'recomposition' (as opposed to de-skilling) and harmonious industrial relations, and argued that this 'Confucian capitalism' radically differed from the western tradition of labour/capital conflict. But contrary to this rosy vision, Gill shows how the Japanese industrial model based on extensive subcontracting, polarises the labour force between a core and a periphery. Core workers – a small fraction of the industrial workforce – enjoy stable employment, high wages and harmonious working relations. But the vast majority of casual workers and day labourers live in extreme poverty and depend on their very employers for credit, food and accommodation. Like the Indian workers from Gujarat, these Japanese workers are trapped in relations of neo-bondage. Gill spent a year and a half in the *yoseba* of Yokohama, an urban area hosting the market for causal labourers and controlled by labour brokers (*tehaishi*) from the local mafia (*yakuzas*). In spite of their precarious labour, day labourers seemed to have a relatively stable and meaningful existence. Not many of them missed their previous jobs in the finance sector, or the families and homes that they had left behind after the financial crisis. They slept in small rooms in hostels or lodging houses and lived by the day enjoying the independence coming from the lack of regular working hours and stable bosses.

But the *ninpudashi* system of extensive subcontracting was radically different and trapped workers in relations of neo-bondage. *Ninpudashis* are job recruiters, supervisors, landlords and patrons working as subcontractors of global developers. They decided who would work on the day and 'loaned' to their labourers credit, foodstuff, alcohol, drugs and cigarettes. Under the *ninpudashi* system, casual labourers were totally dependent on them for survival. The work of Gill shows that the modern system of subcontracting creates not only peripheral workforces but also peripheral capitalists: gang leaders, local brokers, drug dealers and petty speculators. It also shows that this form of flexible capitalism is exploitative in a very different way to Fordism. In Fordism, workers are alienated and exploited through a variety of management techniques – supervision, mechanisation, standardisation – that enforce discipline on the shopfloor. It is true that the very efficient human relation management apparatus of Henry Ford extended outside the shopfloor and into the workers' 'homes' through various forms of family financing, leisure clubs and housing led by the company's Sociology Department. But under the regime of flexible production the disciplining of the workers takes place mainly outside the factory and through the control of their basic needs such as housing, credit and food. In this regime, capitalists do not even need to be on the shopfloor in order to discipline labour.[8] Contemporary capitalism, with its system of flexible subcontracting, seems to spread bonded labour throughout the world, from urban Japan to rural India. Indeed, Gill's ethnography was prescient of Japan's peaking level of labour informalisation[9] that followed the economic crisis of the 1990s. This was dramatically brought out into the public in 2009, when 500 homeless people who had been recently made redundant set up a village-tent in the centre of Tokyo.

In Europe, the financialisation of industry associated with the flexible model was accompanied by the 'rescaling' (Brenner 2004) of the state vis-à-vis supranational institutions such as the European Union, the OECD, the World Bank or the IMF. Particularly the European Union – a political entity that people had not chosen and which they did not relate to – became a powerful agency of de-industrialisation and flexibilisation. Unlike national states, the EU had no obligation to abide by the principles of representative democracy and hence, took unpopular and undemocratic decisions that national governments did not dare to take. For instance, the traditional steel and coal industries of central European states were converted into service economies. In turn, these de-industrialised centres in the EU forced southern and eastern European countries into labour and capital deregulation – in exchange for full membership. These New European Countries (NEC) became the unofficial contractors of the old industrial Europe. Regionalisation was also a political process based on the creation of a supranational consciousness that bypassed national ideologies and was rooted in 'regional' identities.[10] Through a combination of policies, cultural propaganda and economic frameworks the EU sparked new regional identities, borders and institutions that destroyed the traditional framework of industrial democracies. Paradoxically, regional transnational agreements often increased xenophobia and nationalistic conflicts.

Regionalisation and flexible production led to the resurgence of the old 'industrial district model'. Economist Alfred Marshall coined the term 'industrial district' after he visited Sheffield's cutlers' district in the 1940s. There, Marshall argued, the tool industry was rooted in 'local culture' that is, in shared knowldge and practices, skilled labour and co-operative institutions – such as families, guilds and workers' councils. In the 1980s, the term 'industrial district' came to refer to the clusters of small-scale manufacturing industries in northern and central Italy, which were generating skilled and stable employment at a time of widespread economic crisis. International scholars saw in the Italian industrial district a new model of political economy. Traditionally, the Italian state had very little power vis-a-vis the aristocracy, workers' guilds, civic associations and extended *famiglie* (not to mention the mafia). They argued that this micro-political texture of civic associations was central for the success of the 'made in Italy'. In the anti-Keynesian climate of the time, the World Bank and the IMF used the model of the industrial district to de-industrialise and deregulate the global economy.

In my own work on the steel industry (Mollona 2009b) I describe 'the return of Marshall to Sheffield' as a process of ideological re-evaluation of the small-scale and exploitative factory labour that emerged under the New Labour government in the 1990s. The policies of de-industrialisation co-ordinated by Tony Blair were as harsh as those of the Thatcher's era. But they were relatively unchallenged because they were dealt with within the EU framework. While steel companies were facing financial difficulties, the EU structural fund 'Objective One' channelled money away from steel and coal and towards the service and cultural industries.[11] The massive Cultural Industry Quarter mythically rose from the debris of ancient steel factories. At the local level, this structural shift redirected funds towards ethnic communities, historical associations, heritage societies and other 'cultural' organisations and away from the struggling working-class neighbourhoods. The residents of those neighbourhoods that were being bulldozed and re-landscaped into leisure parks and gentrified developments shifted political language and strategy. Snubbing wage work in the bankrupt steel companies, they became casual labourers or petty capitalists in the small and semi-derelict steel and engineering workshops sprouting in the ancient artisan quarters of Sheffield. Adapting to the way founding agencies had shifted their targets from 'class' to 'history' and 'culture', they described themselves as 'cutlers', 'indigenous' or 'heritage' workers rather than as steelworkers (ironically, they were truly working in 'heritage' steel workshops). Thus, the Victorian industrial district – made of cutlery, tools and engineering sweatshops – and the informal and semi-slave labour associated with it paradoxically, returned to Sheffield. As in Victorian times the 'new' class of post-industrial artisans was internally divided, stratified and sectionalist.

TOYOTISM IN THE 'COLONIES'

Western multi-nationals quickly adopted Toyota's flexible model externalising most of their operations to subcontractors around the world and keeping only a small core of workers with high-end and mainly intellectual jobs in design, marketing and planning. For instance, in 1999 the Nike Corporation employed 9,000 permanent workers worldwide – in design, marketing and product development – and subcontracted 100 per cent of the production of goods to nearly 75,000 independent subcontractors. These small subcontractors – located in Singapore, Thailand, Malaysia and Brazil – use child and female labour often in exploitative and unhealthy working conditions as it was recently exposed by various international labour organisations.

Flexible capitalism informalised and deregulated labour globally co-opting those relations of slavery that had continued to exist under post-colonialism. For instance, the development of agro-businesses in the rural region of Gujarat, West India, resurrected the *hali* system of indentured labour. The small village of Chikhligam, where anthropologist Breman conducted fieldwork in 1980s, was organised along caste lines. The high-caste Brahmins controlled most of the land of the village and merchants, barbers, oil pressers, shoemakers, agricultural labourers and untouchables (usually weavers) worked for them. Up until the 1950s under the *hali system* labourers worked for free for their landlords and these in return, offered shelter and political protection for them and their families. Besides working on the land, farmers were also the personal servants of the landlord. They baked, cooked, washed clothes, anointed the master's body with oil and guarded the door of his house. In exchange, the master gave to them an allowance of grain that varied according to the size of their family or even a piece of land. For Breman (1999) the *hali* system insured farmers against the instability of agricultural production in South India. Agricultural labourers without patrons faced destitution and starvation. But the spread of capitalism in the region made the system more contractual and impersonal. Now Brahmins considered labourers as wage workers rather than protégées, and remunerated them in cash and not in kind or with protection. They felt no moral obligations towards them but only economic ones. This made the workers extremely vulnerable. For Breman the transition from servitude to capitalism in Gujarat was not a transition from un-free labour to free labour but rather 'from one form of unfreedom to another'. Against Breman's argument that capitalism disintegrated the *hali* system, Brass (2000a,b) argues that capitalism on the contrary, had resumed it. The relationship of patronage between landlords and peasants made available a flexible pool of informal labourers that were used for a tenth of the salary of wage workers in times of economic crisis. The discussion surrounding the *hali* system mirrors the one on the informal economy. For Hart and Breman the informal economy and patronage are forms of insurance against the new capitalism, for Meillassoux and Brass they are functional to it. Flexible production allows capital to move to those sites where patronage and asymmetrical relations slash real wages and labour standards.

Indeed, the strength of flexible capitalism is to use 'the point of view' of the people it exploits to legitimise their exploitation. As in the slogan of the credit giant HSBC, flexible capitalism can 'act globally and think locally'. Smart and Smart (2006) describe several ethnographic cases of interlocking relations between global capitalists and local Petty Commodity Producers (PCP). In most of these cases global corporations outsource exploitative work to small-scale and family-owned firms rooted in local communities. The petty capitalists running these small firms are individuals with high status and power vis-à-vis their workers. Based on their moral superiority, these high status individuals devalue the labour of their employees (poorer relatives, followers or low-caste villagers) and force them to accept low wages or even to work for free. In other instances, children and women are kidnapped and forcedly separated form their families and put to live with bosses in adjacent villages. But because workers and capitalists are part of the same family or community, there is little conflict between them. For instance, Harriss-White (2010) argues that, in fact, much of India's economy is based on informal and indentured labour constructed on such 'identity factors' as ethnicity, gender and caste. Global corporations co-opt high-caste individuals, community leaders, patriarchs or gang bosses into their production chains and these in turn, extract labour surplus from lower caste and community members. For Basile (2008) the spread of the industrial district for silk in Arni, South India, depicted as a success story of development, is an example of such 'identity capitalism'. The Green Revolution in the 1970s pressurised the rural farmers of Arni to produce luxury saris based on a putting-out system controlled by entrepreneurs/brokers – usually specialised weavers and merchants – in charge of a huge army of underpaid women, children and low-caste workers. The textile industrial district of San Cosme, Mexico described by Rothstein (2006) is based on a structural inequality between global retailers and local small firms surviving on unpaid family labour.

But if in the North labour activism declined due to the violent attack on the working-class by the post-Keynesian state, in the South new grass-roots movements and activist agendas are spreading. For instance, Kearney (1996) discusses how the community of San Jeronimo, in the Oaxaca region of southern Mexico, reacted to global capitalism. On the surface San Jeronimo is a traditional peasant community. All households have access to farm-land, which is communally owned by the town. Almost all production is for self-consumption, produced with simple technology, powered by human and animal energy and regulated though a complex set of social and economic relations that include sharecropping, labour exchange and hired labour. Nevertheless, San Jeronimo is totally dependent on the market for food consumption. Since the 1950s local farmers do not produce beans and corns but work as seasonal workers in the large agro-export operations, especially tomato production, developed on Mexico's north-west coast. This pattern intensified in the 1970s and 1980s when the majority of the young and male population of San Jeronimo worked in agro-businesses in northern Mexico and California. In addition to wage work, the people of San Jeronimo worked in a variety of informal jobs (cleaners, cooks and domestic workers) in big American or Mexican towns.

Is San Jeronimo still a 'peasant community'? From the economic point of view, it is not, because 80 per cent of its subsistence needs are covered with cash and wage labour from American and Mexican agri-businesses and from the service sector. Nevertheless, from the social point of view, it is. Land is still communal, labour is not commodified and endogamic marriage rules ensure that the community stays connected. According to Kearney, the people of San Jeronimo are neither peasants nor proletarians. Making a similar argument to that of Meillassoux, he claims that transnational capitalism and circular migration dissolve the very distinction between rural and industrial labour. The people of San Jeronimo live in transnational spaces, in which notions of land, labour power, finance capital, the household, transnational profits and ancient Mixtec knowledge are mixed together. But the story of San Jeronimo differs from the story of the Guro. Transnational capitalism, according to Kearney, creates transnational workers, with fluid identities and contextual political consciousness. In their community, they develop equalitarian forms of livelihood and oppose foreign companies through the language of indigenous rights and ecological consciousness. In the context of Californian and Mexican agribusiness, they are migrant workers fighting for higher wages and better working conditions through trade union militancy. In the context of the shanty towns of Mexican cities, they are urban dwellers and express political resistance through neighbourhood activism. As informal workers along the Mexican–American border they develop illegal strategies and even forms of violence. In the American cities, they are assimilated in the urban life and become, petty traders, civil servants or gang leaders. For Kearney flexible capitalism fosters flexible political strategies based on a mixture of working-class, ethnic and indigenous, human rights and environmental activism. This is true of many revolutionary movements that have sprung up in the rural South, such as the Landless movement in Brazil (MST), the Zapatista Army of National Liberation (EZLN) in Mexico or the Karnataka farmers' movement (KRRS) in India. These movements have developed indigenous self-government, communal land management, workers co-operative, eco-friendly technologies and non-market distributions. In parallel to these rural developments, urban trade unions in the South have built broad anti-capitalist coalitions of peasant, working-class, women and indigenous and black organisations. Unlike the African anti-colonial movements that I described earlier – which opposed labour commodification with informalisation – these new peasant movements refuse this ethnocentric dichotomy and construct notion of value based on mutualistic rather than dialectical relations, including with the environment.

But these cross-sectional movements do not always succeed, partly because flexible production as I have highlighted above, cuts across the labour capital divide and forces the very workers to collude with or even to become capitalists. Besides, anti-capitalist movements are often co-opted by middle-class or high-caste elites and populist parties. Tom Brass (2000a,b) describes these anti-capitalist movements as 'populist' because they propose 'soft' forms of land redistribution, advocate a return to the rural economy (often based on patronage) and essentialise their political identity in terms of 'peasantry'. Paradoxically, some of these anti-capitalist movements end up being co-opted by right-wing and reactionary organisations as in the case of the *Land Grab* movement in Gujarat, the Maoist Communist Centre in the state of Jharkhand or even the *Sendero Luminoso* movement in rural Peru. The surge of anti-capitalist Islamic organisations in the free trade zones of South East Asia is another instance of such reactionary anti-capitalism. For instance, programmes of rural development and export-oriented industrialisation in Malaysia in the 1980s stirred a violent Islamist backlash. These programmes attracted Japanese, American and European transnational corporations through tax-free zones and an endless supply of female labourers of rual background. In such context, anthropologist Ong (1987) focuses on three Japanese semiconductor factories located in the free trade zone of Kuala Langat, in the Southern part of Malaysia. There, women's employment in industry conflicts with the values of their traditional Muslim communities (*kampung*), where men embody reason and self-knowledge and women are said to be influenced by carnal desires and to be spiritually polluted. But when young women find employment in the new multi-national corporations these traditional values are broken. Becoming economically independent, they leave their family-homes, refuse arranged marriages and embrace the new urban lifestyle associated with foreign capitalism. But this freedom has a price. Emancipated from their fathers, they become the 'factory daughters' of male managers who use the same male *kampung* discourse to exploit them on the shop floor, forcing them to perform wearing and under-remunerated tasks. At the time of Ong's fieldwork, militant Islamic organisations were mounting a moral campaign against foreign capitalism, claiming that its exploitative factory work and immoral values were destroying the rural community.

TAYLOR RETURNS TO THE BRICS

China, India and Brazil were heavily industrialised during the Cold War following the Soviet or American versions of Taylor's scientific management that clashed with these countries' corporate tradition (more labour intensive and less de-skilling than in the North)[12] and the way in which political elites and family oligarchies historically controlled firms preventing the formation of a strong managerial class. In the 1980s India and Brazil and, to a certain extent, China, were forced into a 'second market shift' (Burawoy 2010) involving flexible production, the financialisation of the economy and labour downsizing and deregulation. But in recent years, while the North deregulated, de-skilled and downsized labour according to the flexible production model, Brazil, India and China were following the opposite model of state-led multi-divisional, conglomerate and family-owned capitalism (Goldstein 2007). This economic shift was accompanied by substantial social reforms, especially on welfare and labour security which, for some, constitutes a form of 'globalisation 'from above' (Dong, Bowles and Chang 2010). But interestingly, these reforms focused on the informal or unorganised labour sector whereas labour relations in the formal sector overall worsened (Harriss 2010). To a sceptical eye, these forms of state socialisation of the informal sector are more evidence of the crisis of global finance than of a crisis of state sovereignty. With the financial system in crisis, labour externalisation is more costly than wage labour. During the recent economic crisis, while flexible companies in the North went bust, the conglomerate that I was researching in Brazil survived thanks to its internal credit lines, diversification and flexible *internal* labour markets[13] – meaning the power of firing and hiring workers in line with the economic cycle. I argue that this new production regime, which might be called 'new Taylorism', represents a new form of capital re-organisation, this time led by the South. Indeed the cost of industrial labour in these countries is extremely low, with wages falling relative to GDP. For instance in China, as growth accelerated, the share of wages in national income fell for 22 consecutive years, from 57 per cent of GDP in 1987 to 37 per cent in 2005 (Standing 2011: 28). Partly, this situation is due to China's massive surplus of labour supply, especially in rural areas, which contain 40 per cent of China's labour force. For many economists, China's and India's labour surplus keep wages low and labour vulnerable worldwide. But recent increases in social welfare and wages in China point in another direction.[14] By increasing its workers' power China is rebooting the global economy and consolidating its world power (Marazzi 2011: 105). This does not mean that there are no flexible companies in newly industrialised countries (NIC). Indeed, many household name American and European multi-nationals have expanded into these countries using local contractors (often ruthless brokers) and precarious labour. It means that the long trend of marketisation of the firm (embodied by the flexible production model) is being replaced by a new trend of corporatisation of the market, let by the South.

Indeed the return of Taylorism to China is sparking a new wave of working-class activism (Ngai et al. 2010). In her compelling ethnography of factory work under Hu Jintao's market socialism, Pun Ngai (2005) describes how rural women learn to become 'factory workers' (*dangomei*) through a mixture of capitalist discipline and state oppression. Her fieldwork is based in Meteor, a microelectronic company owned by Hong Kong businessmen and located in the rich Nansghan district of Shenzhen, pullulating with skyscrapers, luxury hotels and department stores. In this anarchic and heterotopian district the new middle class cohabits with petty capitalists, state bureaucrats and a multitude of migrant labourers. The disciplining of the rural 'lazy' labourers of Meteor happens not only through Taylorist forms of work organisation but also by denying to them the status of permanent residents, thus keeping them in a state of permanent fluctuation between their factories and their home towns. Without the permanent resident visa (*hukou*) from the governmental Shenzhen Labour Service Control (LSC) these migrant workers are forced into permanent precarious labour. The *hukou* registration system forces the 200 million Chinese rural migrants into precarious factory work and to an urban existence without schooling, healthcare, housing and state benefits. And yet, these rural migrants are the motor of China's industrial power.

Pun's study documents the harshness of the lives of this precarious workforce made up primarily of women of rural background. Indeed, of the 500 employees of Meteor, 75 per cent work on the production line and 90 per cent of this number are women. Work starts at 8 am and finishes at 10 pm when overtime is considered. 'Becoming *dangomei*' is a relenting and painful process of sensory and emotional adaptation to the production line. Flashing lights indicate different stages of the production process; popular Cantonese music is played in-between shifts to clear the workers' minds; plastic curtains are sealed on the windows to prevent them form being distracted from the outside world; English letters are posted on the walls to allow them to decipher the meanings of the words printed on the components to be assembled; illustrations of the production tasks are scattered all over the line. In the semiconductor assembly room women with nimble fingers handle small dies, wires and printed circuits using microscopes and in artificial light and temperatures that give them chronic headache, dizziness and pains. As in the case described by Ong, these women wage workers escaped the patriarchal organisation of the village only to become factory daughters and sexualised bodies in these newly emerging Taylorist factories. But like the Malay women described by Ong, these women are not passive victims. They enjoy window shopping, pop Cantonese music and flirting with company managers and engage in 'minor genres of resistance', sabotaging machines, joking and gossiping about the management and slowing down production by 'acting out' their menstrual pains, headaches and other bodily pains on the shop floor.

It could be argued that Chinese capitalism is the worse case scenario because it combines labour precariousness and Taylorism. Unlike the entrepreneurial Fafras, Yokohama's daily labourers or the Sheffield 'neo artisans', these Chinese factory workers have no agency. But for Pun the 'half-rural and half-proletarian' condition of the working class in China is conductive to a new form of political consciousness. The Chinese *dangomei* are 'floating people' – suspended between the rural and the urban, the modern and the backward and the individualism of western capitalism and the collectivism of Chinese socialism. Exposed to multiple forms of oppression they develop 'a new cartography of transgression'. Indeed, there is enough evidence that the Chinese working class is getting organised.[15] In 2009 and 2010, a series of suicides among the workers of Foxconn, the world's largest contract manufacturer, assembling 40 per cent of the world's consumer electronics, brought the Chinese working class to worldwide attention. The 70,000 employees of

Foxconn City work on continuous 12-hours shifts, dealing with poisonous chemicals with no protection and low wages.[16] At night they are crowded in the unhealthy company dormitories. Western media commented on the suicides and strikes at Foxconn focusing on the backwards nature of Chinese capitalism but were silent on those powerful customers such as Apple, who ignored the exploitative working conditions at Foxconn.[17] Indeed the suicides at Foxconn and the discussions surrounding them showed that these workers had a personal involvement in their jobs that exceeded the impersonal wage relation.

Chinese labour activism differs radically from labour relations in Volta Redonda, the Brazilian steel town surrounded by the tropical forest where I conducted fieldwork between 2008 and 2009. The city's economy, and consequently its citizen's lives, revolves around the *Companha do Aco* (CA), the biggest steel mill in Latin America. Volta Redonda's steel industry was founded in 1930s by dictator Getulio Vargas as a powerful symbol of Brazilian modernisation. Although the glory days of CA have long passed, the company still controls life in Volta Redonda today, creating as much poverty and marginalisation as industrial wealth for the community. Throughout the day a din of mechanical noise, clouds of industrial chemicals and the sound of workers' labour pour out of the CA's factory and into the surrounding city and forest. The hierarchy of CA is inscribed in the city's geography. Working-class labourers and company management live in quiet American-style suburbs on the hills. The city's marginal people, and they are many, live in favelas at the periphery. Most families in Volta Redonda depend on CA, which employs 8,000 direct and 20,000 indirect workers. But the town's once strong tradition of working-class identity is being eroded by a burgeoning service economy, favelisation and gentrification. In the past, the company had a paternalistic relation with the local residents. CA was considered 'the mother' of Volta Redonda (while the dictator Getulio Vargas was the city's 'father') and its recruitment, career and promotions system were organised along seniority and kinship lines. The residents of Volta Redonda considered themselves as a 'steel family' (*familia siderurgica*). But the privatisation of CA in 1992 led to many redundancies, subcontracting and dismantling of welfare provisions. The Metalworkers Union (SMVR) stepped up its militancy through a series of strikes, high profile campaigns and legal actions against the company, especially against its exploitative subcontracting. Reacting against heightened labour activism and high political costs of tertiarisation CA is currently re-internalising jobs, but lowering wages and harshening industrial relations.[18] Today CA's wages are among the lowest in the world, low even by Brazilian standards. Why do the workers put up with this? Some steel workers and their unions argue that factory labour is both more secure and more defendable than labour in the service and public sectors. Some mention the prestige of the company. Working at CA, they build up a high profile for accessing more profitable jobs and increase their status in their communities. Even if CA is organised according Taylorist principles, the management allows and even encourages employees to take on second jobs and to get involved in extra-curricular activities, typically evangelicalism or CA's in-house cultural and financial training. CA is a dystopian space, in which Tayloristic discipline and lax rules, internal labour markets and externalisation, high tech and obsolescence blur into each other.

It would be a mistake to map flexible production and new Taylorism along the North–South divide, because the two systems are often interwoven. Nonetheless, it is important to highlight the differences between North and South models. Flexible production is a movement of commodification of social relations taking place outside the realm of work. It valorises precisely that kind of reproductive labour – the labour of carers, educators, entertainers and therapists – that most societies consistently devalue. But filtered through the mono-dimensional lens of economics, this valorisation ends up commodifying those intimate relations – of love, care, sex and death – that in most societies are organised along non-market principles, creating a new class of affective and domestic labourers. In new Taylorism the situation is inverted. Informality is internalised inside the factory and the economic dimension of the wage contract is devalued vis-à-vis the non-economic dimensions of religion, race, kinship and party politics. Partly, this has long historical roots. In these countries the capitalist class had to deal with colonial dynasties, populist leaders, party oligarchies and strong domestic economies so that the corporate form emerged as a compromise between the market, the party and the family. Unlike the dispersed capital structure of western capitalism, the concentration of industrial capital in the hands of industrial families, tycoons and oligarchs in emerging countries is a stabilising factor, especially in times of crisis. It could be argued that these two models complement each other and that the rebirth of the multi-national model in the South has a stablising role on the global economy by siphoning industrial profits from the South to the struggling financial markets in the North.

My ethnographic overview shows a great diversification of forms of capitalist organisations worldwide – Taylorist factories, global sweatshops, Toyotist transplants, lean production and industrial districts – that does not match the hypothesis of global convergence towards the flexible production model. Besides, this overview shows that, as Tony Elger and Chris Smith have elegantly argued (Elger and Smith 1994; 2005) Taylorism and Fordism globally overlap in several ways, including the 'loaning of labour' between transnational corporation and their subcontractors (Kamada 1994); hybrid forms of Japanese and UK management in UK plants (Elger and Smith 2005) and TNC turned into 'dream factories' made up exclusively of subcontracted and informal labour in Brazil (Abreu, Beynon and Ramalho 2000). From such diversified economic landscape, the only recognisible pattern is that of increased informalisation and precarisation of labour – whether inside or outside the factory. Informalisation is strictly connected to labour migration and mobility, which is at the heart of the mechanism of labour brokerage.[19]

CONCLUSION

Capitalism is a mechanism of labour alienation based on the added value of human separation. Anthropologist James Carrier shows how the factory system is one such technology of human separation between people, objects and the environment. Carrier highlights four historical stages of capitalist production and corresponding forms of labour 'separation' or alienation. In the *cottage industry* production was based in homes and controlled by family members who owned tools and raw material. Parents and children were team-workers sharing a mixture of utilitarian and affective relations. This system of production was not alienated because labour was embedded in family relations and the objects produced were not sold but were used by those who produced them. At the other extreme, *modern factory production* labour is entirely standardised, de-skilled and repetitive. Workers stand alone in front of their machines, immersed in webs of highly bureaucratised and impersonal rules and relations and corporate values, communications, target, positions and protocols. In this modern production system, people think about themselves as being split into parts. One part is made of separations between objects, persons and places, of impersonal forces called profit, utility, success. Generally this part is associated with the workplace. And the other part is made of intimate connections – between objects, people and places – personal and meaningful social relations and of a benign environment, generally associated with the realm of 'home'. Carrier shows a form of capitalist valorisation based on separating people from each other and from their objects and environment. But I have argued here and elsewhere (Mollona 2009a) that the flexible model works in the opposite way, by blurring and confusing work and leisure, family and factory, formal and informal and the personal and the impersonal. Historically, it can be argued that in times of industrialisation, nationalism, mass production and state centralisation, the realm of society appears separated from the realm of the economy. In times of globalisation, financialisation, petty capitalism and regionalisation, economy and society tend to blur into each other.[20]

But the dynamics of labour alienation (or separation) must be read also in the context of the broader division of labour between the North and the South. Up until the 1980s, European and American capitalists reacted to cyclical overproduction and labour struggles at home by opening factories abroad where labour was cheaper and commodity markets expanding. But the factory was a cumbersome apparatus and, with time, factory workers tended to get organised and to demand higher wages and better working conditions. The flexible production system eliminated altogether the costs of direct production and labour activism by de-territorialising capital and making the factory 'moveable' towards those marginal locations where labour is cheaper and less organised. In terms of bio-political geography the old factory system fixated capital to the 'factory walls' (Tronti 1962) and contained the forced migrations of labour within the urban space. The flexible system unleashed capital from fixed locations forcing workers to 'follow it' in longer-distance and riskier migrations. Without fixed employment and stable incomes the workers became nomads and their labour turned into 'capital' – an internalised force that follows the movements of debts and speculation. Unlike this flexible system, 'new Taylorism' holds the movements of capital and the movements of labour in balance, functioning like a permeable membrane that both separates and connects the town and the countryside, work and home, wage work and the informal economy, and 'Economics' and other human cosmologies. In these factories people call upon multiple moralities – collectivism, hierarchy and competitive individualism – that overflow the wage relation.

The global spread of the informal economy shows a scenario in which the morality of people and the morality of money are conflated either outside the factory – as for Toyotism in the North – or inside it – as for the new Taylorism in the South. Today, global proletarians are also agency workers, peasants, illegal workers, daily labourers, 'the poor' and indigenous subjects. Their politics combines factory, community, media and underground activism, riots and direct action. Their livelihoods mix domestic, craft and factory labour. Their consciousness is experienced through the multiple dimensions of class, race, ethnicity and gender. The global corporations that employ them also perform the functions of states, civil society and philanthropy. In the current scenario we have lost track of where labour and capital are located and what form of political engagement is most effective.

Activists and some social scientists, especially anthropologists, working in post-colonial contexts in the 1970s saw the informal economy as a powerful tool for poor and marginalised subjects to fight back against states, corporate bureaucracies, post-colonial elites and new empires. Some are making a similar argument today, arguing for the abolition or de-commodification of work.[21] At the other end of the spectrum, some argue for the re-commodification of labour, especially in those 'immaterial' sectors (such as the media and art sectors, see Lazzarato 2012) heavily relying on precarious, temporary and unpaid workers. These models treat socialisation and commodification as independent movements. Whereas I suggest that human labour consists of two movements – one of socialisation and subjectification connected to the making of people, and one of objectification and formalisation related to the making of things. Given that capitalism thrives on de-coupling these movements in space and time, anti-capitalism might consist in keeping them in synch. For instance, in my article on trade union activism in Britain (Mollona 2009a), I show how a similar polarisation between commodification and socialisation of labour by the top echelons of two industrial trade unions clashed with the everyday practices of activism on the shop floor. In spite of one steel trade union officially embracing the model of 'business unionism' (based on factory activism and the economic interests of the metal workers) the everyday practices of its reps and workers took place in social centres, in collabouration with civic activists and in the language of human rights. On the other hand, the steel union that formally embraced 'community unionism' (a model based on communitarian values, horizontal and direct activism and social services) in *practice* acted hierarchically and following the narrow economic interests of a group of skilled factory workers. In that article I argued that, since the everyday reality of labour always entails struggles taking place both in the workplace and outside it, the political opposition between social and community unionism was self-defeating.

Capitalism never fully colonised society with work, but instead, it always thrived on its uneven movements between work and labour. If capitalism thrives from this oscillatory logic, anti-capitalism can be imagined in two ways. First, as a simultaneous movement of socialisation and anti-commodification, taking place both in the factory and in society – as seems to be the case ,for instance, in the contemporary Chinese labour movement (Lee 2007). The second option is to embrace stillness rather than movement. Indeed the strength of capitalism is that it relies on such institutions as friendship, kinship and 'teams' – and on the informal value generated by them – which are essentially institutions of communism. Activism might consist in the simple gesture of valuing what is already there, finding our *common* hidden in the ruins of capitalism and investing in contingent forms of livelihoods situated in the places and times 'in-between' capital's oscillations. Conceived in this way, as a space of 'diverse economies'[22] informed by non-capitalist places and temporalities, the notion of informal economy might be truly revolutionary.

NOTES

1. Since the 1970s, 60 per cent of the exports of coffee, diamonds and ivory have been smuggled.
2. She defines them as 'states in which the economy is based on politics and not on markets'.
3. The famous philanthropist De Soto was making similar claims for Latin America.
4. I discuss a similar instance in Sheffield (Mollona 2005) and also Fortunati (1989).
5. Their indirect wages (made up of family allowances, unemployment benefits and pensions) are three times lower than the average.
6. In the form of wage and welfare policies.
7. Union set up and controlled by employers.
8. Burawoy calls it 'new despotic capitalism' (1985).
9. By 2010 temps will make up of one third of the workforce in Japan, Standing (2011).
10. For Smith (2006) regionalisation entailed a shift from class alliances towards ethnic and cultural identity.
11. Swyngedouw et al. (2002) makes a similar case for the mining sector in Belgium.
12. For China, see Arrighi (2007) and for Brazil see Dilnius (2011).
13. The company where I conducted fieldwork recently reduced real wages and increased working hours rather than externalise labour.
14. This trend seems to be reversing in China, see 'Manufacturing: The End of Cheap China', *The Economist*, 10 March 2012.
15. In 2008 there were 120,000 strikes in the country (Standing 2011).
16. $22 a day for a highly qualified worker, including overtime.
17. An exception is the *New York Times* investigation into Apple's connivance with Foxconn 'China, human costs are built into an iPad', 25/1/2012.
18. The Brazilian Labour Law explicitly forbids subcontracting.
19. Labour migrants are equally central in the model of extreme subcontracting of Californian agro-businesses and in China's factory system.
20. In this light, sixteenth-century mercantilism and post-Fordism are similar.
21. For instance, Gorz (1999) or Guy Standing's proposal for a universal Basic Income (2011).
22. I am referring to Gibson-Graham's notion of 'diverse economies' (2012).

REFERENCES

Abreu, Alice, Beynon, Huw and Jose, Ricardo Ramalho. 2000. ' "The dream factory": VW's modular production system in resende, Brazil', in *Work, Employment and Society*, vol. 14, no. 2, 265–82.
Arendt, Anna. 1988. *The Human Condition*. Chicago: University of Chicago Press.
Arrighi, Giovanni. 2007. *Adam Smith in Beijing*. London: Verso.
Basile, Elisabetta. 2008. 'From green revolution to industrial dispersal: Informality and flexibility in an industrial district for silk in rural South India', Unpublished manuscript.
Bloch, Maurice and Jonathan Parry. 1989. *Money and the Morality of Exchange*. Cambridge: Cambridge University Press.

Brass, Tom. 2000a. 'Labour in post-colonial India: A response to Breman', in *Journal of Peasant Studies*, vol. 28, 126–46.

——. 2000b. *Peasants, Populism and Postmodernism. The Return of the Agrarian Myth.* London: Frank Cass.

Breman, Jan. 1999. 'The study of industrial labour in India. The formal sector: An introductory review', in J. Parry, J. Breman and K. Kapadia (eds) *The Worlds of* Industrial Labour, New Delhi: Sage, pp. 1–41.

Brenner, Neil. 2004. *New State Spaces. Urban Governance and the Rescaling of Statehood.* Oxford: Oxford University Press.

Burawoy, Michael. 1985. *The Politics of Production.* London: Verso.

Burawoy, Michael (2010) 'From Polanyi to Pollyanna: The False Optimism of Global Labour Studies', *Global Labour Journal*, vol. 1: no. 2: 301–13.

Carsten, Janet. 1989. 'Cooking money: Gender and the symbolic transformation of means of exchange in a Malay fishing community', in Maurice Bloch and Jonathan Parry (eds) *Money and the Morality of Exchange*, Cambridge: Cambridge University Press.

Dilnius, Oliver. 2011. *Brazil's Steel City. Developmentalism, Strategic Power, and Industrial Relations in Volta Redonda, 194–1964.* Stanford: Stanford University Press.

Dong, Xiao-Yuan, Bowles, Paul and Chang, Hongqin. 2010. 'Managing liberalization and globalization in rural China: Trends in rural labour allocation, income and inequality', in *Global Labour Journal*, vol. 1, no. 1, 32–55.

Elger, Tony and Smith, Chris (eds). 1994. *Global Japanization? The Transnational Transformation of the Labour Process.* London: Routledge.

——2005. *Assembling Work. Remaking Factory Regimes in Japanese Multinationals in Britain.* Oxford: Oxford University Press.

Fortunati, Leopoldina. 1989. *Arcane of Reproduction: Housework, Prostitution, Labour and Capital.* Milan: Autonomedia.

Gibson-Graham, J. K. 2012. 'Diverse economies: Performative practices for "other worlds"', in T. Barnes, J. Peck, J. and E. Sheppard (eds) *The Blackwell Companion to Economic Geography*, Oxford: Wiley Blackwell, pp. 33–46.

Gill, Tom. 2000. '*Yoseba* and *Ninpudashi*. Changing patterns of employment on the fringes of the Japanese economy', in J. S. Eades, T. Gill and H. Befu (eds) *Globalisation and Social Change in Contemporary Japan*, Melbourne: Trans Pacific Press, pp. 123–43.

Goldstein, Andrea. 2007. *Multinational Corporations from Emerging Economies: Composition, Conceptualization and Direction in the Global Economy*, Basingstoke: Palgrave Macmillan.

Gorz, Andre. 1999. 'A new task for unions: The liberation of time from work', in R. Munck and P. Waterman (eds) *Labour Worldwide in the Era of Globalisation*, Basingstoke: Macmillan, pp. 41–63.

Harriss, John and Harriss, Barbara. 1989. 'Agrarian transformation in the Third World', in D. Gregory and R. Walford (eds) *Horizons in Human Geography*, Basingstoke: Macmillan, pp. 25–46.

Harriss, John. 2010. 'Globalization(s) and labour in China and India: Introductory reflections', in *Global Labour Journal*, vol. 1, no. 1, 3–11.

Harriss-White, Barbara. 2010. 'Globalization, the financial crisis and petty production in India's socially regulated informal economy' in *Global Labour Journal*, vol. 1, no. 1, 152–77.

Hart, Keith. 1973. 'Informal income opportunities and urban employment in Ghana', *Journal of Modern African Studies*, vol. 1, 61–89.

Kamada Toshiko. 1994. 'Japanese management and the loaning of Labour: Restructuring in the Japanese Steel and Iron Industry', in T. Elger, and C. Smith (eds) *Global Japanization? The Transnational Transformation of the Labour Process*, London: Routledge, pp. 91–115.

Kearney, Michael. 1996. *Re-conceptualising Peasantry: Anthropology in Global Perspective*, Boulder and Oxford: Westview Press.

Lazzarato, Maurizio. 2012. *La Fabrique de L'Homme Edette'.Essai sur la condition néolibérale*, Paris: Éditions Amsterdam.

Lee, Ching Kwan. 2007. *Against the Law: Labour Protests in China's Rustbelt and Sunbelt*, Berkeley and Los Angeles: University of California Press.

Marazzi, Christian. 2011. *The Violence of Financial Capitalism*, Cambridge, MA: The MIT Press.

MacGaffey, Patricia, 1987. *The Real Economy of Zaire*, London and Philadelphia: James Currey.

Meillassoux, Claude. 1981. *Maidens, Meal and Money*, Cambridge: Cambridge University Press.

Mollona, Massimiliano. 2009a. 'Community unionism versus business unionism: The return of the moral economy in trade union studies', in *American Ethnologist*, vol. 36, no. 4: 651–66.

———. 2009b. *Made in Sheffield. An Ethnography of Industrial Work and Politics*, Oxford: Berghahn.

———. 2005. 'Factory, family and neighbourhood. The political economy of informal labour in Sheffield, UK', in *Journal of Royal Anthropological Society (JRAI), (N.S.)* vol. 11, 527–48.

Ngai, Pun. 2005. *Made in China Women Factory Workers in a Global Workplace*, Durham and London: Duke University Press.

Ngai, Pun, Chan, Chi, King, Chris, and Chan, Jenny. 2010. 'The role of the state, labour policy and migrant workers' struggles in globalized China', in *Global Labour Journal*, vol. 1, no. 1, 132–51.

Ong, Aihwa. 1987 *Spirits of Resistance and Capitalist Discipline: Factory Women in Malaysia*, Albany: State of New York Press.

———. 2006. 'Labour arbitrage: Displacement and betrayals in the Silicon Valley', in *Neoliberalism as Exception. Mutation in Citizenship and Sovereignty.* Duke University Press, pp. 157–95.

Parry Jonathan, 1989. *Death in Benares*, Cambridge: Cambridge University Press.

Roitman, Janet. 2005. *Fiscal Disobedience. An Anthropology of Economic Regulation in Central Africa*, Princeton: University Press.

Rostow, Walt, 1960. *The Stages of Economic Growth: A Non-Communist Manifesto*, Cambridge: Cambridge University Press.

Rothstein Frances. 2006. 'Flexibility for whom? Small-scale garment manufacturing in rural Mexico', in Alan Smart and Josephine Smart (eds) *Petty Capitalism and Globalisation*, Albany, NY: State University of New York Press, pp. ??–?.

Sennett, Richard. 2008. *The Craftsman*, London: Allen Lane.

Smart, Alan and Smart, Josephine (eds). 2006. *Petty Capitalism and Globalisation*, Albancy, NY: State University of New York Press.

Smith, Gavin. 2006. 'When the logic of capital is the real Background which lurks in the background: Programme and practice in European "regional economies"', in *Current Anthropology*, vol. 47, no. 4, 621–39.

Standing, Guy, 2011. *The Precariat. The New Dangerous Class*, London: Bloomsbury Academics.

Swyngedouw, Eric, Moualert, Frank, and Rodriguez, Arantza 2002. 'The neoliberal urbanisation of Europe: Large-scale urban development projects and the new urban policy', in N. Brenner and N. Theodore (eds), *Spaces of Neoliberalism*, Oxford: Blackwell, pp. 195–229.

Tronti, Mario. 1962. *Operai e Capitale*, Torino: Einaudi.

9

NEW FORMS OF LABOUR CONFLICT: A TRANSNATIONAL OVERVIEW

Gregor Gall

INTRODUCTION

Open the pages of the *Yearbook of Annual Statistics* of the United Nation's International Labour Organisation (ILO) at the section on strikes and it quickly becomes apparent that not only has the level of strike activity fallen massively in countless countries over the last 30 years but that it was never that high in the first place in many others. This should make the observer ponder at least two points. First, if the strike is declining or even withering away, and if workers are far from contented in their wage-labour, what means are replacing the strike? This would be to anticipate a 'displacement effect' (see Gall and Hebdon 2008) for discontent will, surely, be expressed by other means as it cannot and will not be suppressed indefinitely by employers (or even workers themselves). Second, was the strike tool actually ever the main tool of the workers' movement? This at least indicates that other collective forms of what is called 'industrial action' (and especially 'industrial action short-of-a-strike') like the overtime ban, the work-to-rule, the work-to-contract and so on, do exist. Moreover, they should not be overlooked for although the strike has proved its reliability and endurance, it is far from ideal in all or other situations.

Accordingly, this chapter will seek to provide a transnational overview of forms of labour conflict, paying particular attention to the issue of the expression and resolution of grievances over time by variations in the use of different tools. By transnational, it is meant that the chapter does not engage in international or comparative analysis, but rather seeks to construct an assessment of dominant trends across and throughout the economies and societies of developed economies. In doing so, four propositions are explored. The first is that in examining 'new' forms of labour conflict under – and within – capitalism it becomes evident that little is likely to be fundamentally new in the sense of 'never before having occurred'. This should not strike any social scientist as particularly surprising for capitalism is not a new system of organising society and the very continuity of this societal system is likely to give rise to a continuity of response from wage labourers in the forms that labour conflict takes. The second is that as capitalism is now a more globalised system of society than ever before the prospect exists that forms of labour conflict between workers and capitalists over the terms of wage labour may be variations and replications on already well-established themes. In this sense, we may view forms of labour conflict as new in that they have been (a) used by particular groups of workers for the first time in one part of the world, and (b) rediscovered by different groups of workers for the first time in a long time. Collectively, the forms are re-occurring phenomena but now on a global scale. The third is that some minor innovation *within* existing forms should be anticipated for the way in which capital has globalised itself and the way it organises – sometimes in response to challenges from labour – may find its match in the way labour organises itself and responds to capital. This would be to anticipate new spatial and temporal dimensions of labour conflict rather than new forms of labour conflict per se. The fourth is that because capitalism has not become truly standardised in the way it operates on a global scale different countries and regions retain something of their own particularities by virtue of varying political cultures and this impacts upon forms of labour conflict. Consequently, while a tendency towards convergence of forms of labour conflict is apparent, divergence is also possible and probable.

The term 'labour conflict' in this chapter denotes how the two sides in the employment relationship, namely, workers and employers, organise the antagonistic side to their relationship. This is based upon configurations for each side of their material interests, ideology and power resources, leading to intentions, processes and outcomes of conflict. Thus, conflict is neither irrational nor dysfunctional for either side because it concerns the prosecution of their interests. While conflict is not the only side to the employment relationship, it is a major one and the focus of this chapter. However, the specific focus is to examine the repertoire of contention – or armoury of tools – that the workers' side has in engaging in conflict with employers over the collective prosecution of their collective interests. The stress on the collective is because while individualised forms of labour conflict are not unimportant, they are not as sharp and strong challenges to the managerial prerogative and the rights of capital as collective ones are. But that does not mean they shall be disregarded entirely in the chapter, for there is no Chinese Wall between the individual and the collective. Rather than being seen as binary opposites, they are better viewed as two ends of the same spectrum with the forms of semi-individual and semi-collective standing in between them. This is because there are times when individual workers can take individual actions but these can only be understood in a collective context, namely, their significance and contribution to a collective process or outcome of struggles. And when the right and ability to strike is infringed upon, such types of action take on greater significance.

The underlying perspective adopted in this chapter is a Marxist or radical one whereby it is assumed that there is a continual and unceasing conflict of interest between capital and labour over the terms of exploitation of labour by capital and the oppression that is involved in maintaining this exploitation. In the words of Edwards (1986), there is a 'structured antagonism'. This means, notwithstanding the countervailing tendency towards co-operation, conflict is always latent. However, conflict may not always be easily observable, that is, overt, for, on the one hand, strikes and the like are merely the expression of conflict and not the substance of the conflict itself while, on the other, it only seems that conflict is apparent when there are visible symptoms of it like strikes. Thus, quiescence should not be mistaken for harmony and co-operation, especially as conflict is mostly observable through its overt signs. In seeking to establish that conflict is endemic, inherent and often latent in its expression as a result of exploitation of labour by capital, two other dimensions are crucial. One is, to borrow a phrase from Burawoy (1979: 194), the anarchic nature of the free market additionally leads to despotism in the workplace as capital uses the wages and conditions of workers as shock absorbers to cope with this anarchy. The other is that the need for capital to translate purchased labour time into profitable labour power and output creates the arena for bargaining over effort and the need for managers to manage labour for capital. This leads to further grounds for contesting capital's regime of exploitation and oppression by labour.

METHODOLOGICAL CHALLENGES

In presenting a transnational overview of new forms of labour conflict, there are significant problems concerning the existence of data, and where it does exist, its reliability. Although data on strikes does exist for most countries, being compiled from national governments into the aforementioned ILO Yearbooks (http://laboursta.ilo.org/), it is notoriously lacking in robustness in terms of completeness and standardised inclusion criteria. For example, many countries do not include public sector strikes and for Greece, which has experienced the highest level of general strikes of any country in the world in recent years, there are no data from 1999 onwards. But at least there are data, however inadequate, and that cannot be said of many other forms of labour conflict. For example, the University of Kansas' 'European protest and coercion data', covering the period 1980 to 1995 for many western and eastern European countries and containing data from newspaper reports, is one of the few exceptions here. It covers a number of forms of industrial action short-of-a-strike (like a work-to-rule) and workers' protests and demonstrations concerned with work and employment. But it still does not cover forms like sabotage and output restriction because these are relatively hidden and not reported upon by newspapers. Nonetheless, it stands out as an oasis in a desert until 1995. Surveys do exist that cover other forms of labour conflict but these are episodic rather than periodic and do not allow much in the way of inter- and trans-national analysis. Therefore, the social scientist is left conducting rather unscientific science by relying upon a host of media reports and other assorted bits and bobs in trying to build up, at best, a rather anecdotal overview of forms of labour conflict. Clearly, both breadth and depth are, thus, very much in short supply but so too is the ability to judge entirely what is new and what is not because of the inability to have longitudinal series data. Consequently, what can at best be offered is an impressionistic and anecdotal overview that would need significant data generation to confirm, vary or repudiate.

NECESSITY—THE MOTHER OF INNOVATION?

A significant but qualified aforementioned proposition was that as the terrain upon which labour struggles takes place changes, so too would the tools workers deploy in these struggles. The most obvious senses of this pertain to developments in the application of technology and automation of the means of production, distribution and exchange, and changes in the organisation and structure of capital. However, there seems to have been relatively little innovation in forms of workers' labour conflict here, and so it may be more a case of adaption than innovation.

Legal fragmentation and separation of units of capital – often to act as a subterfuge to the *de facto* common linkages and patterns of ownership – has posed a grave challenge to workers' ability to act collectively. Thus, de-merging, subsidiarisation, outsourcing, offshoring and the like have meant that legally and physically workers are separated from their (former) workmates. This then has consequences for the structures of industrial relations and collective bargaining, and the processes and structures of power relationships between workers and employers. The effect has been to 'divide and rule' so that workers are challenged to reconfigure and re-organise their collectivity. One stark example is in manufacturing, where workers in a company's different plants are often forced to compete for investment to stave off closure. Given that production, distribution and exchange remain necessarily highly integrated under globalised capitalism – and in horizontal and vertical as well as spatial and temporal ways – but that these systems are now also more fragile than ever before, this provides the potential lever for workers. Take for instance, vehicle manufacturers or supermarket retailers. In the former, and *within* some companies, their different plants will produce different parts of the vehicle for assembly elsewhere while in other adjacent or more distant plants external units of capital will supply components. In the latter, supermarkets tend to act monopsonistically with regard to their (external) suppliers. Although the supplier is totally reliant almost upon pain of death to sell to the single buyer, suggesting a completely asymmetrical relationship, this cuts both ways as the buyer does not usually have more than one supplier. Both vehicle manufacturers and supermarket retailers also use lean and just-in-time (JIT) supply chain systems where stock levels are cut right down to only what is needed in the here and now. The effect of this is to create situations where groups of workers downstream from either the assembly of the vehicles or the sale of goods and produce in the supermarket are in a strategic position. These could be workers making or transporting gearboxes just as they could be processing or transporting chickens. A union that organises car workers could then try to hold the company to ransom on an issue that covers all its members by bringing out – or threatening to – a particular group of strategic workers on strike rather than all its members and, if need be, use contributions from its non-striking members to fund the strikers' loss wages. The degree of susceptibility of production and supply chains to strategic groups of workers' exercising leverage in this way has all the more been heightened by the concentration of production and distribution facilities into super-centres as it has done with outsourcing of key functions like IT services to specialist providers.

Yet, despite all this, instances of the actual use of this leverage do not seem to have been much in evidence. The 1988 and 1990 Ford strikes in Britain had a sharp impact upon production in Belgium and were successful for this reason. But they did not set an influential and widespread precedent. Thus, two of the few known recent examples concern construction and poultry processing. In the former, in a dispute over the ultimatum to 'sign up or be sacked', electricians at seven major companies in Britain used the tactic of blockading construction sites from the outside to resist the new inferior contracts. Construction sites are supplied with materials on a JIT basis so being able to gather together electricians (and others) not employed at the site to blockade it to stop the entry of supplies can create delays, the significance of which is magnified by the contractual completion deadlines which incur financial penalties if missed. In the latter, again in Britain, the Unite union has used public pressure and collective actions upon supermarkets like Marks and Spencer to use their influence on their suppliers to better the terms and conditions that Unite's members have at the supplier companies. So in addition to actions by the workers themselves at the supplier companies, this form of action, which damages brands and reputation, has been used as a supplementary tool. This form of pressure has also successfully been used by the Service Employees' International Union in the USA, LHMWU in Australia and New Zealand and Unite in Britain in the contract cleaning centre by targeting the clients to put pressure on the contract companies (see Crosby 2009).

What is it that explains the rather infrequent usage of these types of action? Apart from the importance of the general decline in union density given that unionisation is the key form of collectivism and collectivism is necessary to take collective action, has this been because workers have been financially and ideologically 'bought off' in order to dissuade them from doing so? There is a bit of this but more important as an explanation has been employers seeking to either de-collectivise these workers through de-recognising their unions and using personal contracts or gain 'sweetheart' no-strike or 'partnership' agreements which neuter the unions and their use of this potential leverage (see Gall (1998, 2000) on the printing industry). On top of this, certainly in Britain and the United States, it is the legal regulation of industrial action that bars the use of lawful solidarity action by which it might be expected to see some groups of workers acting on behalf of themselves and others.

Given the prevalence – indeed, now centrality – of information technology to both the organisation of units of capital and the organisation of work itself, it might be expected that workers would engage in cyber and virtual wars with employers, especially in terms of acts of sabotage (see Brown 1977). This becomes all the more pertinent with the hegemony of Human Resources

Management (HRM). It can be seen as a form of mind control, essentially putting the supervisor inside the workers' head so that they supervise themselves. However, while there has been some attention given to examining the extent of 'organisational misbehaviour' (Ackroyd and Thompson 1999) defined as subversion and which included the use of critical humour (see also Taylor and Bain 2003), not only are these not evidence of a new form of labour conflict but there is also little in them that suggest new genres of existing forms of labour conflict, either. Indeed, the little that can be outwardly observed concerning new technology is that it has been used to organise old and existing means of labour conflict. ACAS (2010) noted the social organisation of strikes was beginning to deploy the means of 'new' or 'social' media and that the engineering construction workers' strikes of 2009 in Britain showed that grass-roots workers could use these means without recourse to official union structures and resources. To ACAS, this meant unofficial strikes were due to make a comeback but there was no evidence of this (Gall and Cohen 2013). The theme of variations on existing themes can also be seen with the 'mass sickie' where workers call in sick en masse to their work. This was used by British Airways cabin crew in 1997 and Turkish Airlines staff and Air Canada and Air India pilots in 2012. Although an innovation, the mass sickie is a de facto strike based on the withdrawal of labour. Only in the case of police officers and other public servants who are lawfully barred from striking has this tactic constituted a genuine innovation. In their case, it is called the 'blue flu' and is practised in the USA in particular.

NEW ARENAS AND TERRAINS OF CONTESTATION?

The considerable expansion of private service sector work has placed an ever increasing premium upon emotional and aesthetic labour. 'Smiling down the telephone', among others, is an example of the way in which the heart has to be managed. Displaying the right 'look' as per 'lookism' is another manifestation for carrying out a task in a way the employer sees fit. This then becomes one of the new arenas or terrains upon which labour conflict could take place, and may give rise to new forms of labour conflict from the workers' side. Certainly resistance has taken place in regard of this form of labour in call centres and retail and leisure (Bain and Taylor 2000, Taylor and Bain 2001, Warhurst and Nickson 2009). But again it seems nothing is but what is not. Take the issue of appearance and body shape. In the 1960s, the Hotel Employees and Restaurant Employees (HERE) union organised Playboy 'bunny girls' in Detroit and other cities. In the process of collective bargaining, underpinned by strikes, the women and their union successfully contested Hugh Hefner's sole right to determine what attractiveness was in terms of body shape, age, costume specification and so on (Cobble 1991). This was part of a fight to prevent the perpetuation of the idea that women should be obscene but not heard, according to the strike organiser, Myra Wolfgang. Turning the clock forward some 30 or more years, exotic dancers contested the right of club operators and owners to determine what their body shapes are, what they wear, whether they have tattoos on show and so on (Gall 2006) and, on one occasion, dancers engaged in a 'no pink' – no showing of female genitalia – form of industrial action as part of a campaign for union recognition (Gall 2012). This forms part of a wider and long history of women contesting employers' definitions – and imposition – of femininity which date backs to the early twentieth century in service work, especially in waitressing (Cobble 1991).

The weakening of workplace unionism's ability to take more than just small demonstrative actions may be the explanation for the development tactics of labour conflict which could be said to be symbolic or publicity stunts. The sense of atrophy here is heightened because many of these actions are held in the extra-workplace arena of public spaces. For example, bus drivers working for Luxembourg's private bus companies held a two-week protest in 2011, in which they grew beards or wore green wristbands to visibly signal their discontent with working conditions, namely, long working hours and a lack of toilet facilities. The protest, called 'Operation La BARBE!', was intended to attract the attention of employers and the public, without disrupting services. It took place as negotiations on a new collective agreement were taking place. Another instance was in 2010 when workers under threat of redundancy at Vinyls and Eurocoop in Sardinia occupied an abandoned prison on the island of Asinara, proclaiming it to be 'The Island of the Redundant' in a parody of the TV programme, 'The Island of the Famous'. Indeed, examples of union publicity-grabbing stunts using animals (pigs, camels, donkeys and the like) at company AGMs have been fairly commonly used in Britain while flashmob tactics have been used in Britain and Germany. These are, at best, attempts to generate 'soft' power, and often involve 'workers as citizens' as much or more than they do as 'workers as workers'.

RETURN OF THE GENERAL STRIKE?

The first ever general strike was organised in Britain in 1842 by the Chartists. Since then, general strikes have become a well-known, if statistically rather infrequently used, form of *political* striking in countries of the global North and South. They have been used in countries as diverse as Brazil, Egypt, Indonesia, Poland, South Africa and South Korea to remove authoritarian regimes since the Second World War. The weakening of union movements in Western European countries since the 1970s has not seen a commensurate decline in the ability to mobilise these forms of protest. Indeed, in a sign of their weakening political influence – traditionally through corporatism and social democratic parties – general strikes have become proportionately more common and, since the crisis of neo-liberalism in 2007, general strikes in many of these countries have become increasingly frequent (albeit not at the level of those in Greece, which experienced seventeen between 2010 and 2011) (see Gall 2013). Yet seldom have general strikes been called against employers even though they are often called against measures that benefit employers (like reductions in corporation tax or further restricting the lawful ability to strike). This is because general strikes are political strikes against governments first and foremost. Sometimes, they are offensive actions of insurrectionary significance. But only when a strike across the public sector becomes a de facto general strike (because of the contemporary atrophy of union membership in the private sector) does the dispute directly become a direct form of labour conflict because the government is the ultimate employer.

Nonetheless, the increasing dissolution of union movements into the public sector means that public sector strikes are of more prominence now that private sector strikes are few and far between. Given that private sector strikes are essentially economic strikes, aiming to impose costs upon profit-seeking organisations, strikes in the public sector are essentially political, aiming to apply leverage on the government. Moreover, given also that greater scales of action are needed in political strikes in order to achieve the necessary amount of leverage (compared to the economic strike), such strikes then become more political still. But compared to economic strikes, they remain protests aimed at feeding into processes of political exchange rather than attempts to completely halt the provision of goods and services as in the private sector. Yet of late, strikes in the private sector have become more like strikes in the public sector in that they try less to choke off the supply of revenue and profit and more to politically pressure the employer into giving concessions or to return to the bargaining table. The quintessential example of this is the one-day strike (even if part of a series of one-day strikes) or the 'smart' strike of rotating strikes by different parts of the same workforce (rather than all striking together simultaneously). With this form of striking dominating the ever declining number of strikes in the private sector, if appears that in the kingdom of the blind, the one-eyed man – the public sector political strike – is king. The one exception to this would seem to be found in Germany, where the 'warning' strike continues to be heavily used in the private sector as part of the collective bargaining process.

Moreover, the weakening of organised labour in western economies since the 1970s, coupled with the tightening of the legal regulation of lawful, protected industrial action from the 1980s, has also seen the decline of the 'wildcat' strike in many countries. So the erosion of previously powerful workplace unionisms which were capable of organising such wildcats and the centralisation of control within unions over the deployment of strike action (as a result of the changed legal regulation) have been the major contributors to the decline. Yet for certain types of workers which exercise significant amounts of strategic influence like transport, distribution and communication workers, this form of action has been maintained as a key tool in their armoury against their employers in most European countries. The same cannot be said of where wildcat strikes were most common some 30 or more years ago, namely, in manufacturing. Yet outside of Europe, the strike (including wildcats) has either returned or been deployed in a way that is clearly at odds with the trajectories of many established economies. The most obvious examples are China (Cooke 2013), Egypt (Alexander 2013) and Indonesia (Ford 2013).

INDUSTRIAL ACTION SHORT OF STRIKING

When industrial action takes places and it grabs the news headlines, it is usually strikes that do so. This is because they are more visible and high impact forms of collective action than many others workers are able to take. However, little attention – especially media attention – is then paid to the more subterranean forms of industrial action short-of-a-strike. The one exception is where industries and organisations run on such habitually high levels of overtime or goodwill that overtime bans or work-to-rules can have a significant and immediate impact upon the availability of a good or service. But those are exceptional cases so, again, this turns attention back to these more subterranean forms. An infrequent number of one-off surveys have shown in Britain (Milner 1993), for example, that the various forms of industrial action short-of-a-strike up to the early 1990s were more frequent that one might have first thought. This tendency to more industrial action short-of-a-strike than meets the eye was continued in Britain, for the Workplace Industrial Relations

Survey (WIRS) and the Workplaver Employment Relations Survey (WERS) both showed that although the frequency of industrial action short-of-a-strike had fallen since 1990 from 10 per cent to 2 per cent in workplaces with more than 25 employees (Millward et al. 2000: 178), it had increased more recently, whereby between 1998 and 2004 in workplaces with 10 or more employees and was the sole preserve of the public sector (Kersley et al. 2005: 209), marking a noteworthy development. There is no particular reason to believe that other western economies would not have experienced similar trajectories in workers' use of industrial action short-of-a-strike (even if each began from a different starting point as per strike activity). In Britain, the number of ballots with 'yes' mandates for industrial action short-of-a-strike has remained relatively high at around 500 per annum from 2002 to 2010 (Gall and Cohen 2013).

OCCUPATIONS

Workplace occupations are far from being new. Indeed, the first modern occupation or 'sit-down' strike was recorded in 1906 at General Electric and undertaken by Industrial Workers of the World (IWW) or Wobbly union members (Kornbluth 2011) and the tactic was famously used in the 1930s in the US to gain union recognition from major vehicle manufacturers. The tactic was also used in revolutionary times in Italy (1919–21), Spain (1936), Chile (1972) and Portugal (1974), among others). However, with the continuing spate of industrial restructuring and closures leading to redundancies, and the pace of this being accelerated by the crisis of neo-liberalism since 2007, it might have been expected that the occupation tactic would have been widely used to either try to stop redundancies – or at least better their terms. This is because seizing control of the means of production, distribution and exchange arguably puts workers in the strongest position to bargain with employers (even in cases of white-collar workplaces – see Cullinane and Dundon 2011). In the global North, this has not proven to be the case, except in France (Contrepois 2011, Gall 2010, 2011). By firstly comparing Britain to France and Greece, some insight may be gained into why this is the case.

Although occupations have continued at the pace of two to three minor ones per annum in Britain (Gall 2011) since they were lasted used in a major way in the 1970s (see Tuckman 2011), this has not been sufficient to make them part of the contemporary repertoire of contention for workers in Britain. By contrast, in the run up to the crisis of neo-liberalism, there were major instances in France like those at the Cellatex chemical plant in

2000, Moulinex in 2001 and at Schneider Electrics in 2004. This more active sense of historical collective recall, along with the more direct action traditions in France, has meant that the number of workplace occupations since 2008 has been over 100. Indeed, while occupations (alongside the use of 'bossnap-pings' (see Contrepois 2011) which has marked itself out as innovative) can be traced back to the Popular Front of 1936, this set of closely related tactics was infrequently used until the mid-1970s and over obtaining better working conditions and wage increases (Communisation 2011, see also Contrepois 2013). After that, and with the threat of mass unemployment, they were used against workplaces closures and collective redundancies but not on the scale seen since 2009. Alongside bossnapping, workers in France have also used the tactics of threatening to blow up the factories they were occupying (with materials found in the occupied factory) or pollute rivers (again with materials found in the occupied factory). Yet even though these acts were not organised by unions or even unionised workers, they remain essentially militant actions for moderate means because the issue of taking over the factories and putting them under workers' control with production of more socially useful alternatives was never ventured. Nonetheless, such tactics based around the occupation were relatively common. By contrast in Britain, there have been just nine occupations since 2007 and the tool has been more used by students and community campaigners as citizens than by workers as workers. Even in Eire, with similar a industrial relations system to Britain but a population more than 10 times smaller, there have been 10 occupations since 2007.

By the same token as France, a 23-day occupation of a major power plant in Greece in 2008 became a cause célèbre and was likely to have been an important point of reference for civil servants in 2011 undertaking the occupation of their ministries in order to prevent the 'troika' audit team of the European Central Bank/European Union/International Monetary Fund doing their work to enable cuts in public services (including massive redundancies in the public sector) in return for further bailouts. They were supported by street blockades while local authority workers occupied town halls. Given the preponderance of general strikes in Greece against austerity measures since 2009, indicating that in the declining purchase of each general strike, the use of the occupation tactic was a key innovation in this circumstance for it forced the rescheduling of the troika visit. Its greater purchase was that such an indefinite occupation becomes sustainable while an indefinite general strike is not. However, the occupation tactic was not widely used elsewhere in Greece at this time, suggesting that the specificity of the political situation was more important than the industrial situation (of likely job losses) facing the civil servants. But that the occupation tactic was more used by students and farmers than workers – with the exception of bus and shipbuilding workers – in the preceding 30 years also means that there was a limit to the extent that the 2008 occupation was a spur to others.

That said, South Korea is the country where the occupation tactic has most been used most and in by far the most spectacular manner. Dating from the 1970s as the independent workers' movement struggled against the powerful chaebol (conglomerate) employers (backed by the authoritarian and military state), workers in heavy engineering and shipbuilding routinely have engaged in occupations of many weeks and months to stop redundancies, fight for higher wages and gain union recognition. When police and para-military forces were deployed against the occcupations at the chaebols' behest, the strikers organised themselves in mass numbers and in military style to construct barricades and fight back with metal poles. In these instances, it became clear that the state no longer had a monopoly of the means to organised violence. Workers were prepared to fight fire with fire. Even after the removal of the military regime in 1987, these means of labour conflict on the workers' side remained in use because of the continuation of violent repression of the workers' actions. Only of late has the ferocity of the workers' response lessened due to less aggressive stances by employers and weakened unions. And, as highlighted above, occupations by individuals of key, strategic components such as cranes can form part of a collective resistance to employers. In one case, the crane occupation was part of an 11-month occupation by fellow workers of other ground-level facilities.

It seems that one of the true innovations in the 1970s – the Upper Clyde Shipbuilders' (UCS) work-in of 1971–72 – has almost never been repeated despite its potency. The work-in is a particular form of occupation where production is continued under workers' control. The basis of the tactic is to either show that workers are capable of running an operation without conventional – capitalist – management or to demonstrate to another capitalist (or potential investor like a government) that there is a viable business. While many occupations have often then become workers' co-operatives in Western Europe or taken over on a permanent or semi-permanent basis – so-called 'recovered factories' – in some south American countries (see Kabat 2011, Saria de Faria and Novaes 2011), there have not been work-ins. The absence of the work-in after UCS' work-in is not because workers have not been faced with the prospect of mass redundancies and workplace closure. Rather, it is because of the absence of a sizeable and credible radical left milieu espousing practical – as opposed to ultra-left – means of mounting immediate challenges to the control of individual capitalists.

INDIVIDUAL ACTS AS PART OF A COLLECTIVE STRUGGLE

Suicide, sometimes through self-immolation, in non-work situations as a result of non-work issues is often viewed as the action of a lone individual. No matter that the reasons may collectively reflect a deep alienation from society, these acts are usually seen as those of deviant loners. But in the case of workplace suicide, this is not so because it is primarily a direct response to exploitation and oppression found there. Thus, nearly 60 suicides of France Telecom workers have taken place between 2007 and 2011, either at work or at home, but with notes left explicitly linking suicide to their jobs (*The Guardian*, 9 September 2009, 27 April 2011). These were individual symptoms of a collective protest – found in not just the number of suicides but union agitation over a climate of bullying, extreme pressure, poor management methods and restructuring cuts that forced people to repeatedly change jobs. More overtly in China, Foxconn, manufacturer of iPads and iPhones, has been plagued by some 20 suicides between 2009 and 2011 in protest at working conditions including excessive overtime, a ban on talking to co-workers during 12 hour shifts, low wages, and living in massive dormitories. In 2012, strikes and the threat of mass suicides by 300 workers jumping off a roof helped resolve a dispute in the workers' favour. The China Labour Bulletin (http://www.clb.org.hk) indicates that suicides have been widely used by other workers, too, not least suppliers to Foxconn. Indeed, these suicides may reflect the absence of independent unions and the lawful right to strike, thereby, shutting down these collective means for expressing and resolving grievances. But neither independent unions nor the right to strike were absent in France, although the considerable weakness of unions in the private sector there – including in the manufacturing sector – may account for the exercise of the suicide as a supplement or alternative. In the case of South Korea, self-immolation is used more than elsewhere (and often as a form of suicide). It is part of an array of forms used alongside strikes, protests and occupations (Doucette 2013). In modern times, self-immolation has been used as a form of political protest, for example, by Tibetan monks against Chinese occupation. But in South Korea, it is part of the collective means of expressing and resolving grievances, albeit these modern-day roots may come from its use as a form of protest against Japanese occupation in the early twentieth century (Sang-Hwan 2004). This same is true for occupations by individuals of key machinery and equipment in order to stop its use. For example, a worker occupied a crane of Hanjin Heavy Industries and Construction for 309 days against 400 redundancies in 2011.

But suicide and self-immolation are not the only manifestations of what prima facie seem like atomised, individual actions but are, in fact, individualised actions and expressions of a wider collective phenomenon and a collective process of taking action. For example, a combination of the continuing juridification of individual rights and the longstanding existence of these rights in law throughout many western countries has helped make a significant impact upon how conflict is expressed and resolved. It would be easy to read the growing use of individual means of conflict resolution as bearing the imprint of the decline of worker collectivism and the concomitant growth of worker individualism (as well as the decline of collective conflict itself). While it would be wrong to juxtapose both means as representing an 'either or' situation, it is also not the case that the two categories of means are necessarily incompatible and detrimental to each other (see Kelly 1998). In acknowledging this, it then becomes possible to see the extensive usage of such individual means in a number of countries (McCammon 2001, Jefferys 2011) as a way to express and resolve collective conflict in two ways. The first is where test cases are taken in order to set precedents for others to use in its wake. The second is where individual claims on the same issue are lodged en masse. In such ways, the individual claim is a collective tool in the same way that the suicide and self-immolation are.

CHARACTERISTICS AND INTER-COUNTRY DIFFERENCES

Parts of the aforementioned propositions concerned a number of aspects of the temporal and spatial dimensions of labour conflict. The final proposition specifically concerned the tendency towards the standardisation of labour conflict across the globe. This section further examines a number of particular issues contained therein.

The first concerns the nature of the workers' collective action, especially the strike. While it is true that no two strikes are exactly alike, the quintessential generic nature of the strike as a tool can vary considerably across time. Consequently, strikes can have different social significance. In addition to the distinction made earlier between strikes that are primarily economic or primarily political in intent and effect, a second aspect can be identified within this particular dichotomy. This concerns the question of whether strikes are offensive or defensive in terms of the relationship between capital and labour, and movements in the frontier of control between the two. So for the most part, the conflict that workers have engaged in since the 1980s has been *defensive*. This means it has been attempting to stop employers worsening – in real terms – terms and conditions of employment. Strikes against redundancies, speed-ups and de-skilling are obvious examples, as is striking against a pay offer (rather than for a pay demand). This compares with action taken by workers in the period up to the early 1970s when workers took *offensive* action by not just striking to demand higher wages and pay awards but also critically by challenging managerial control over the organisation of work and work process. These struggles were often successful in encroaching upon that managerial control which previously had seemed inviolable and sacrosanct. With further control, workers were able to beneficially increase the terms they received from the wage-effort bargain albeit these were not always reducible to the cash nexus. However, there are times when defensive action can become offensive action. Occupations of workplaces to stop closures and redundancy offers, especially on a scale seen in the likes of Argentina in the early 2000s, provide one such instance when they result in takeovers of facilities and their running under self-management. The UCS work-in was a stand-alone example of this, as was the Lip clock factory work-in in France from 1973–4 and 1976–7 (see Contrepois 2013 and wikipedia entry http://en.wikipedia.org/wiki/LIP_factory).

Second, another important distinction concerns a particular spatial dimension of actions. Depending on the nature and tempo of workers' struggles, spatial forms of action can be either more or less sectional – in other words more or less generalised. So, for example, a strike can take the form of a specific group of workers acting to defend themselves or of many different groups striking together in a general or generalised strike because they have common cause. Objective material circumstances concerning the number of workers' material interests being attacked or eroded is the key but not sole variable here. Such circumstances tell us how many workers are potential strikers but it is only the state of workers' collective organisation and consciousness that will tell us whether it is probable that few or many will strike. Collective consciousness is the cognitive ability to see the issues at hand in different ways – in other words, the subjective way of seeing what appear to be the same objective conditions in different ways. It is this that determines the extent to which 'an injury to one is an injury to all' and 'unity is strength' to quote the two key dictums of the workers' movement. It was a hallmark of many struggles in the post-war period that sectionalism was dominant, particularly where unions were organised as unions of trades. More latterly, however, the decline of *trade* unions' hegemony of general and industrial unions provides the basis – subject to the influence of the dimensions of bargaining units – for more generalised actions to be taken. This is particularly so in political strikes and strikes in the public services.

Finally, the ways in which labour conflict is expressed varies considerably depending upon, inter alia, the legal regulation of industrial conflict and traditions of protest of different countries. Although convergence towards a tighter regulation of industrial and related action due to the hegemony of neo-liberalism can be detected, this is not a uniform trend in that the tightening of the regulation has taken place at different paces and in different forms. Thus, the spaces for and stimuli to industrial action continue to present evidence of difference (if not also divergence). For example, with the development of a more assertive and growing working class but no lawful right to strike and the absence of lawful independent unions, workers are liable to use rioting as a means to express grievances and seek their resolution. This has been the case in both Indonesia and China in the last 20 years, and in South Korea in a pre-ceding period. Recent rioting in European countries like Britain, France and Greece has not directly had its roots within the workplace (even if unemploy-ment was one of its causes). And, although workers rioting in Egypt has not been unknown, the same conditions as those of China and India have led to the strike becoming a major tool of the working class there (Alexander 2008, 2011, 2013). Yet, in southern European countries like France, Greece, Italy, Portugal and Spain, particular forms of more organised direct action are far more a significant part of the repertoire of contention in these countries than their northern European neighbors. Actions such as blocking motorways and railways and blockading ports and areas of public social spaces feature rela-tively frequently in these countries. This is likely to be because existing patterns of Protestant behaviour developed against authoritarian regimes and subse-quently the influential communist parties in these countries were excluded from the process of political dialogue so that they sought to mobilise workers in extra-parliamentary actions. But on top of this, there are also specific dif-ferences. For example, the extremely low level of union density in France over many years has inclined workers to use such highly visible and immediately effective tactics.

CONCLUSION

Four propositions on workers forms of labour conflict were expounded at the outset; little is fundamentally new; variations and replications take place on already established themes; minor innovation takes place within existing forms; and varying political cultures impact upon forms of labour conflict. All four were found to be supported by a transnational survey of available evi-dence. Thus, notwithstanding the methodological difficulties in researching the issues, organised labour has seldom sought to reinvent the wheel – or even develop an alternative to it. What may make forms of labour conflict look 'new' is the context, way and frequency in which they are used as well as the way in which workers use them. Thus, one of the first recorded uses of transport workers working but not collecting fares as a form of industrial action took place in the United States in the early part of the twentieth century (Kornbluth 2011). Without knowledge of that, the few cases of such action in recent times would seem to be radical innovations (particularly given their usage as part of alliances with members of the travelling public). In this sense, we are locked into both 'back to the future' and 'forward to the past'. So, but for the historical amnesia of those that report (or do not report) on these events, the historical antecedents and precedents would be far more easily seen. Yet, because of the methodological difficulties in accessing or generating reliable data on a range of different forms of workers' labour conflict over any extended or longitudinal time frame, it is hazardous to make any solid or definitive statements about the relative propensities and incidences of any or all of these means. Yet, it seems safe to conclude that workers' forms of labour conflict continue to be based, not unnaturally, on the withdrawal of willingness to work and to work as directed. But, for those concerned with the transformation of capitalism into socialism, the rare occurrence of the violation of the managerial prerogative becoming also a violation of the property rights of capital must be of concern. It is only through such a transformation that observers could legitimately talk of a qualitative change in the nature of workers' forms of labour conflict.

REFERENCES

ACAS (2010) *Riding Out The Storm: Managing Conflict in a Recession and Beyond*, Advisory, Conciliation and Arbitration Service, London.

Ackroyd, S. and Thompson, P. (1999) *Organizational Misbehaviour*, Sage, London.

Alexander, A. (2008) 'Inside Egypt's mass strikes', *International Socialism*, vol. 118, available at http://isj.org.uk/index.php4?id=428&issue=118.

Alexander, A. (2011) 'The growing social soul of Egypt's democratic revolution', *International Socialism*, vol. 131, 77–105.

Alexander, A. (2013) 'Egyptian workers rediscover the strike' in Gall, G. (ed.) *New Forms and Expressions of Conflict at Work*, Palgrave Macmillan, Basingstoke, pp. 130–51.

Bain, P. and Taylor P. (2000) 'Entrapped by the "electronic panopticon"? Worker resistance in the call centre', *New Technology, Work and Employment*, vol. 15, no. 1, 2–18.

Brown, G. (1977) *Sabotage – A Study in Industrial Conflict*, Spokesman, Nottingham.

Burawoy, M. (1979) *Manufacturing Consent: Changes in the Labour Process under Monopoly Capitalism*, University of Chicago Press, Chicago.

Cobble, D. (1991) *Dishing it Out: Waitresses and their Unions in the Twentieth Century*, University of Illinois Press, Urbana.

Communisation (2011) 'On the desperate struggles in France', available at http://thecommune.co.uk/2011/12/09/on-the-desperate-struggles-in-france/.

Contrepois, S. (2011) 'Labour struggles against mass redundancies in France: Understanding direct action', *Employee Relations*, vol. 33, no. 6, 642–53.

Contrepois, S. (2013) 'Direct action in France: A new phase in labour-capital conflict' in Gall, G. (ed.) *New Forms and Expressions of Conflict at Work*, Palgrave Macmillan, Basingstoke, pp. 152–70.

Cooke, F. (2013) 'New dynamics of industrial conflicts in China: Causes, expressions and resolution alternatives' in Gall, G. (ed.) *New Forms and Expressions of Conflict at Work*, Palgrave Macmillan, Basingstoke, pp. 108–29.

Crosby, M. (2009) 'CleanStart – fighting for a fair deal for cleaners' in Gall, G. (ed.) *The Future of Union Organising – Building for Tomorrow*, Palgrave Macmillan, Basingstoke, pp. 114–30.

Cullinane, N. And Dundon, T. (2011) 'Redundancy and workplace occupation: The case of the Republic of Ireland', *Employee Relations*, vol. 33, no. 6, 624–41.

Doucette, J. (2013) 'Minjung tactics in a post-Minjung era? The survival of self-immolation and traumatic forms of labour protest South Korea' in Gall, G. (ed.) *New Forms and Expressions of Conflict at Work*, Palgrave Macmillan, Basingstoke, pp. 212–32.

Edwards, P. (1986) *Conflict at Work – A Materialist Analysis*, Blackwell, Oxford.

Ford, M. (2013) 'Violent industrial protest in Indonesia: Cultural phenomenon or legacy of an authoritarian past?' in Gall, G. (ed.) *New Forms and Expressions of Conflict at Work*, Palgrave Macmillan, Basingstoke, pp. 171–90.

Gall, G. (1998) 'Resisting the rise of the non-union employer; the case of the press workers' *Capital and Class*, vol. 64, 43–61.

Gall, G. (2000) 'Employment relations and the labour process in the newspaper industry: Is there the potential for the return of the NUJ?', *New Technology, Work and Employment*, vol. 15, no. 2, 94–107.

Gall, G. (2006) *Sex Worker Union Organising – An International Study*, Palgrave Macmillan, Basingstoke.

Gall, G. (2010) 'Resisting recession and redundancy: Contemporary worker occupations in Britain', *Working USA: The Journal of Labour and Society*, vol. 13, no.1, 107–32.

Gall, G. (2011) 'Contemporary workplace occupations in Britain: Stimuli, dynamics and outcomes', *Employee Relations*, vol. 33, no. 6, 607–23.

Gall, G. (2012) *An Agency of Their Own – Sex Worker Union Organising*, Zero, London.

Gall, G. (2013) 'Quiescence continued? Recent strike activity in nine western European economies', *Economic and Industrial Democracy* (forthcoming), available at http://eid.sagepub.com/content/early/2012/08/30/0143831X12453956.full.pdf+html.

Gall, G. and Cohen, S. (2013) 'The collective expression of workplace grievances in Britain' in Gall, G. (ed.) *New Forms and Expressions of Conflict at Work*, Palgrave Macmillan, Basingstoke, pp. 86–107.

Gall, G. and Hebdon, R. (2008) 'Conflict at work' in Bacon, N., Blyton, P., Fiorito, J. and Heery, E. (eds) *Sage Handbook of Employment and Industrial Relations*, Sage, London, pp. 588–605.

Jefferys, S. (2011) 'Collective and individual conflicts in five European countries', *Employee Relations*, vol. 33, no. 6, 670–87.

Kabat, M. (2011) 'Argentinean worker-taken factories: Trajectories of workers' control under the economic crisis' in Ness, I. and Azzellini, D. (eds) *Ours to Master and to Own: Worker's Control from the Commune to the Present*, Haymarket Books, Chicago, pp. 365–81.

Kelly, J. (1998) *Rethinking Industrial Relations – Mobilization, Collectivism and Long Waves*, Routledge, London.

Kersley, B., Alpin, C., Forth, J., Bryson, A., Bewley, H., Dix, G., and Oxenbridge, S. (2005) *Inside the Workplace: First Findings from the 2004 Workplace Employment Relations Survey*, DTI, London.

Kornbluth, J. (2011) (ed.) *Rebel Voices: An IWW Anthology*, Merlin Press, Pontypool.

McCammon, H. (2001) 'Labour's legal mobilization: Why and when do worker file unfair labour practices?', *Work and Occupations*, vol. 28, no. 2, 143–75.

Millward, N., Bryson, A. and Forth, J. (2000) *All Change at Work? British Employment Relations 1980–1998, as Portrayed by the Workplace Industrial Relations Survey Series*, Routledge, London.

Milner, S. (1993) 'Overtime bans and strikes: Evidence on relative incidence', *Industrial Relations Journal*, vol. 24, no. 3, 201–10.

Sang-Hwan, J. (2004) 'Continuing suicide among labourers in Korea', *Labour History*, vol. 45, no. 3, 271–97.

Saria de Faria, M. and Novaes, H. (2011) 'Brazilian recovered factories: The constraints of workers' control' in Ness, I. and Azzellini, D. (eds) *Ours to Master and to Own: Worker's Control from the Commune to the Present*, Haymarket Books, Chicago, pp. 400–17.

Taylor P. and Bain P. (2001) 'Trade unions, workers' rights and the "frontier of control" in UK call centres', *Economic and Industrial Democracy*, vol. 22, no. 1, 39–66.

Taylor P. and Bain P. (2003) 'Subterranean worksick blues: Humour as subversion in two call centres', *Organization Studies*, vol. 24, no. 9, 1487–509.

Tuckman, A. (2011) 'Workers' control and the politics of factory occupation in 1970s Britain' in Ness, I. and Azzellini, D. (eds) *Ours to Master and to Own: Worker's Control from the Commune to the Present*, Haymarket Books, Chicago, pp. 284–301.

Warhurst, C. and Nickson, D. (2009) ' "Who's got the look?" From emotional to aesthetic and sexualised labour in interactive services', *Gender, Work and Organisation*, vol. 16, no. 3, 385–404.

10

LABOUR MIGRATION AND EMERGENT CLASS CONFLICT: CORPORATE NEO-LIBERALISM, WORKER MOBILITY AND LABOUR RESISTANCE IN THE US

Immanuel Ness

INTRODUCTION

The chapter examines the contemporary influence of corporate-driven migration on the US labour movement. It does so by analysing the relations between fluxes of labour migrations, corporate strategies, US government policies and trade unions and workers' responses to these. The US far and away maintains the most highly developed and largest migrant labour force in the world and might be considered a good representative example of global trends both in terms of understanding the logics behind business strategies on migration and the labour movement responses to it.

Since the inception of capitalism, migrant labour has been used by capital to undermine wages and working conditions and with this the overall mobilising capacities of workers and their class-based organisations. The function of migrant labour has been historically documented by Friedrich Engels and theorised by Karl Marx as a force that is used to expand surplus labour by reducing the cost of production (Engels 1844/2009; Marx 1867/1990). Following on from this tradition, more recently, authors such as Duménil, Lévy and Harvey, among others, argue that the instrumental and growing use of migration by global capital continue to be the main reason for the erosion of wage standards, contributing to the expansion of the reserve army of labour (Duménil and Lévy 2004; 2011; Harvey 2005). Yet literature on migration has often been ambiguous on the role of migrants within the labour movement. Some scholars view migrants as integral to advancing working-class consciousness and call traditional labour unions to a more pro-active and receptive approach in organising the newcomers. However, as labour unions have lost density and influence from the 1960s to the present, migrant labour is also frequently shunned by traditional unions as a drag on the wages of what Lenin referred to as a 'labour aristocracy'.

This ambiguity on the role of migrants within the labour movement has been further increased in the US by government's contradictory policies on immigration, which have openly favoured, depending on the economic context, only those forms of migration beneficial to the interests of corporations. In this sense while the 1980s saw a rapid expansion of undocumented migration and the flourishing of multilateral policies encouraging labour mobility across borders, more recently US legislative and corporate efforts, in an attempt to regulate labour flows for capitalist demands, have on the one hand established a system of guest workers, and on the other hand have criminalised those who entered the country without legal documentation. As a whole, these policies have weakened labour unions and working-class power. However, despite the impediments to class-based organising, migrant workers have most often engaged in self-organising to defend their interests. As labour migration grows under twenty-first-century neo-liberalism, and organising efforts expand, transnational solidarity campaigns for migrant labourers are becoming increasingly important to defend workers' interests. Established trade unions offer lukewarm support for immigrant organising. As a result, migrant workers are often even more militant than native-born workers who often do not display the same bonds of community and solidarity (Ness 2005; Nevins 2002).

Since 1990, migrant labour has emerged as a fundamental element of the global labour market; by 2010 migrant workers constituted on average about 10 per cent of all workers countries of the Global North. While labour migration is an enduring feature of capitalist production, from its origins in the mid-eighteenth century, the form that emerged in the 1990s has taken however on a new parameter of marginality and inferiority. Migrant labourers are more and more foreign labourers temporarily authorised to work in a host country with the knowledge and acquiescence of governing authorities. In Europe and North America, as well as Oceania, employers 'restructure' industries by recruiting migrant workers for skilled and unskilled jobs.

These workers sign contracts with specific companies before migrating temporarily to more developed countries to perform restricted jobs for a fixed duration of time. Because of the nature of their contracts, these migrants face a number of unique challenges, including confinement to one employer, onerous work arrangements, withholding of wages, and lack of access to national employment regulations governing minimum wage and hour standards. Why do so many migrant workers participate in such an exploitive system? Simply put, as economic conditions worsen, workers desperately seek foreign jobs in the Global North as a means to provide for their families and communities through remittances for basic needs such as food, housing, and education. As these guest programmes expand, new migrant workers inevitably form part of the subaltern underside of the Global North labour markets as these are transformed through the expanding use of foreign temporary workers.

While wages and conditions of work contrast significantly, both highly skilled and unskilled temporary workers occupy essential spaces in the labour market but without the prospect of establishing a foundation of power and support, as they have no permanency and are almost always sent home upon completion of their assignments. In a range of occupations, from Internet technology, business services and nursing, to welding, construction and hospitality, countries in the Global North are permitting private businesses to fill positions once held by native-born and immigrant workers with guest workers. In the US, for example, the federal government only requires that the employer 'prove' that either (a) there are no American workers willing to fill the position or (b) there are no American workers trained and qualified to do the particular job. In the US from 1990 to 2005, undocumented migration served the interest of capital, by restricting migrant workers legal rights and permitting primarily Mexican workers entry into the country. More recently, the same targets have been achieved by creating an authorised category of foreign workers and by easing the ability for Mexican workers to illegally cross the border into the US. The overall results of these policies have been that wage demands were dampened among US workers, who were forced to accede to wage cuts or job loss (Fine 2005; Gordon 2007; Milkman 2006; Ness 2005, 2011; Moody 1997; Standing 2011).

The chapter is divided into three main sections. The first focuses on the competing social and political forces in the evolution of US and global guest worker programmes; the second, taking the US as its case, explores the significance of the shift towards temporary labour migration in place of formal immigration and settlement programmes traditionally favoured by capital; the third analyses guest workers' responses.

GLOBAL MIGRATION, US POLICY AND NEO-LIBERALISM

Today the World Bank and international development agencies are turning away from the substandard and ecologically hazardous development policies of the 1960s to 1980s which invested in the economic infrastructure of the Global South and instead they are advocating policies that create poverty and force workers to migrate abroad in order to survive, and produce major sources of revenue through remittances. The World Bank indeed considers remittances essential components of advancing national development and reducing poverty. They finance education and health expenses and provide capital for small entrepreneurs. In Sri Lanka, the birth weight of children in remittance recipient households is higher than that of the children of other households. In countries such as Tajikistan, Tonga, Nepal, Honduras, and Moldova, remittances can be 40 per cent of GDP or even higher. In countries affected by crisis or natural disasters, say in Somalia or Haiti, remittances provide a lifeline to the poor (Ratha 2008).

The neo-liberal capitalist propaganda machine, dominated by the US government and the media greatly exaggerates and overstates foreigners' conviction that they will improve their living standard by working abroad. To be sure, labouring in the hub of the empire might provide help to some workers, but in the unlikely event that economic conditions improve most migrants expect to return to their home countries. Why must global capitalists push, pull, shove or force migrant workers to travel to the Global North just for economic sustenance? Most unauthorised migrants do not enthusiastically accept migration (Bacon 2008; McAdam 2012). Unlike some guest workers, the decision to migrate without authorisation does not represent a significant advance in wages but an economic necessity. Migrants risk life and limb in exchange for a job with low pay, low status and a consequent lack of voice. It is not the job that degrades the worker but, rather, the powerless and poor conditions under which they labour.

The US is leading the way in hiring foreign contract workers en masse even before it negotiates a new General Agreement on Tariffs and Trade (GATT) treaty through the World Trade Organization (WTO), where widening the market for global service workers is negotiated and ratified. The insatiable urge of policymakers is to ease the way for corporations to create a new body of contract workers unprotected by US labour laws, and thus unable to organise into unions or to protest wages and conditions, an attitude punishable by deportation. The US is at the forefront of negotiations with the WTO to do away with trade barriers that impede importing and exporting professional and unskilled labour through the General Agreement on Trade and Services Mode Four–GATS-4 (hereafter GATS-4) (Bhagwati, Panagariya, Srinivasan 2004; Maimbo and Ratha 2005; Mattoo and Carzaniga 2003).

Even while actively negotiating a global labour migration agreement, right-wing governments find that foreign workers are useful scapegoats that allow them to garner votes from workers fearing job loss. In 2006, US president George W. Bush sent 6,000 troops to the US border with Mexico followed by the building of a barrier between the US and Mexico in order to show that he was tough on undocumented immigration, and to deflect working-class attention from his 2007 plan to reform immigration through expanding guest work programmes. The policies were a delusion intended to neutralise right-wing, populist, xenophobic policy-makers who sought to gain traction with primarily white workers who had been dissuaded from countering avaricious multi-national corporations through organising resistance. Therefore, some US workers are easily convinced that foreign workers and the relocation of industry are leading sources of unemployment. Barack Obama followed with an extension of migration controls and detentions for unauthorised workers.

Both liberal and conservative politicians who benefit from foreign labour conveniently blame undocumented migrant workers for taking away jobs, even if those very same officials are actively establishing and advancing guest worker programmes to promote business interests in their states and districts. The corporate-dominated mass media in the US and Europe do not consider inequality and immiseration caused by the imposition of neo-liberal policies in the South as triggers for the growing migration of impoverished workers and peasants (Dobbs 2004; Faux 2006; Ginsborg 2005). Overall, corporations have always supported unregulated migration in the US, so Congress and the president must walk a thin line to create the popular false impression that they are restricting immigration, while responding to business demands for cheap foreign labour. For example, relaxing restrictions on immigration almost immediately after the elections, as it happened in November 1990 (USCIS 2010b).

Much of the present debate in the US on immigration policy revolves around the failure and unintended consequences of utterly inconsistent government policies to establish and regulate the flow of authorised and unauthorised migrants. Ineffectual regulatory policies have bifurcated migrant workers into two groups – undocumented labourers and guest workers. Focusing on guest workers rather than on undocumented labourers foreshadows the potential prospects and pitfalls of the programme for foreign workers as well as US nationals, and the potential influence of such a programme on the broader labour movement. This chapter shows that if government and corporate efforts to replace undocumented labourers with an established guest worker labour force succeed, conditions for all workers will significantly diminish.

However, as we have seen in past immigration bills, government programmes are plagued with uncertainty and doubt. Can the government seriously address the status of the more than 12 million undocumented migrants living in the US that most employers welcome in flagrant defiance of the 1986 immigration law? Since 2000, the AFL-CIO and most major unions adopted a policy for repeal of this immigration law, which sanctions 'employers who knowingly hire undocumented workers' (USCIS 2010). But if a new comprehensive bill is enacted repealing the most harmful provisions of existing law for undocumented immigrants, most proposals have called on a new guest worker law that will institutionally marginalise temporary workers. Furthermore, if the new legislation moves most undocumented workers into a guest worker programme, many unions that have grown by organising low-wage service workers conceivably could suffer significant loss in membership.

Global advocates for expanding migration by temporarily hiring guest workers do not make known the way that the decline of education programmes in destination countries plays a part in the shortage of nurses, IT professionals, engineers, and even truckers. If we are witnessing a severe shortage in high-technology jobs, why are more and more employers cutting jobs that pay decent wages and reconstituting them as low-wage employment? Essentially, we are witnessing the comprehensive erosion of the employer–employee compromise that survived from the mid-1930s to the early 1980s providing for decent wages, unemployment insurance, social security, pensions and social welfare benefits. That relationship is rooted in the class compromise of the New Deal in the 1930s, which frequently obligated US employers to continue to retain workers even if business slowed, and that also provided health and pension benefits to workers through the workplace (Faux 2006; Piven and Cloward 1993; Uchitelle 2006).

The erosion of wages and working conditions through guest work in the private sector is part of a much broader dynamic of the neo-liberal era that extends beyond immigration and guest work. The new assault on workers' rights is an essential part of a corporate effort to expand surplus value through the process of production. An extensive examination of management and business publications by Boltanski and Chiapello (2007) show that US and European employers have shifted emphasis from traditional forms of production to extraction of profits from independent workers, who have few or no ties to corporations. These independent workers are essentially self-employed and thus responsible for their own health insurance and for paying their own taxes. Thus, they are technically independent, but that is not always necessarily a positive situation. Guest work might be seen in a similar light and certainly as part of a broader strategy by capitalists to undermine wages and conditions on the job.

A new migration policy must be developed that addresses the authentic reality of the dramatic growth of foreign migration to the US in the neo-liberal era. The failure to develop a consistent migration policy over the past 25 years in part is an extension of the enduring conflict between capital and labour. The weakening of the institutional and economic power of organised labour has contributed to growing nativist sentiment that ironically prevents capital from permitting unfettered migration. The growth of nativism obstructs comprehensive immigration reform that would legalise undocumented immigrants.

THE BOOM IN TRADING WORKERS

Since the proliferation of market reforms in the late 1970s, global barriers to trade liberalisation have been systematically demolished. Finance capitalists and business support the de-territorialisation of work but not the free movement of workers. In the meantime, the global market economy resembles a Lego building under construction to prevent the resurgence of social protections. The new wall of the building replacing government protections is a sturdy and essential component of market liberalisation, one that expands trade in goods and services to promote the trade in workers between countries, without offering genuine worker mobility and rights. Resistance to the neo-liberal programme will build a wall around any country that seeks to moderate the market. The trade in labour – as opposed to the free movement of workers – is the next round of negotiations under a (GATS-4) that will from time to time fill spot shortages in skilled and unskilled labour that supporters believe are inevitable in the global trade regime. In contrast to the European Union, where workers in the region may migrate freely, GATS-4 will not mandate lifting restrictions on the mobility of workers in North American Free Trade Agreement (NAFTA) and other regional trade blocks. Thus, rather than employing workers, GATS-4 will allow General Motors, for example, to contract workers from the Global South to fill spot shortages at significantly lower costs than full-time workers and without the obligation to pay for healthcare, unemployment insurance, pension benefits, or even workers' compensation.

A completely new perspective is emerging among corporate and government managers in the Global South. In the 1970s and 1980s, national leaders viewed relocating skilled labour from the South to the North as a *brain drain* that deprived developing nations of professional workers, a resource that would otherwise improve their standard of living. Now, China, India, the Philippines, and countries of the Caribbean Basin view workers as profitable commodities for export to the Global North. In the early 1970s, Arghiri Emmanuel saw workers as an international commodity only protected by the power vested in national unions in his conceptualisation of *unequal exchange* (1972). Today, corporate and government leaders promote labour as an export component in the creation of capital through foreign remittances, and potentially a source of good will that will encourage multi-nationals to relocate subsidiaries to their countries.

We are observing that the economic standards of the majority of workers in the Global South is warping through exporting services to the North as new development policies direct disproportionate funding to IT, business services and nursing, as well as infrastructure, construction, hospitality, and other services for global exports, ignoring other key components of their burgeoning economies. Ostensibly, in GATS mode 4 negotiations over the expansion of service guest work, the WTO is arguing that temporary labour migration is as vital to developing countries' economic growth as goods and services are to advanced economies. Explicitly, the Global South considers the expansion in the movement of people from poor to advanced countries to perform services an important source of exports and revenue (Mattoo and Carzaniga 2003, 1–19).

THE RISE OF TEMPORARY LABOUR MIGRATION IN THE US

Essential to the growth of temporary work under advanced capitalism is a dialectical relationship between capital and labour. Capital almost always requests open migration to enlarge the reserve army of labour and increase competition with native-born workers as a means to lower wages and job standards. In opposition, organised and unorganised labour has historically opposed new immigrants entering labour markets to compete for jobs at lower wages. As largely unregulated migration to the US since the late 1980s to the first decade of the early twentieth century has expanded the immigrant working-class, labour unions have sought to restrict migration to shield native-born workers who are most vulnerable to labour migration.

US immigration policy plays an important role in this story. The US policy toward migrant labour is a politically sensitive issue for policy-makers. Since the passage of the 1965 Immigration Act, the political debate in the US has shifted from ensuring the rights of foreigners from formerly excluded regions of the Global South to training a US workforce equipped for the new neo-liberal economy. Neo-liberalism is set apart from preceding eras of capitalism, as it promotes free trade and deregulation as well as accentuates financialisation and privatisation at great cost to workers and the environment throughout the world (Duménil and Lévy 2004). As more workers have migrated to the United States from 1986 to 2010, immigration policy has become a significant arena of political struggle between supporters and opponents of restrictions on the flow of foreign labourers.

The passage of the Immigration Reform and Control Act (IRCA) in 1986 and the implementation of the NAFTA were decisive in greatly expanding the unauthorised entry of migrant workers in the US. These workers were compelled by large and small employers to work for significantly lower than prevailing wages. As a result, by the late-1990s, a growing number of capitalist labour markets that once provided decent employment and wages had been eviscerated through outsourcing and insourcing of documented and undocumented labour. Central to the 1986 act are provisions that use employer sanctions to ban businesses from hiring immigrants deemed illegal, a stipulation that was requested by organised labour in the US. However, federal and state authorities did not generally enforce these provisions from the time of the law's passage until the draconian enforcement Immigration and Customs Enforcement (ICE) raids began in 2005–06. As a result, the pace of migration has accelerated even more rapidly in the ensuing two decades, as undocumented workers have inundated old and new labour markets, creating an oversupply of low-wage labour in a growing number of manufacturing, service and agricultural industries.

In 2000, responding to the dramatic growth of mostly undocumented workers in the US in large labour markets, the AFL-CIO, spurred by service sector unions, initiated a dramatic policy shift. They began calling for repeal of the 1986 immigration law that uses 'employer sanctions' to penalise employers who hire undocumented workers. This meant that the same labour unions that had supported the sanctions began requesting that the government not enforce the legislation. On balance, employers were rarely, if ever, penalised for hiring undocumented immigrants anyway, and employer sanctions had only served as a means for employers to evade unionisation by threatening immigrant workers who sought to organise. Realising this, unions re-evaluated their stance and started undertaking efforts to facilitate the organisation of immigrant workers. From 1995 to 2005, organising campaigns contributed to increasing wages, often above the minimum, and improved conditions in labour-market niches where immigrants were employed. In the late 1990s, more labour unions sought the re-organisation of growing industries where membership nearly vanished, including building services, hotels and restaurants, food and retail trade, security, along with the rapidly growing healthcare sector.

Employers were not so enthusiastic. The unions were trying to find a way to circumvent corporate efforts to keep wages for undocumented workers in check through threats and coercion. Seeing their grip on immigrant workers loosening, employers responded by calling for expansion of temporary worker programmes.

Supporters of businesses engaged in contracting temporary workers contend that a comprehensive programme of legal migration is necessary to bolster the economy, filling a shortage of professional workers in modern industry and providing a pool of low-wage workers for menial jobs that US workers do not want. Corporate advocates for formal guest work programmes see new migrants as essential to expanding profitability through replacing higher-wage workers in the labour markets. Many of these occupations once provided decent wages to US workers but were re-organised by business officials and transformed into low-wage migrant labour markets. Once migrant workers move into the jobs they remain solidly working class – only as temporary workers, their capacity to organise is severely compromised. When workers do engage in collective action, owners frequently dismiss and deport them (Ness 2005). While labour shortages have not directly compelled the US government to allow more migrants, it is undeniable that a whole range of formerly 'good' jobs in once solidly working-class industries that were organised by unions – such as hospitality, building services, retail services, food processing, and transportation – are now filled by guest workers and undocumented migrants at lower wages and drastically inferior working conditions. By organising new immigrant workers who were part of the fabric of major communities throughout the US, unions sought to improve wages and conditions in a range of labour markets. Organising immigrant workers would reduce the incentive for employers to hire foreigners and, in so doing, raise standards for US-born workers as well.

A new configuration of industry has transformed the traditional institutional forms of labour organisation that took shape through the industrial unions established from the 1920s through the 1950s. The institutional form of labour–management relations, based on recognition and collective bargaining, is inadequate for today's migrant labour force, because it does not facilitate new forms of labour activism leading to improved conditions. At the same time corporate propaganda creates a great deal of anxiety and distress among US workers by making them believe that they will lose even their poor jobs if they protest.

Further complicating this already bleak situation, over the past two decades the extraordinary growth of documented and undocumented migrant labour has transformed state and national labour regulatory systems, thereby creating new challenges for workers and their unions in maintaining wages and labour standards. In some cases, migrant labourers have replaced workers and their unions throughout entire labour markets. The demand to expand and institutionalise migrant labour systems will further erode the capacity of unions to organise workers typically employed for foreign contractors in professional and less-skilled labour markets. Simultaneously, efforts to enlarge the migrant labour programmes leave immigrants themselves defenceless against corporate despotism. In the new global labour commodity chain, migrants in a growing number of service industries are considered factors of production to be dispensed with when no longer considered necessary (Gereffi and Korzeniewicz 1993).[1]

DOES THE GLOBAL NORTH NEED FOREIGN MIGRATION?

Western Europe and the US had been hastily expanding low-wage and flexible labour migration even before completing negotiations aimed at ratifying an international agreement on migration by the WTO framework that regulates global trade. Prospects for a massive non-immigrant labour force in the developed world through temporary worker visas will surely further erode labour power as corporations assert an inability to find workers at home for more and more jobs – or maintain that native-born workers are disinterested in working them. Such a policy will undercut native-born and migrant workers, and intensify poverty in emerging capitalist countries in the Global South.

The prevailing assertion on work shortages in the labour policy and human resources literature that predominates in Western Europe and the US is contradictory. On the one hand, supporters of expanding migrant labour contend there is a shortage of workers in the Global North. Further, they argue that fewer students are graduating from higher-skilled professions, contributing to the need for expanding legal temporary labour programmes from the Global

South. For instance, India and the Philippines train significantly higher levels of Internet technology workers and nurses than in North America. In the Philippines, government provides training in skills specifically for those planning to work abroad, rather than those seeking to stay (Rodriguez 2010, 32–9). Conversely, other writers argue that the US has a labour shortage of unskilled service and even manufacturing workers in a range of industries. Due to the shortage in skilled and unskilled labour, the United States must reluctantly recruit skilled workers from abroad to meet the demands of high technology and business services on the one hand and hospitality workers on the other (Friedman 2005; Levy and Murnane 2004; National Research Council 2001; Papademetriou and Yale-Loehr 1996; Saxenian 2006). In some instances, advocates of expanded migration concurrently assert both opposing perspectives (Jacoby 2006). Since the world financial meltdown, academic discourse on labour shortages has declined dramatically, even if corporate business lobbies continue to argue that there is a pressing need for foreign labour, and labour contractors continue to press businesses to replace existing workers with foreign labour, especially in the hospitality and tourism industry (Chase 2009).

A large and growing concern among these academics and policy-makers is that the American labour force may not be prepared to compete with equally skilled foreign workers willing to work at lower wages for longer hours. This chapter challenges the predominant view that an expanding global skilled labour market represents a threat to American dominance in new technological development, but suggests, rather, that capital's search for profit directs government efforts to expand guest worker programmes that will diminish wages in new labour markets.

Finance capital and business have historically engaged in an open strategy to downgrade worker standards in a range of occupational labour markets. Large multi-national corporations with no demonstrated interest in educating workers in the Global North argue that they are facing a critical crisis of engineers, medical workers and highly skilled professional workers. For example, proponents in the US argue that they have too few high-technology workers; the primary cause is the nation's failure to promote education and training in new and emerging sectors. While professional training institutions have declined in the US since the 1990s, over the past two decades, native-born skilled workers have been replaced by migrant workers to fill skilled positions at lower cost. As Grace Chang contends:

> immigration from the Third World into the United States doesn't just happen in response (4) to a set of factors but is carefully orchestrated – that is, desired,

planned, compelled, managed, accelerated, slowed, and periodically stopped – by the direct actions of US interests, including the government as state and as employer, private employers, and corporations.

(Chang 2000: 3–4)

In Western Europe, Canada, and Oceania, migration laws have been enacted from 2000 to 2010 to regulate border crossings in accordance with the needs of capital with minimal participation of organised labour. In the US similar legislation has not been enacted due to political polarisation and the growth of nativist sentiment that seeks to curb foreign workers. Business and capital in the US prefer unregulated migration to a comprehensive reform that would limit the supply of foreign labour that is instrumental in keeping production and service costs low. Consequently, business operates through undocumented workers who are trafficked illegally across the US border and guest work programmes that are supported by federal elected officials. Thus, both undocumented migration and guest worker programmes are essentially a means to enlarge the reserve army of labour, and used as a means of expanding profits in both skilled and less-skilled occupations through exploiting foreign workers (Gonzalez 2006; Mandel 1995; Vogel 2006).

In the 1990s and 2000s, with attention drawn to the outsourcing of manufacturing jobs to the Global South, the growth of skilled guest workers in the IT sector went largely unnoticed, below the radar screen of public scrutiny. New skilled and unskilled immigrants, conventionally portrayed as assiduous and eager to work long hours at low pay, have entered an array of industries, which are often dominated by low-wage US-born workers. In reality the plan is to further reduce wages and working conditions. Academic and popular discourse suggests that these foreign labourers are working in low-wage unskilled menial jobs in the service economy that have been vacated by US workers without taking into consideration the fact that many workers have been forced out by the replacement of US-born workers with foreign-born workers on local, regional, and national levels. For example, many unionised African–Americans labouring in the public sector, building services, hospitality, and other industries were replaced by even lower-wage foreign labour.

Federal lawmakers have expanded guest worker programmes in the United States in ways that allow them to control the flow and restrict the rights of these workers. The US system of guest work programmes are divided into three general types: (1) seasonal agricultural labourers; (2) low-wage service and manual labour in hospitality, construction and welding; (3) highlyskilled labour in business services, Internet technology and engineering. Such government programmes, if implemented widely, as conceived by congressional legislation and broadly supported by both the Democratic and Republican parties, could create an international contingent of temporary and seasonal migrant labour that will come and go to the Global North, as multinational corporations need them. This scheme could trigger a downward spiral in labour rights throughout the world.

TEMPORARY WORKERS: ORGANISING AND GLOBAL LABOUR SOLIDARITY

Recent evidence disproves the thesis that migrant workers are less likely to organise into workers' organisations than native-born workers. The scale of migration to the US from Mexico and Central America and entry into traditionally low-wage jobs has contributed to greater trade union recognition of the necessity to consolidate the power of immigrants into unions (Bacon 2008; Milkman 2006; Ness 2005). These unions include the Service Employees' International Union (SEIU) which represents hospital and healthcare workers, UNITE-HERE, the hotel, restaurant and hospitality worker union; LIUNA (Labourers International Union of North America, representing construction workers; and UFCW (United Food and Commercial Workers), representing workers in food markets and retail establishments. While workers seek representation, the traditional structures of US labour law inhibit immigrant worker efforts to organise unions. Despite this restrictive legislation, migrant workers in the US have engaged in significant self-activity and protests to convey their aspiration to organise and improve their wages and working conditions. In the winter and spring of 2006, millions of immigrants participated in demonstrations for legal status and equal rights, culminating on 1 May, when 1.5 million workers engaged in a one-day general strike throughout the US. Migrant workers in and out of trade unions walked off the job to publicly protest against discrimination and inequality in US workplaces and civil society. The Mayday general strike and protests revealed the high level of organising within migrant communities that contributed to the revival of Mayday as the official labour holiday of all workers in the US. The major demand was for legislative immigration reform that would legalise 12 to 14 million undocumented immigrants residing and working in the country but protests and manifestation also helped to raise the voice of workers over their wages and working conditions (Archibold 2006).

The remarkable general strike exposed the high level of organisation within immigrant communities throughout the US and the inadequacy of traditional labour unions to mobilise workers outside their unions due to employer and government opposition. Subsequently, even as the US government has engaged in mass deportations of undocumented workers, migrant workers have become emboldened to form organisations with the support of local community groups to defend their interests through autonomous and traditional labour unions. Most notably, from 3 to 8 December 2008, more than 200 mostly immigrant manufacturing workers who were members of United Electrical Workers UE Local 1110, a militant rank-and-file union, went on a sit-down strike at the Republic Window and Door factory in Chicago after the company declared bankruptcy, demanding payment of back wages and the re-opening of the plant (Lydersen 2009: 38–42). The workers gained back-pay and the plant was purchased by Serious Materials and re-opened until 2013, when the firm planned on closing the factory again. On 23 February 2012 workers again staged a sit-down strike against the shutdown. In the fall of 2013, with the support of the UE and co-operative funders, the workers formed a unionised co-operative.

Guest workers have also self-organised to improve their status and working conditions. In the spring of 2008, some 500 Indian guest workers employed at Signal International, an oil services company in Pascagoula, Mississippi, staged a sit-down strike claiming poor conditions that were equivalent to indentured servitude. The workers, mostly welders, gained support from Indian and US workers and organisers who engaged in sympathy hunger strikes in December 2008 to support the workers who paid contractors to work for Signal at a higher rate of pay (Ness 2011). The workers gained support from the Southern Poverty Law Center and the newly formed New Orleans Workers Center for Racial Justice (NOWCRJ). In 2011, NOWCRJ helped form the Guestworker Alliance as a national organisation to represent and defend US guest workers. The organisation represents workers throughout the economy, including workers employed at a Louisiana seafood processor for Walmart, who successfully struck against the contractor for improved wages and working conditions in October 2012.The strike by temporary guest workers was followed by walkouts of workers at Walmart warehouses and superstores, in protest over low wages, poor conditions, and employer intimidation (Eidelson 2012). As migrant organising increases, the significance of transnational solidarity has become crucial. Increasingly segments of foreign labour movements from Mexico, India and elsewhere are supporting migrant workers through solidarity activities.

To argue that guest workers are not to be permitted to stay in the US like other immigrants, while at the same time embracing undocumented workers – as many unions have until August 2009 – was a contradictory pathway to the further diminution of organised labour. While the AFL-CIO union federation has taken a clear position opposing guest worker programmes that create a subordinate class of 'indentured servants', some unions have not unambiguously opposed the plan (AFL-CIO 2009). This chapter argues that organised labour and the working class must advance a policy that defends both undocumented labourers and guest workers to resist corporate exploitation through developing alliances with progressive unions and labour movements in poor countries.

The Farm Labour Organizing Committee (FLOC), an AFL-CIO affiliate, offers a good case study of a possible solution for transnational migrants. This union is negotiating with agri-business in the US to establish standards for guest workers who otherwise do not have the right to organise to defend their interests. In September 2004 FLOC reached a precedent-setting agreement with the North Carolina Growers Association to unionise 8,000 guest workers, ending a five-year boycott against Mt. Olive products. The success of FLOC in unionising contract agricultural workers in North Carolina in the early 2000s stems from a dedicated policy of organising workers both in the US and Mexico. The initial victory of FLOC demonstrates that a more militant and anti-racist labour movement is capable of resisting draconian capitalist labour-migration programmes (Gordon 2007; Hill 2008; Smith-Nonini 2009).

As a consequence, migrant workers have tended to join workers' centres that seek to represent workers in back wage claims in specific industries and locations (Jayaraman and Ness 2005; Fine 2005). But workers' centres do not build lasting union organisations among taxi drivers, restaurants, domestic workers, as well as guest workers employed in agriculture, fisheries and hospitality industries, and day labourers, typically in construction. Consequently, some have transformed into unions that have gained status with official labour bodies on the local, state and federal level. In June 2010, the new labour organisations organised into the Excluded Workers Congress (EWC) at the US Social Forum, the EWC seeks to organise immigrant and native-born workers in low-wage industries who are seeking improved wages and working conditions, but have been largely ignored by traditional unions (Harvey 2012). However, in many instances, the power and effectiveness of these labour organisations representing low-wage precarious workers remains untested and dependent on support from non-profits or traditional labour unions.

CONCLUSIONS

Labour unions must form to consolidate the power of migrant working-class militancy. Most migrant worker resistance on the job is sporadic and unsystematic, as in the case of Republic Window and Door, Signal International and Walmart and, while frequently not publicised, they are gaining greater national attention as the economic crisis deepens. While hospitals and educational institutions in the US resist unionisation, some labour organisations are compelling foreign labour contractors to ensure that temporary workers join their unions with identical wages and benefits. But these superficial organising victories must be expanded in order to address the needs of the broader working class in the Global North and South. Now that capital is increasingly integrating globally, US unions must formalise a system of standardised wages, benefits and conditions, and engage in cross-border organising to advance the standards of workers throughout the world (Gordon 2007).

But business is using prospects for guest worker programmes to do away with decent – and in some cases prestigious – jobs and as a means of supplying a steady source of highly competent skilled IT workers and low-wage labourers working in the US hospitality industry. The corporate frenzy to restructure the workplace to reduce prevailing standards will not stop without a vigorous challenge from a new labour movement that transforms into a social movement capable of pushing government and business to advance the wages and human rights of working people in the US and throughout the world.

While the International Trade Union Confederation (ITUC) has initiated more expansive efforts to defend migrant labourers, as an ossified organisation representing general union federations, most of its proclamations are formalities. The human rights route through the International Labour Organization (ILO) has also fallen short of passing resolutions acceptable to the US. ILO conventions on the rights of workers are a step in the right direction, but without a base rooted in labour, they are unlikely to expand the rights of workers. Similarly, efforts by university students to eliminate sweatshops globally may represent a model for the treatment of guest workers. However earnest the efforts of activist organisations, for example, Jobs with Justice, and United Students against Sweatshops (USAS), little will become of their endeavours without sustained union support (Ansley 2008; Featherstone 2002; Kabeer 2004).

The expansion of a larger temporary worker programme, a fait accompli for international corporations, inauspiciously inaugurates a new era in US labour policy that transforms workers into disposable commodities and disciplines them by establishing new laws to facilitate temporary migration. On a global basis, The WTO has yet to enact a global labour trade accord for workers, but the US is the world's leader in promoting foreign labour through formal guest worker programmes that are viewed as the wave of the future.

To respond effectively to a capitalist offensive against the labouring classes on a global scale, the workers and poor must win tangible organising victories and must unify across borders by struggling for the right to join unions. Many foreign manufacturing jobs pay poverty wages even by the standards of the Global South (Elliott and Freeman 2003). Therefore, for an accurate understanding of the shortage of workers, we must follow the *job* and not the *worker* in order to assess the degree to which decent-paying jobs in the US and Europe are transforming into poverty-wage jobs in the Global South. Due to restrictions imposed on temporary workers, and employers' efforts to circumvent laws that seek to equalise wages among immigrant and US-born workers, guest workers may be among the least-protected workers in the nation. This chapter thus maintains that organising guest workers into labour unions would help to staunch the decline in worker power in the Global North and throughout the world. However, the potential of the power of migrant workers must also take into account the fact that conditions are declining for all workers. As such, native-born and migrant workers must strive toward a revolutionary transformation of capitalist society that is necessary to appreciably transform the dynamic of labour exploitation.

NOTE

1. Gereffi and Korzeniewicz (1993) examine the emergence and growth of the service sector commodity chain in the international economy and its effect on national economies (see Essay 6, pp. 123–42).

REFERENCES

AFL-CIO (XXXX). 2009. RESOLUTION 11: 'The Labour Movement's principles for comprehensive immigration reform'. Available at: http://www.aflcio.org/aboutus/thisistheaflcio/convention/2009/upload/res_11.pdf. Accessed 3 December 2009.

Ansley, Frances. 2008. 'Doing policy from below: Worker solidarity and the prospects for immigration reform', *Cornell International Law Journal*, vol. 41, 102–14.

Archibold, Randal. 2006. *Immigrants Take to the U.S. Streets in Show of Strength. New York Times*. 2 May, 2. P. A1.

Bacon, David. 2008. *Illegal People: How Globalization Creates Migration and Criminalizes Immigrants*. Boston: Beacon Press.

Bhagwati, Jagdish, Panagariya, Arvind, Srinivasan, T.N. 2004. 'The muddles over outsourcing', *Journal of Economic Perspectives*, vol. 18, no. 4, Fall, 93–114.

Boltanski, Luc and Chiapello, Eve. 2007. *The New Spirit of Capitalism*. London: Verso.

Chang, G. 2000 *Disposable Domestics: Immigrant Women Workers in the Global Economy*. Cambridge, MA: South End Press.

Chase, Katie Johnston. 2009. 'Hundreds attend rally for fired Hyatt housekeepers: Politicians urge boycott of the hotel', *Boston Globe*. 18 September.

Cornelius, Wayne A. and Lewis, Jessa M. (eds). 2006. *Impacts of Border Enforcement on Mexican Migration: A View from Sending Countries*. Boulder, CO: Lynne Rienner.

Dobbs, Lou. 2004. *Exporting America: Why Corporate Greed is Shipping American Jobs Overseas*. New York: Warner Books.

Duménil, Gérard and Lévy, Dominique. 2004. *Capital Resurgent: Roots of the Neoliberal Revolution*. Cambridge, MA: Harvard University Press.

——. 2011. *The Crisis of Neoliberalism*. Cambridge, MA: Harvard University Press.

Eidelson, Josh. 2012. 'Guest workers who sparked June Walmart supplier walk-out hail strike wave's spread', *The Nation*. 30 November. Website accessed 11 August 2013.

Elliott, Kimberly Ann, and Freeman, Richard B. 2003. *Can Labour Standards Improve Under Globalization?* Washington, DC: Institute for International Economics.

Emmanuel, Arghiri. 1972. *Unequal Exchange: A Study of the Imperialism of Trade*. New York: Monthly Review Press.

Engels, Frederich. 1844/2009. *The Condition of the Working Class in England*. New York: Oxford University Press.

Faux, Jeff. 2006. *The Global Class War: How America's Bipartisan Elite Lost our Future – and What it Will Take to Win it Back*. Hoboken, NJ: Wiley.

Featherstone, Liza. 2002. *Students Against Sweatshops*. London and New York: Verso.

Fine, Janice. 2005. *Workers Centers: Organizing Communities at the Edge of the Dream*. Ithaca, NY: Cornell University Press.

Friedman, Thomas. 2005. *The World is Flat: A Brief History of the Twenty-first Century*. New York: Farrar, Straus, Giroux.

Gereffi, Gary and Korzeniewicz, Miguel (eds). 1993. *Commodity Chains and Global Capitalism*. Westport, CT: Greenwood Publishing Company.

Ginsborg, Paul. 2005. *Silvia Berlusconi: Television, Power and Patrimony*. London: Verso.

Gonzalez, Gilbert. 2006. *Guest Workers or Colonized Labour? Mexican Labour Migration to the United States*. Boulder, Colorado: Paradigm Publishers.

Gordon, Jennifer. 2007. 'Transnational labour citizenship', *University of Southern California Law Review*, vol. 80, 508–87

Harvey, David. 2005. *A Brief History of Neoliberalism*. New York: Oxford University Press.

——. 2012. *Rebel Cities: From the Right to the City to the Urban Revolution*. New York: Verso.

Hill, Jennifer. 2008. 'Binational guestworker unions: Moving guestworkers into the house of labour', *Fordham Urban Law Journal*, vol. 35, 307–48.

Jacoby, Tamar. 2006. ' "Guest workers" won't work: A path to permanent citizenship would benefit everyone', *The Washington Post,* 26 March, p. B7.

Jayaraman, Sarumathi and Ness, Immanuel. 2005. *The New Urban Immigrant Workforce: Innovative Models for Labour Organizing*. Armonk, NY: M.E. Sharpe Publisher.

Kabeer, Naila. 2004. 'Globalization, labour standards, and women's rights: Dilemmas of collective (in)action in an interdependent world', *Feminist Economics*, vol. 10, no. 1, March, 3–35.

Levy, Frank and Murnane, Richard J. 2004. *The New Division of Labour: How Computers Are Creating the Next Job Market*. Princeton: Princeton University Press.

Lydersen, Kari. 2009. *Revolt on Goose Island: The Chicago Factory Takeover and What it says about the Economic Crisis*. Brooklyn, NY: Melville House.

Maimbo, Samuel Munzele and Ratha, Dilip. 2005. *Remittances: Development Impact and Future Prospects*. Washington: The World Bank.

Mandel, Ernest. 1995. *Long Waves of Capitalist Development: A Marxist Interpretation* (revised edn). London: Verso.

Marx, K. 1867/1990. *Capital: A Critique of Political Economy* (Volume I). New York: Penguin Books.

Mattoo, A. and Carzaniga, A. 2003. *Moving People to Deliver Services*. Washington, DC: World Bank/Oxford University Press.

McAdam, Jane. 2012. *Climate Change, Forced Migration, and International Law*. Oxford: Oxford University Press.

Milkman, Ruth. 2006. *L.A. Story: Immigrant Workers and the Future of the U.S. Labour Movement*. New York: Russell Sage Foundation.

Moody, Kim 1997. *Workers in a Lean World: Unions in the International Economy*. New York: Verso.

National Research Council. 2001. *Building a Workforce for the Information Economy*. Washington, DC: National Academy Press.

Ness, Immanuel. 2005. *Immigrants, Unions and the New U.S. Labour Market*. Philadelphia: Temple University Press.

———. 2011. *Guest Workers and Resistance to U.S. Corporate Despotism*. Urbana/Chicago: University of Illinois Press.

Nevins, Joseph. 2002. *Operation Gatekeeper: The Rise of the 'Illegal Alien' and the Making of the U.S.–Mexico Boundary*. New York: Routledge.

Papademetriou, Demetrios G., and Yale-Loehr, Stephen. 1996. *Balancing Interests: Rethinking U.S. Selection of Skilled Immigrants*. New York: International Migration Policy Program of the Carnegie Endowment for International Peace.

Piven, Frances Fox and Cloward, Richard A. (2000). 'Power repertoires and globalization', *Politics & Society*, vol. 28, no. 3, 413–30.

———. 1993. *Regulating the Poor: The Functions of Public Welfare*. New York: Vintage.

Ratha, Dilip. 2008. 'As the economic crisis deepens, migration and remittances has become even more important for development', World Bank. 18 December.

Rodriguez, Robyn Margalit. 2010. *Migrants for Export: How the Philippine State Brokers Labour to the World*. Minneapolis: University of Minnesota Press.

Saxenian, Anna Lee. 2006. *The New Argonauts: Regional Advantage in a Global Economy*. Cambridge: Harvard University Press.

Smith-Nonini, Sandy. 2009. 'H2A guest workers and the State of North Carolina: From transnational production to transnational organizing', in Fran Ansley and Jon Shefner (eds) *Global Connections and Local Receptions: New Latino Immigration to the Southeastern United States*. Knoxville: University of Tennessee Press.

Standing, G. 2011. *The Precariat: The New Dangerous Class*. London: Bloomsbury.

United Nations. 2005. The Population Division of the Department of Economic and Social Affairs. *Trends in Total Migrant Stock: The 2003 Revision*. New York: United Nations Press Office.

———. 2006. Department of Economic and Social Affairs, Population Division. "International Migration and Development." Thirty-Ninth Session, April 3–7. http://www.un.org/esa/population/cpd/comm2006.htm.

———. *Trends in Migrant Stock: The 2008 Revision*. Data in digital form. New York: United Nations.

USCIS. 2009. 'Cap count for H-1B, H-2B and H-3 workers for fiscal year 2010'. Available at: http://www.uscis.gov/portal/site/uscis/menuitem.5af9bb95919f35e66f614176543f6d1a/?vgnextoid=138b6138f898d010VgnVCM10000048f3d6a1RCRD&vgnextchannel=91919c7755cb9010VgnVCM10000045f3d6a1RCRD. Accessed 3 December 2009.

———. 2010a. 'Immigration reform and control Act of 1986 (IRCA)'. Available at: http://www.uscis.gov/portal/site/uscis/menuitem.5af9bb95919f35e66f614176543f6d1a/?vgnextchannel=b328194d3e88d010VgnVCM10000048f3d6a1RCRD&vgnextoid=04a295c4f635f010VgnVCM1000000ecd190aRCRD. Accessed 5 March 2010.

———. 2010b. Immigration Act of 1990. Available at: http://www.uscis.gov/portal/site/uscis/menuitem.5af9bb95919f35e66f614176543f6d1a/?vgnextoid=84ff95c4f635f010VgnVCM1000000ecd190aRCRD&vgnextchannel=b328194d3e88d010VgnVCM10000048f3d6a1RCRD. Accessed 2 August 2010.

Uchitelle, Louis. 2006. *Disposable American: Layoffs and their Consequences.* New York: Knopf.

Vogel, Richard D. 2006. 'Transient servitude: The U.S. guest worker program for exploiting Mexican and Central American workers', *Monthly Review,* vol. 58, no. 7, 1–23.

World Migration 2005. *Costs and Benefits of International Migration.* Geneva: IOM.

———. 2008. *Managing Labour Mobility in the Evolving Economy.* Geneva: IOM.

INDEX